SEX/GENDER AND SELF-DETERMINATION

Policy Developments in Law, Health and Pedagogical Contexts

Zowie Davy

First published in Great Britain in 2021 by

Bristol University Press
University of Bristol
1–9 Old Park Hill
Bristol
BS2 8BB
UK
t: +44 (0)117 954 5940
e: bup-info@bristol.ac.uk

Details of international sales and distribution partners are available at
bristoluniversitypress.co.uk

British Library Cataloguing in Publication Data
A catalogue record for this book is available from the British Library

ISBN 978-1-4473-4427-8 hardcover
ISBN 978-1-4473-4565-7 paperback
ISBN 978-1-4473-4567-1 ePub
ISBN 978-1-4473-4566-4 ePdf

Cover design: Robin Hawes
Front cover image: SERGEY MELNIKOV / Stocksy.com
Bristol University Press uses environmentally responsible print partners.
Printed in the United Kingdom by CMP, Poole

To all those siblings who have passed in pursuit of

self-determination, TDOR & IDOR

Contents

Introduction

The concept of self-determination has a lengthy scholarly history. The concept has motivated a range of bioethical concerns; as such, the interpretations and thus the effects that result from utilizing the concept vary. This book considers key personal, political and pedagogical approaches to trans, sex/gender expansive and intersex people in various policy fields such as sex/gender recognition legislation, medical diagnoses, medical interventions and educational policies. This book also contemplates how self-determination relates to sex/gender productions, transitions and expressions, and how they correspond to current debates around binary sex/gender embodiment. I will consider throughout how diverse cultural practices and systems may still be (de)limiting trans, sex/gender expansive and intersex trajectories to self-determination. These are not dead ends though but produce new virtualities. This is because trans people are always becoming-trans, sex/gender expansive people are always becoming-sex/gender expansive and intersex people are always becoming intersex-people. This is the same for cis people too, who are always becoming-cis people. The relevant qualities that everybody has are not inherent, archetypal or phylogenetic but are desired in specific assemblages of becoming-human and/or becoming-social (Deleuze and Guattari, 2004).

We will ask if (self-)determining sex/gender is an effect of desire connected to coercive effects, and what this looks like. We will explore how legal, medical and pedagogical policies have more in common with each other than we may think and ask does each of these policy areas co-produce and affect human and non-human bodies? The basic response from a new materialist perspective, which I draw on throughout, must be 'of course'. Affect, according to Siegworth and Gregg (2010: 1), 'is found in those intensities that pass body to body (human and nonhuman), in those resonances that circulate about, between and sometimes stick to bodies and worlds'. Affect is the ability to affect and be affected and corresponds to the passage from one experiential state to another (Deleuze and Guattari, 2004). Medico-legal, bioethical and pedagogical bodies (human and non-human) stick together in particular ways, or, in new materialist terms, assemble through them in multiple, interconnecting and affecting ways. Deleuze and Guattari (1984) insist in *Anti-Oedipus* that our drives are continuously circulating and are simply desiring machines that never exist in a free and unbound state, nor are they ever merely individual; they are always arranged and assembled through social formations. Desires circulate in a multiplicity of ways in competition with each other. Human and non-human affect produces unconscious drives/desires that can account for changes and inventions. For without the capacity to exceed the given, the subject is trapped in repetition in predetermined rather than co-produced systems of the real (Duff, 2014: 38). Changes and inventions, I will go on to show, can be viewed as cultural minoritarian turns (Braidotti, 2006a), through which the desire of self-care allows us to understand 'self-determination' in relation to trans sexing/gendering, sex/gender expansivity and intersexuality, in their singularities. I would like to stress that this book was written in a climate of anti-gender ideology, which originated in anti-feminist and anti-trans discourse among right-wing Christians, particularly in Catholic denominations (Careaga-Pérez, 2016; Kuhar and Paternotte, 2017). These people launched worldwide attacks on minorities, such as trans and sex/gender expansive and, to a lesser extent, intersex people, in an attempt to territorialize social hierarchies and 'traditional' values. Using anti-gender tactics, such as the reaffirmation of a sex/gender binary and its partnership with heterosexuality, trans and sex/gender expansive and intersex people are refused acknowledgement. Anti-gender ideology attacks trans, sex/gender expansive and intersex people's right to bodily integrity, autonomy and self-determination. As such, the subject matter of this book is an important area of social, cultural and policy inquiry, and this analysis is timely.

The book will look to immediate pasts, present contexts, and potential future directions of being able to self-determine sex/gender within the different policy domains mentioned earlier. Key areas of consideration will be the debates surrounding the medico-legal, bioethical, and pedagogical policy contexts. These contexts at first glance may seem disconnected; however, by drawing on new materialism, and particularly Deleuzian empiricism, each of the chapters is connected through material bodies, both human and non-human, in policy, health and pedagogical assemblages (see Sellar, 2012; Duff, 2014). As such, this book, while drawing on DeleuzoGuattarian concepts and ideas, attends to (self-)determining sex/gender.

My approach to sex/gender self-determination will be to show how a variety of human and non-human forces may be enrolled in the promotion of an equitable ethical framework that acknowledges potential relationships between trans, sex/gender expansive and intersex people, physicians, teachers and others through a 'nomadic ethics' (Braidotti, 1994). The first chapter develops the DeleuzoGuattarian framework by situating the debates surrounding sex/gender as a key motif that travels through the rest of the book. I look at key feminist and new materialist debates, and explore sex and gender, trans, sex/gender expansive and intersex people, notions of biologism and bioethical encounters to comprehend the contexts in which particular bodies are producing desires for sex/gender self-determination. I will argue that sex/gender assemblages help us to understand the complex ways in which humans are continuously produced through, rather than determined by biological, material, affective, social, semiotic, political, and economic forces. In the latter part of the chapter, I briefly explore the notions of sex/gender autonomy and bodily integrity in the context of legislative human rights so that I can demonstrate that the affect produced circulates about, between and sometimes sticks to trans, sex/gender expansive and intersex bodies, developing a minoritarian set of forces that co-produce self-determination claims based on sex/gender.

In Chapter 2, I explore the conceptual frameworks developed in the self-determination literature. I acknowledge how large bureaucratic agencies, such as government, the United Nations and the National Health Service (NHS), have promoted self-determination, and observe how de jure state functionaries, such as educators, scientists, physicians, psychiatrists and group representatives, institutionalize boundaries around good and bad practices, language use and identifications. Abulof (2016: 539) aptly calls these functionaries 'norm entrepreneurs'. Norm entrepreneurs, I argue, however, can curb self-determination for trans, gender expansive and intersex people. This curbing attempts to delimit biopolitical assemblages by administering norms, resulting in me questioning whether the desire for self-determination can be really called self-determination at all.

Norm entrepreneurs can wittingly or unwittingly territorialize the assemblages trans, gender expansive and intersex people momentarily find themselves in, by folding their power into social structures, but despite this, there are always movements – or what Deleuze and Guattari (2004: xvii) call 'lignes de fuite'. The concept of 'lignes de fuite' has been translated into English as 'lines of flight' and can signify the acts of fleeing, eluding, flowing, leaking and disappearing into the distance.

Chapter 3 will look at a range of medico-legal policies in order to draw distinctions between international and UK contexts in relation to patient centredness, autonomy, bodily integrity and self-determination. Here we will observe institutional lines of flight. I will explore the development of medical governance, particularly (but not exclusively) in the UK, to understand whether the relational field and all its relevant parts implicated in the medical-patient-policy assemblage continue to be fit for purpose in assigning a sex/gender at birth. We will question whether sex/gender assignments as norm-entrepreneurial acts have a medical purpose and what challenges can be levelled at the practice in light of human rights declarations surrounding the rights of people in relation to bodily integrity, autonomy and self-determination. This detour into medico-legal policy domains will also point to the ways that trans, sex/gender expansive and intersex people are treated differently to cis sex/gender people in many parts of the world, and continue to be unnecessarily pathologized. Additionally, in the case of some intersex people, I will suggest that they are unnecessarily surgically operated on because such decisions rest on the historical development of the norm-producing psychiatric and psychosexual frameworks. I will simply highlight that all bodies are affected and affect differently the ethical arguments about bodily integrity, autonomy and self-determination. This difference, however, demonstrates the inequity in healthcare practices and highlights the refusal to apply the same ethical standards to trans, gender expansive and intersex people as to cis sex/gender people.

As mentioned earlier, norm entrepreneurs fold their power into social structures; understanding this through a Deleuzian lens, however, allows for movement rather than endless repetition. Chapter 4 then will briefly explore the burgeoning debates from the international trans and intersex depathologization movement, folding in their desires and power in relation to medico-legal sex/gender self-determination. I will go on to describe the different degrees to which sex/gender self-determination has made inroads into medico-legal frameworks in Europe, Asia, and South America, and assess whether these developments are underpinned by self-determination. As such, this chapter deals with the micro-challenges and movements producing new medical practices for trans, sex/gender expansive and intersex people through political activism. This activism argues for a patient-centred, self-determination model to be implemented. I will demonstrate that in some countries, psychiatrists' power over trans, sex/gender expansive and intersex people's bodies is being questioned, and highlight how far the self-determination model has succeeded in changing the planes of immanence for them in various jurisdictions. In this chapter, I deal with intersex people separately due to the timing of interventions that usually take place in assigning a 'true sex'. I will, however, show the connection between claims to self-determination for intersex people and how they have been incorporated into the political discourse of trans and sex/gender expansive people. I will conclude that, in order to understand self-determination and sex/gender health in the wake of depathologizing demands, it is important to probe the discursive claims for a politics of self-determination of the trans, non-binary and intersex depathologization health movement. I suggest that the informed consent model in medicine is emerging, albeit slowly, into medical care for trans, sex/gender expansive and intersex people and is a line of flight that may enhance their self-determination.

In the fifth chapter, I will continue with the theme of advocacy for self-determination from a different cultural angle. Drawing on empirical data from parents of trans and sex/gender expansive children in the UK, I will explore how they attempt to reassemble policy and practice in schools in relation to who has the right to determine sex/gender for their children. I demonstrate that parents are at the forefront of establishing a minoritarian turn within schools. I will however demonstrate that the limit-situations imposed try to halt these processes of becoming. Nonetheless, I will argue that despite these limit-situations, parent-advocates are establishing new ways for trans and sex/gender expansive children to co-produce (rather than self-determine) their place (in nomadic ways) in school cultures.

To recap, this book will be focusing on three seemingly separate, but interrelated, areas of society: politico-legal arenas, medico-legal systems, bioethical and pedagogical environments. Self-determining sex/gender is now in international public consciousness due to numerous media commentaries, governmental debates and the corresponding and relatively fast-paced shifts in legal and policy constructions regarding trans, sex/gender expansive, and intersex people in law and medicine, and in universities and schools (see Agius et al, 2015; Davy et al, 2018).

One other area that will be considered in this book is the academic publishing that touches and affects all the areas considered through transferences of epistemological 'tastes' and 'evidence'. Publishing by, and prominent positions of, academics and researchers within knowledge-production processes concomitantly support policy development. Parts of this book then involve a critique of conventional representations of 'self-determination', especially where (academic/professional) disciplines have a strong hold over the knowledge making that surrounds trans, sex/gender expansive and intersex bodies. To this end I do not intend to offer a definitive version of 'self-determination', but suggest that it alternates, sticks to and shifts with other human and non-human bodies through co-productive forces, which are multifaceted and complex, despite us often referring to a quest for self-determination. First though, as already noted, I turn to the topic that seems so fundamental to us as humans: sex/gender.

1

The scope of sex/gender embodiment and self-determination

Introduction

The term 'sex/gender self-determination' will be important throughout the book. Scholars have been exploring self-determination in relation to individuals' minority and majority identities, colonial and postcolonial nation building, citizenship, healthcare, pedagogy and more. These fields of literature are not impervious to theoretical changes. One stark omission in earlier debates has been in relation to sex/gender self-determination. It is as if this is an impossibility and that sex/gender is an inherent given. However, the concept increasingly crops up in the literature about intersex bodies, and also in relation to sexed/gendered bodies, in medicine more generally. When intensities of power shift through human and non-human bodies, that are either supportive of, or a challenge to, (a) people's self-determination, we begin to see nuanced conceptual changes in the literature. We can use these analytical conceptualizations as 'types' within a particularly Deleuzian form of empiricism and ethics to talk about differing levels of 'self-determination' as 'desire' if, indeed, we believe that there is such a thing in the first place. The 'types' of literature help us attend to an examination of the principle of self-determination on micro and macro planes of immanence and at all the levels between.

This chapter takes as its starting point the ways in which our bodies are produced and are sites of production. The dimensions of 'sexual difference' have been key cornerstones in how we produce, and how particular people are given, the power to sex/gender bodies, resulting in a context that has come to be understood as essential to life itself. While many think sex/gender is fixed and unchanging, many others argue that sex/gender is mutable, an ever-changing, relational product, with connections manifested within productive assemblages. As such, I discuss the Deleuzian framework that I will draw on throughout the book in this chapter, while working through several ways that sex and gender, and sex/gender, have been conceptualized and related to cis, trans, gender expansive and intersex people. Sexual difference and sex/gender is, as Braidotti (1994) suggests, a game of priorities played out in relation to our own cultural survival. The network of issues that have historically and contemporaneously manifested around sex/gender continue to be sites of battle, as well as production, in contemporary societies throughout the world. My intention in this chapter is to highlight some key debates and show some paradoxes in some arguments when we take the concept of sex/gender and connect it to self-determination.

Sex/gender assignments

My selection of the sex/gender concept has several motivations, which has led me to develop a new materialist understanding of self-determination. In 'Immanence: A life', Deleuze (1997), explains that the reality of the/a life is virtual. What he means by this is that life in general or the life of a certain living subject passes through and is affected by regulating objects or bodies (both human and non-human), which affects them on a virtual plane. Life in general, or a life of a living subject, are not relatively separate spheres from, for example, industry, law or pedagogy, but produce life through desiring it. Similarly, each sphere of human organization desires something from the living subject. Each event in a/the life coexists and mingles unintentionally in its singularity; such events neither come together nor divide in the same way for all. Deleuze (1997: 5–6) states:

> A life contains only virtuals. It is made of virtualities, events, singularities. What we call virtual is not something that lacks reality, but something that enters into a process of actualization following the plane that gives it its own reality. The immanent event actualizes itself in a state of things and in a lived state which bring the event about. The plane of immanence is actualized in an Object and Subject to which it attributes itself. But, however hard it might be to separate them [Object and Subject] from their actualization, the plane of immanence is itself virtual just as the events which people it are virtualities. The events or singularities give all their virtuality to the plane, just as the plane of immanence gives a full reality to the virtual events.

Hence, Deleuze and Guattari (2004: 4, emphasis in original) state that: 'everything is production: *production of productions*, of actions and of passions; productions of recording processes, of distributions and of co-ordinates that serve as points of reference; *productions of consumptions*, of sensual pleasure, of anxieties, and of pain'. For instance, national, class, ethnic, gender and sexual identifications, among numerous others, are separated and then combined in many ways and serve us as points of reference. These events produce forces, which are desiring machines producing, in our case here, sex/gender assignments. There is no inherency in these sex/gender assignments and eventual identifications, but they are ontologically differentiated, constituted and produced because of the relational connections manifested within productive assemblages. Looking at a large area of theoretical work through this lens can provide us with exemplary insights about the historical and geographical specificity, the social forces that are working through, and the multiple reconfigurations produced surrounding sex/gender and self-determination.

The theoretical significance of the concept of sex/gender assignment to self-determination, at different levels, is especially important to marginalized people who are often besieged by multiple forces that produce inequalities in contemporary societies. As noted earlier, the groups of people I am considering in this book are those who are assigned one sex/gender at birth, but who identify and reconfigure themselves in another sex/gender or without a sex/gender at all, whom we generally refer to as trans (gender) or sex/gender expansive, respectively. Cordoba (2020) suggests that 'trans', as a linguistic marker, is used as an umbrella term to describe those who identify within a binary sex/gender system and those who identify beyond it. There have been several labels produced by those who identify beyond the system, for example, genderqueer, pangender, bigender, agender and neutrois, to show that it is not complex enough for them (Barker and Richards, 2015). The social context in which all these identifications are produced are not in distinction to nature but through the production of nature (Deleuze and Guattari, 1984).

Additionally, intersex people are assigned a sex/gender shortly after birth and either legally retain it throughout their life, or for part of it and then produce it differently, or, like some trans and sex/gender expansive people, wish to move socio-legally beyond their assignment and the binary sex/gender system altogether, and maintain their intersex status. Very few de jure states administer this socio-legal position as standard. I do not wish to infer that there are two sexes/genders or even a 'third', but that many de jure states systematically administer only two sexes/genders, and occasionally a 'third', to house the natural, material infinitude of '*n sexes*', which is a term that Deleuze and Guattari (2007) use to indicate that sexes/gender are reconfigured in multiple ways. Trans (gender) and sex/gender expansivity, and to a lesser extent intersex (albeit no less important), have emerged as subjects of increasing social, cultural and social scientific interest in recent years. This is so much so in relation to trans and sex/gender expansive people that it has been claimed that a 'transgender tipping point' has been reached (Steinmetz, 2014). The tipping point is signified by a rise in focus on trans and sex/gender expansive people within the media and popular culture and ever-shifting attitudes – some progressive and some regressive – towards trans and sex/gender expansive people in international legal administrations and national sex/gender recognition legislation worldwide (see Davy et al, 2018). Intersex people are minimally considered in popular culture and political circles, and are rarely accounted for in policy directives; however, there have been some notable shifts, which I will consider in more depth later. Sex/gender expansive people are also rarely considered, but again there are some shifts.

Implicated in sex/gender assignment and self-determination negotiations are the physicians who first assign and thus attempt to determine sex/gender at birth, and those who interact with trans, sex/gender expansive and intersex people during and post any transitioning procedures and sex/gender affirmation interventions. Davis and colleagues (2016) demonstrate that physicians initially 'engage in a process of "giving gender," but they do so by "giving sex"', which forms the fundamental basis of a normative framework of sex, gender and sexuality. While I agree with this theorization, I suggest that 'giving sex/gender' is a better term as it connects the two heuristic devices of sex and gender on the virtual planes that medicine and people produce. An initial sex/gender assignment, unwittingly perhaps, eventually supports the production of pathologies surrounding trans, sex/gender expansive and intersex people's bodies. Recently, physicians and policy makers have produced revisions for several psychiatric and health policies for trans, sex/gender expansive and intersex people (APA, 2013; NHS, 2016; WHO, 2018), in which the assignment of sex/gender at birth contributes to the pathologizing language in each of the texts. These diagnostic shifts nonetheless continue to connect trans, sex/gender expansive and intersex people to diagnosis and treatments, through the production of (new) 'symptomologies' – in different degrees – which helps to diffuse affect towards the sex/gender healthcare systems across the globe.

Moreover, there has been a small increase in the relatively recent phenomena of producing university and school policies for trans, sex/gender expansive and intersex academics and students (Agius et al,

2015; Cannon and Best, 2015; De Montfort University, 2017), which firmly situate them as having viable lives in their own right. These human and non-human 'desiring machines', as Deleuze and Guattari (1984: 1) call them, are 'flow-producing machines' and connect to others, producing a producing/product identity. Here 'identity' is a productive category rather than the opaque and oft used notion of (sex/gender) 'identity' with its essentialist connotations. Nor indeed is 'identity' used here in the way that some social constructionists' do, who have a somewhat unworkable usage 'identity' as being fluid or multiple, due to its conceptual and analytical ambiguity (Brubaker and Cooper, 2000). 'Identity' cannot be both a category of practice and an analytical category to best understand life or understand the productive nature of it. Therefore, following Brubaker and Cooper (2000), I will use the term 'identification', which I will explore in more depth a little later.

Cultural productions and their affect, such as diagnostic revisions, pedagogical policies and the media, produce virtual fields of movement that trans, sex/gender expansive and intersex people of all ages are invoking, co-producing and sometimes challenging. For example, in fields of policy production which alludes to a set of social problems for these groups of people, trans, sex/gender expansive and intersex people are suggesting that they are not the problem, but that the individual is often being denied a seat at the production table through the restrictions imposed in the policies. They often want to challenge the representations of sex/gender assignments, transitions, expressions and roles. The problems that manifest in society are produced in the infrastructure and in the policy process of representations and differentiations, which cast shadows over the actual problem itself in the virtual fields, that of their own production. Remember the virtual fields do not determine matter, they help to produce new matter. These fields are part of the enfolding assemblage that produces new sexes/genders. The biological, material, affective, social, semiotic, political and economic forces, which affect body singularities that bind these groups to a particular series in the policy assemblage, highlight the virtual event that these human and non-human bodies instantiate. The affective becomings that these encounters produce momentarily apprehend the body but do not determine it. The policy does not simply represent these body singularities but, as Duff (2014: 12) suggests, the policy condition is produced in the body's 'condition'. He says:

> To misunderstand the virtual in this [representative] way
> is to reduce immanence to mere potential or possibility,

suggesting that all matter, all life, is prefigured in some underlying set of essences or identities that simply await their expression [in the policies], their actualisation, in life [... We must start] positing difference and differentiation as the genetic conditions by which individual forms emerge and settle into entities capable of being identified as such.

Nonetheless, recent policy produces (legal, social and medical) flows through which the 'self-determination' of sex/gender differences can be actualized or denied in much more diverse ways than have been previously represented. For example, since the 1972 Swedish act, which acknowledged trans people's 'new' sex/gender if they were sterilized, numerous de jure states have produced legal frameworks establishing their own parameters of recognition. For example, trans and intersex people in the UK can change their name and sex marker from male to female or female to male on nearly all relevant records through a process of self-determination without changing their birth certificate. Official changes can be performed with the NHS, Driver and Vehicle Licensing Agency and the Passport Office. A physician's letter is required to change the sex/gender marker on passports. For trans people, in order to have their birth certificate amended they must use the Gender Recognition Act 2004 (GRA, 2004) if they wish to go from one sex/gender marker to the other. However, the Gender Recognition Act policy route to sex/gender affirmation opposite to the one that was assigned at birth works on the basis that people are diagnosed with gender dysphoria or can provide evidence of 'transitioning' medical interventions. I am not asserting whether this is right or wrong but acknowledging two different virtualities that these different policy relations instantiate, and the affective becomings that these encounters can produce. I will explore these affective parameters in more depth in Chapter 4. Suffice it to say here that, before the implementation of the Gender Recognition Act (GRA, 2004), legal sex/gender recognition for trans adults was partly denied in the UK and based on a different virtuality. One could not legally change sex/gender on a birth certificate but you could on a driving licence. These sets of policy relations instantiated and affected sex/gender becomings differently in relation to driving, travelling or marrying. The point is that the medico-legal-assemblage produces different material actualities by producing virtualities that can be used both to empower and to disempower, to privilege or to inhibit bodily productions. We can see that the medico-legal assemblage connecting trans people creates different material actualities if we compare it to, for example, the medico-legal assemblage for cis and intersex people.

Let us look at the situation of intersex people in light of what I have just said. There are several medically recognized forms of intersex people, all with materially different bodies. Intersex people have different chromosomal make-ups, for example XXY, XYY, XO and XX/YY with varying numbers of karyotypes and some with XY and XX chromosomes with endocrinological differences, such as partial androgen insensitivity syndrome, complete androgen insensitivity syndrome, congenital adrenal hyperplasia and 5-alpha-reductase deficiency, Klientfelter's and Turner's syndrome. For the diversity of intersex people in the UK, legal sex/gender assignment of either male or female is based on different criteria to those of cis sex/gender or trans people. One of the first decisions made by the parent(s) and the attending medical team is the child's sex/gender that they will be socialized into. The socialization process is often accompanied with surgical and endocrinological interventions, some necessary to prolong life and some unnecessary, carried out so that the child can aesthetically conform to socially ideal bodies. Despite many surgical interventions being therapeutically unnecessary to prolong life, they are widely used to manage the so-called medical emergency and assign a sex/gender at birth (see Horowitz and Glassberg, 1992). Both Preves (2005) and Kessler (1998) argue that surgical interventions are underpinned by medical policy based on the assumption that it would be psychosocially and psychosexually beneficial for the child to grow up with a genital appearance that resembles other children of the 'same' chosen sex/gender. This has been commonly called the 'optimal gender policy' (Meyer-Bahlburg, 1999). The problem with the notion of 'optimal' is that it is empirical nonsense due to the impossibility of generating baseline data that is required to test the assumption. The 'optimal gender policy' must then be understood as a tacit form of medicine that merely hopes that intersex people will be thankful that they were genitally 'normalized', and that the chosen male or female sex/gender for their birth certificate does not cause them any dysphoria.

Moreover, in these cases, there are different sets of matter that are considered by the attending medical teams and parents that produce them as 'male' or 'female', resulting in a set of arrangements that disregards the sex/gender-producing factors that are applied to cis, trans and sex/gender expansive people. As Chandler (2013: 520) suggests, we are: 'reborn or born-again in a world in which we appear to be without the signposts of modernity [...] where "the arrow of time" ensures that circumstances are never stable for repeatable cause-and-effect relations, destabilising any possibility of acting on the basis of knowable eternal or fixed "natural" laws'.

In these examples, the affective forces are not equally distributed, but nor do they determine anything. The affective properties function through people co-producing them in society. My point is not about whether the policy and practices are right or wrong – many others have argued both in favour of and against both – but to point to the ways in which policy and medical practice co-produce sex/gender in ways that are claimed to be empirical sureties, but are in fact empirical obscurities. All this directs me to the ethical dilemma of whether sex/gender assignment is required at birth or if it should be left to be self-determined at a later date.

Health and social policy, medico-legal and cultural developments, in different degrees, reflect the assorted ways in which trans, sex/gender expansive and intersex people acquire visibility beyond the dominant western medical models that previously encouraged stealthiness, requiring such conditions to be hidden and thus making them into something to be ashamed of. In many parts of the world, trans, sex/gender expansive and intersex people are now producing their worlds on complex planes of immanence and in ways that Braidotti (2006a: 79) calls 'becoming-minoritarian'. Becoming-minoritarian, she suggests, is a desire through and upon which undervalued people are reconceptualizing their subjectivities through processes of becoming that are embodied, relational and on the move. They are becoming un-undervalued within dominant culture while also 'using' the prescribed shame as a productive desire to foster human connection and effectively write 'a minoritarian memory experience into existence' (Stafford, 2012: 311).

A critical reflection on the undervalued past journeys and present practices, and on the systems affecting trans, sex/gender expansive and intersex people in their societies, has enabled them to find gaps in the negative discourses surrounding their bodies, to challenge in-group and out-group norms and their points of weakness, while getting to know where resistance and new articulations can occur through practices of self-care (Foucault, 1994a). As Patricia Clough (2008) points out, 'subjects' should not be thought of as being produced by the system they are found in or that they will inevitably internalize social norms. Rather, in neoliberal capitalist systems, bodies are materially produced and emerge within biopolitical relations. Pitts-Taylor (2016: 163) describes this as bodies functioning in 'biomediated capitalism [where] biology both drives production and is the resource mined, excavated and produced'. Contemporary biomedical culture now identifies (trans, sex/gender expansive and intersex) bodies, from the surface level of flesh and beyond to the molecule, neuron and gene, but in different ways that matter. All bodies are now key sites for the practice of self-care and the refinement of what Pitts-Taylor (2016: 163) calls 'deserving biomedical citizenship'. These cultural minoritarian turns and practices of self-care mark sex/gender self-determination in relation to trans sex/gender, sex/gender expansive and intersex identifications, in their singularities, as important and timely areas of social, cultural and policy inquiry. In order to do this, we need to understand a little more about the concept sex/gender that I am using and the reasons for this.

Sex and gender

Sex and gender stick together, though many have tried to split them up to do particular theoretical and analytical work. To understand this better, there is a need to establish the specifics of the terms 'gender' and 'sex' and offer some examples of how they have been employed, and highlight the issues with their deployment. Academics and lay people, particularly in western societies, tend to understand sex and gender in terms of mutually exclusive hierarchical categories (Carrera et al, 2012). By splitting sex and gender they produce an incomplete understanding of cis, trans, sex/gender expansive and intersex people. General usage of the term 'gender' gradually materialized from the late 1960s in psychosexology and the social sciences. This term was argued to differentiate aspects of life that were interpreted to be emerging from social rather than biological foundations (Diamond, 2000). Milton Diamond's (2000: 47) argument in his article 'Sex and gender: Same or different?' was that 'males and females, as biological entities, were accepted as essentially similar cross-culturally, but men and women, by virtue of the multitude of different roles they played in diversified societies, were not so easily catalogued [...] sex would refer to biological traits while gender would refer to social/cultural ones', even though, still to this day, 'sex' and 'gender' are often used interchangeably. Diamond (2002: 321), a few years after he had posed the question of whether sex and gender were different from each other, answered 'yes', but suggested also that the distinction was more useful for those analyses involving transsexuality and intersexuality. He added, further, that we should be encouraging the distinction in our analytical work. I would not be so sure about why it is analytically useful, or why we need to encourage this for transsexuality and intersexuality in particular, or indeed for any human body. I also contest the arbitrary splitting of cis people and trans, sex/gender expansive and intersex people.

'Sex' is often heuristically different to 'gender' in the way it is used in much of the literature. 'Sex' is produced in biopolitical, interpersonal and personal domains and is problematically essential to gender when the term is required discursively either to undermine, or make claims for, gender recognition rights around being an autonomous and authentic sexed/gendered subject. For instance, some (lesbian) feminist separatists have produced the sexed female subject position of a 'womyn born womyn' (see Browne, 2011). The 'womyn born womyn' concept was developed during second-wave feminism, signifying women who were sexed female at birth, raised as girls, and continue to identify as womyn. They rejected 'men' from the word 'women' in order to demonstrate the existence of an autonomous group of sex/ gender subjects. Feminists who use this term draw on 'female' as an essential biological category and 'womyn' as an autonomous gender subject, and mark it in opposition to the essential notion of 'male'. It was hoped that reiterating 'womyn' would engender a reworking of power relations between men and womyn, and enable the creation of what many saw as utopian womyn-only spaces and entry policies (Browne, 2009).

Simone de Beauvoir (1997), in *The second sex*, describes the power relations between men and women and argues that, in civic life, the management of (a) people is organized through a dualism between those sexed male and those sexed female. This dualism, she asserts, does several things: it provides social entitlements, prestige, entry into crucial areas of life for men and denies or restricts them for women. The primary sex/gender assignment dualism also sets up other dualisms based on positive and negative (sexed/gendered) characteristics, such as rationality/irrationality, reasoned/unreasonable, powerful/passive in a sustained defamation of those sexed female (Braidotti, 1994). The sexed body and the gendered characteristics attached to it were skilfully manufactured, albeit aggregated artificially. In DeleuzoGuattarian terms the nomadic intensities of 'sex' and 'gender' collide in civic society on multiple planes of immanence, not as separate objective entities, but as productive assemblages with forces. I argue that sex/gender are always connected and affective, albeit having different intensive forces within different assemblages and produced through different (human and non-human) bodies. These affects are characteristic of the distinctive abilities of human and non-human bodies and produce what Deleuze calls 'desires'. In *Anti-Oedipus*, Deleuze and Guattari (1984) reject the exteriority/interiority parallelism by reformulating desire as affecting and being affected, which forms part of the infrastructure itself.

Braidotti's concept of nomadic ethics disrupts the infrastructure of 'sex' and 'gender' as separate entities and can be employed to explore wanderings beyond the established dictates of sexual differences, through reassembling bodies, technologies, habits, affects and texts in ways that transform the human beyond a naïve understanding of binary sex or gender, female and male. This is unlike the individualizing aspects we often see in other stories being told. For example, in some biopolitical domains, binary sex and gender are separated or merged, often unwittingly and sometimes knowingly, to assert power over others' desire, autonomy, bodily integrity and 'self-determination'.[1] 'Sex' is often viewed as being more affective as a biological, and thus a more powerful scientific concept, despite the biological representations being mediated by gendered as well as colonial and racialized norms (Laqueur, 1990). Despite some people distinguishing between 'sex' and 'gender' in legal, biological, medical and policy fields, among others, many scholars and practitioners often talk about 'sex' even though they are referring to 'gender' and vice versa. In relation to trans, sex/gender expansive and intersex people, the concepts of 'sex' and 'gender' are often interchangeably posed as gender conforming when related to the bodies of cis sex/gender people and as non-conforming when related to trans, sex/gender expansive and intersex people's 'true sex'. This I find a strange conceptual framework because I am never sure about what people are (not) conforming to, as there is no archetypical sex/gender. As such, I find this fundamentally misleading and a redundant splitting of sex and gender albeit one that is not inconsequential for contemporary policy constructions surrounding a person's ethical right to self-determine their sex/gender (at any age).

I have just suggested that when the term 'sex' is used it has powerful biological-esque truth effects on many people's consciousness. As the historian and social philosopher, Foucault (1980a: x) says, in the introduction to *Herculine Barbin: Being the recently discovered memoirs of a nineteenth-century French hermaphrodite*: 'the idea that one must indeed finally have a true sex is far from being completely dispelled' (unlike the dismissing of gender expressions as mere social constructions, parody, or being inauthentic). He continues: 'Whatever the opinion of the biologists on this point, the idea that there exist complex, obscure, and essential relationships between sex and truth is found – at least in a diffuse state – not only in psychiatry, psychoanalysis and psychology, but also in current [public] opinion.'

Even though Foucault wrote the introduction to this text 40 years ago about an intersex person in the 1800s, the debate that is acknowledged within it rears its head again and again in contemporary times when the question of somebody's 'sex' is raised in public (and sometimes in private) spaces. In particular, questions arise in the case of 'non-passing' cis, trans, sex/gender expansive and intersex people in sex-segregated spaces, such as toilets and changing rooms, sporting competitions and so on. As an example, in sporting competitions we may want to consider how people sexed/gendered female, and who develop 'hyper-androgenization' because of polycystic ovaries, are often questioned about their 'true sex' (see for example Santos, 2020), especially when they win the competition. Opponents of sex/gender self-determination position them as the 'sex' that they were assumed to truly be at birth and accepts the assignment made by medical practitioners, who are sanctioned across the world to provide a 'true sex' for a birth certificate.[2] For the ardent critic of sex/gender self-determination, this assignment is immovable.

'Passing' (through) as unremarkable men and women, by relying on verbal and non-verbal signs and signifiers such as bodily aesthetics in particular spaces, would not provoke any questions nor dislocate the sex/gender self-determination of the person (Davy, 2011b). However, those trans, non-binary and intersex people whose bodily aesthetics defy or do not securely fit the emblematic parameters of a person's or a culture's masculine and feminine (binary) biological sex/gender system are judged in social interactions and spaces, and often face accusations from the angriest opponents of sex/gender self-determination of being sycophantic fantasists[3] and fraudulent illusionists,[4] and are frequently accused of wanting to invade sex-segregated spaces for suspicious, illegal (sexual) or deceitful reasons (see Jeffreys and Davy, 2014). Accusations of sexed inauthenticity underpin all these accusatory suggestions and simultaneously try to deny that sex/gender self-determination is possible because of an underlying medically assigned true sex. This is despite accusers producing their own sex/gender in the ways that they want, through their masculine, feminine, or androgynous bodily aesthetics, roles and, to some degree, their bodily morphology. These angry accusers seem not to recognize that their own embodied characteristics are affected by a desire to self-determine themselves through their unfolding assemblages as a configuration of man/masculine/feminine/androgynous, woman/feminine/masculine/androgynous, and so on in a sexed/gendered, patriarchal and hierarchical world. Moreover, these critics are not automatically positioned in an undesirable position as fantasists, frauds, or potential sexual assaulters if their own masculinity or femininity does not 'fit' with their bodily morphology.

An instance of this in the UK, featured in a BBC Radio 4 (Jeffreys and Davy, 2014) debate I had with Sheila Jeffreys about her then latest book. In the debate she suggested that she does not have a gender and then went on to describe that she does not actually do femininity, because it is a 'social construction', stating that it was developed by men and the patriarchal system to subjugate women, inferring femininity's (and presumably masculinity's) inauthenticity. It was unclear what she meant here. The whole premise of social constructionist thought about sex/gender has never suggested that the doing of sex/gender was inauthentic. Whether one produces it or not is irrelevant to the social constructedness of masculinity or femininity. They do not suggest that one thing is real and the other is socially constructed but that everything we see, do, hear is socially constructed, including sex assignment at birth. Put another way, in social constructionism you cannot pick what is (masculinity and femininity – gender) and what is not (sex) socially constructed, because everything is. Nonetheless, Jeffreys suggested that she presents her sex/gender in contradistinction to femininity, because she says femininity hurts women (and trans people). She seems unaware, however, that she is still accepting the parameters surrounding what femininity 'is' – this so-called social construction – while self-determining her (non-feminine or masculine?) sex/gender presentation, role and form of womanhood as she sees fit in relation to her value system in which she sees 'femininity' as harmful. Implicit in the argument is that those who adopt bodily practices that are regarded (by her) as feminine are inherently harmful. This line of argument has many wider consequences for 'self-determination' practices that (for her) can be divided into simplistic dichotomies of 'good' and 'bad' agency.

Jeffreys' understanding of 'femininity', when done by a trans girl or woman, is seen as even more harmful and even more inferior because those, who she refers to as men and boys, who adopt femininity are attempting to invade women's spaces, metaphorically raping them, by wanting to present themselves as feminine women and girls. Given the fact that she had already asserted that femininity is a social construction and according to her argument not real, it then seems strange to call for women-only spaces unless her framework of recognition of 'woman' is from a different epistemological perspective, such as essentialism. Jeffreys does hold that women are born women – a strange assertion because we are all born as very small people – and then interpolated as boys or girls through a 'biological' assignment by physicians. This interpolation of women that Jeffreys speaks of is first based on morphology, and then on our treatment (by men) in society as second-class citizens, and the way patriarchal society has unfolded. This I cannot deny, as it seems that those both legally and culturally sexed/gendered female do draw the short straw in relation to many social hierarchies, and are subject to violence and infantilization.[5] However, this must also mean that trans women, sex/gender expansive people and intersex people who look and are treated like women will inevitably suffer the same secondary position as those who are sexed/gendered female at birth. Rarely do people look more deeply into the materiality of the body before prejudice is asserted. What this does not mean, however, is that those who were sexed/gendered male at birth are all inherently positioned at the top of the hierarchy of maleness (see for example Connell and Messerschmidt, 2005), or are fraudulent or sexual predators.[6] Westbrook and Schilt call this producing of someone else's sex/gender a 'biology-based determination of gender' (Westbrook and Schilt, 2014: 33). They suggest that this is different to 'identity-based gender' determination, when others recognize people within a sex/gender category with which they identify themselves, and are regarded as legitimately being able to determine that sex/gender. Because Jeffreys has not felt that her assigned sex (cis sex/gender status), and presumably her bodily aesthetics and historical positioning, has been mis-determined at birth, she assumes that that is how everyone ought to feel.

Jeffreys then went on to claim that trans women particularly should not be allowed in sex-segregated spaces established as for 'women only' – changing rooms, women's refuges – because they are men, were socialized as male and are potential sexual predators because of their assigned sex at birth; yet trans (men), non-binary and intersex people who were assigned female at birth, in spite of their current sex/gender identification, role or bodily aesthetics and presentation, would be allowed into these spaces if we followed the logic of her argument. Here it is suggested that being socialized as a female and not a male has more weight in the debate over sex-segregated spaces than sex/gender identification, which is socially constructed and thus, in her terms, unreal.

These arguments have been taken up in the UK in relation to sex-segregated spaces, by illustrating that the arguments against rely on unsubstantiated claims of, among other things, 'men' perpetrating sex-crimes (as 'women') and being able to change their legal sex on demand. The most vocal voices are from a faction of self-determined 'gender critical feminists', who declare that they do not want to be subjected to 'males' who self-determine their sex/genders. One objection to self-determination for those sexed male at birth is a belief that, if there is no procedure to verify that individuals genuinely self-identify with their sex/gender, this may lead to deceitful men claiming a female identity in order to access women-only spaces. In addition, gender critical feminists object to the possibility of sex/gender self-determination because it would create a right for trans women who have no intention to transition medically, to enter locker rooms and public restrooms. And that this possibility of 'deceit' will inevitably lead to increasing the risks of sexual assault, voyeurism and other sex-based crimes in places such as refuges, toilets and changing rooms. Self-determination models of law for trans people, and an increase in safety and privacy violations such as assault, sex crimes and voyeurism, have not transpired in, for example, Ireland, Malta and elsewhere. A recent study, moreover, has flatly refuted gender critical claims of there being evidence from criminal incident reports that they will inevitably increase (Hasenbush et al, 2019). Moreover, the Gender Recognition Act 2004, enacted over fifteen years ago, already accommodates several provisions that undermine these spurious arguments: for example, the law does not force trans people to have surgery or even apply for recognition, but they continue to use appropriate facilities for their sex/gender identifications and have done so for many years before and since the implementation of the law. None of these aspects have correlated with any increase in sexual offence crimes being reported. In fact, in these spaces, they are extremely rare. The point about what I will call non-surgical trans people[7] is important. Even if a trans person has had surgery or has transitioned, there is no decree that they should change their documentation; it is in fact the Equality Act 2010 that facilitates the possibility of those who identify as a particular sex/gender accessing the facilities of sex-segregated spaces (in a limited way) according to sex/gender identification (for a fuller analysis about this see Sharpe, 2020). Another important aspect to note is that, according to the Gender Recognition Act 2004, trans people do not have to have genital reassignment surgery to attain their new birth certificates in their experienced sex/gender. Those people who do not or cannot have any surgical interventions nonetheless do have to present evidence of a diagnosis of gender dysphoria, or information about which surgical operations were planned but could not be actualized in order for them to be assessed according to their 'new' sex/gender. The law also stipulates that the person must live for the rest of their life with the 'new' sex/gender (whatever that means). While these gender critical feminists rarely explain the causal connection between legal facilitation and illegal (and may I say abhorrent) behaviour, it is assumed that the people who may commit these crimes would inevitably be able to use this productive policy to claim that they are within their rights to enter sex segregated spaces, heightening the potential of sex-crimes being perpetrated. As already noted, there is no evidence of this and there is no causal mechanism that can be demonstrated by gender critical feminists to claim such a thing. There have been a few known cases where rapes have been perpetrated by trans women, but there have also been a few known sexual assaults by cis women against cis women. Based on the known cases, none of the trans women were men pretending to be women in segregated places; however women have been convicted for pretending to be men in order to sexually assault cis women. Moreover, we do not hold accountable all cis women and girls for the actions of a few, whereas most of the gender critical feminists seem to want to hold all trans people accountable for the few crimes that have been committed by other trans people. While this is a potentiality among many other potentialities, we may wish to access the empirical data either to evidence such possibilities or to discredit the claims.

This gender critical line of argumentation is paradoxically counter to the arguments of some women too. According to gender critical feminists, sex-segregated spaces should be policed at macro and micro levels. The former through changing legislation to prevent 'men', a category in which they include trans women and girls, from entering these spaces. The latter, they have less to say about, but through new legislation, people will be able to challenge those suspected of not being the 'correct' sex. These same places that are espoused as 'women-only' spaces are often 'troubled' by those also sexed female at birth and who wish to remain so legally. The butch lesbian, masculine lesbian or non-binary lesbian may trouble the sex/gender aesthetic expectations in sex-segregated spaces. The sexing/gendering of spaces requires that the questioned person must, or feels obliged to, (re)assert their sex/gender within a binary categorization in certain spaces: "I am a woman" or "I am a man." Many gender critical feminists paradoxically assert that these women are necessary casualties to avoid a reduction of many other women's and girl's rights. The rights of the butch lesbian, the masculine lesbian or the non-binary lesbian are thwarted for the sake of fears around a few documented crimes. All these gender critical arguments are premised on some selective early 1970s radical feminist teachings, in that medical establishments and their norm entrepreneurs (whether sexed/gendered male or female) gaze over people's bodies and have the professional right awarded to them via their scientific credentials to help produce how that body is seen and connected into society. Broadly, the argument is that all men are potential rapists, which of course is prejudiced thought. They then in turn try to (re)write this representation into contemporary medico-legal policies.

Many feminists, such as Longino and Doell (1983) and others (Martin, 2002; Saini, 2018), have shown how androcentric bias is written into scientific work about sex/gender differences, and how this language works to produce its object of observation rather than discovering, in this case, the biological body. Gender critical feminists ignore the productive nature of science and tend to rely on the sexed assignment of a person (by a physician). From there, assumptions are made about the physiological and biologically determined sex/gender differences, and such feminists feel that this is the only sufficient justification for claiming womanhood and the rights of women and girls. The slogan 'adult human female' that has recently been passed around on Twitter between connected gender critical feminists is meant to convey that to be a woman one must have the potential for carrying a fetus. As such, a difference of interpretation over sex and gender has opened up old fights and created new ones (rather than debates) in feminist circles. The fights are loosely between those who believe that 'biological sex' is immutable and those who believe that transitioning to align a sense of self with a legally binding marker of identity, male or female, is possible. The former suggest that trans, sex/gender expansive and intersex people's rights to determine who they want to become and where they want to go (in relation to sex-segregated spaces) appears to be erasing the hard-won rights of women, so much so that they feel that the legal framework surrounding trans, sex/gender expansive and intersex rights has surpassed the right of women to meet and talk about their own sex-based rights. The real, for these gender critical feminists, is the sex assigned at birth, based on bodily morphology and the later treatment of these bodies in society. It is in situations where questions of access to sex-segregated spaces and sex-based rights arise that identity-based and biology-based determinations ideologically collide (Westbrook and Schilt, 2014).

There are splits, of course, in feminist circles, about who has the right to determine sex/gender and how the intersections of sex/gender desire can either provide a feminist politics that centres on using the category of women while being inclusive of trans, sex/gender expansive, intersex and cis. This approach encompasses all those who experience oppression as women, and in which self-determination is at the sole discretion of that sister. Feminists such as Braidotti (1994, 2002), Colebrook (2015) and Grosz (1994, 2005, 2011) have developed a model for thinking through the experience of sex/gender, without at the same time reifying binary differences. By developing a critique, and helping us look at the ways that sex/gender merge and collide with, for example medico-legal and bioethical policy, and by accommodating difference, they demonstrate how a nomadic ethics is able to produce the affect for self-determination. They also allow for the reconfiguring of multiple bodies and subjects. These theorists interrupt the preservation of essential sexual categories (Duff, 2014) and clear the way for a nomadic ethics of becoming that retains an ontology of difference in their attempts to destabilize sex/gender.

From biologism to feminism to new materialism

While it cannot be denied that being born into patriarchal societies has profound effects on economic, social and sexual lives, and often social status is connected to the biopolitical organization of life itself, the outcomes are not as straightforward or as linear as Jeffreys or the gender critical feminists believe. For instance, intersectionality theory (Crenshaw, 1989, 1991; Davy, 2011a; Hines, 2010; Monro and Richardson, 2011; Meyer, 2012) has shown that sex/gender produces different intensities in relation to 'race', ethnicity, class, sexuality, social value and status, and geography other than genital morphology. To posit behavioural outcomes based purely on genital morphology and socialization is therefore naïve and in contradistinction to the claim that gender is socially constructed and sex is real. Sex/gender is produced in intersubjective relationships through the life course, with measured, appraised and then hierarchized norms being produced in society.

Medically, intersex people are often viewed as biological anomalies.[8] Their bodies, morphologically, chromosomally and intersexually, are described as 'disguising' a 'true sex' underneath *vis-à-vis* medico-legal policies and social norms. However, intersex bodies are possibly the most obvious ones that we can witness that productively flee, elude, flow, leak and disappear from the performative binary registers[9] that much of the world upholds by defining sex – male and female – within legal statutes, medical protocols and policy domains, and within other important documents that categorize people's sexes/genders. These excesses to the norm, however, are continually constrained – and sometimes restrained – in relation to the particular and problematic categorical accounting of sex/gender. It is here, at this intersection, that refusing a distinction between sex and gender has been very productive.

I will appeal for an understanding about sex/gender following what Deleuze and Guattari call a 'multiplicity of molecular combinations bringing into play not only the man in the woman and the woman in the man, but the relation to [...] a thousand tiny sexes' (cited in Linstead and Pullen, 2006: 1301). Sex dimorphic assumptions upon which sex/gender is based, problematically leave many theoretical arguments going around in circles. Research on binary sex/gender differences has too often hesitated on the difficult questions of how and where these sex differences manifest, or the largely obstinate question (in humans) of the source of such differences. It is no small task to ascertain where sex/gender differences come from by looking purely at the biological, molecular body, for with humans controlled experiments are and always have been impossible, and thus any conclusions can only ever rely on quasi-experiments with deductive ontological assumptions about dimorphic sex/gender, which are easily contestable through a methodological or social critique. Nonetheless, the pervasiveness of these 'biological' arguments surrounding sex/gender differences continue and are often buttressed by what Jackson and Rees (2007: 918) call a particularly western understanding of sociality. They state:

> Evolutionary psychology is the most pervasive of these new naturalistic theories and the broadest in scope. Here gender and sexuality are not only presented as natural facts, given by our evolutionary heritage, but they occupy centre stage as the motor of evolution and the basis of all human conduct. The entirety of human social life is made reducible to the heterosexual, reproductive imperative: the drive to pass on our genes to the next generation. A corollary of this privileging of heterosexual reproduction is that competition – for mates and offspring – is envisaged as the foundation of human social relations.

The 'biological fact' of 'differences' between the sexes is only a 'fact' of any interest because of the social, medical and legal importance attached to it (Chau and Herring, 2002), and that as a result privileges some people more than others – men more than women, cis sex/gender people more than trans, sex/gender expansive and intersex people, able-bodied people more than people with disabilities, white people more than black and brown people, reproducing people over non-reproducing people and so on. Jackson and Scott (2001) argue that binary sex differentiation is just as much a cultural practice as gender differentiation and, thus, just as socially constructed as the production of gender roles, expressions and 'differences.' Sex/gender differentiation tends to support the myth that sex/gender roles and expressions are somehow appropriate for one sex/gender and not for the 'other'. Anne

Fausto-Sterling (2000), Elizabeth Grosz (1994) and Donna Haraway (1991: 149) have all shown how 'nature and culture are reworked', co-constructed and co-emerge, and, as Fujimura (2006: 49) argues, produced within a shared terrain where:

> many differences emerge both within and between [the methodological/scientific and the social literatures] on the questions of how to theorize the social in the scientific and about the scientific in the social, and how to create a language that does not separate science from society.

We are all born into a world in which we are affected by and embody scientific and social features that become what Merleau-Ponty (2002) calls 'habits'. However, habits have no essence and morph over time, like Wittgenstein's 'family resemblances'. People who share a particular language game engage in repetitive usages, although imperfectly. As such, the arbitrariness of, in our case biological science, that purports to describe 'natural' and 'neutral' terms such as 'male', 'female', 'femininity', 'masculinity' and so on, is evident since, as Anna Marie Smith (1998: 161) notes, these terms: 'only have that appearance thanks to the concealed effects of power. If it appears that only one form of "femininity," "masculinity", "marriage" or "the family" is "natural", then what we are dealing with is concealed power'. Any explanation that suggests an invariant core and ideas about inherent behaviours is already 'pregnant' with social meaning and conceals the molecular connection between the person and their world.

A binary formation of sex/gender has for many years been problematized at a societal level. For instance, in a number of cultures – in Samoa, India, Pakistan, Bangladesh, the US, Albania, Papua New Guinea and Nigeria, for instance (Croall et al, 1999; Pettan, 2003; Nwoko, 2012; Hossain, 2017, 2018) – de jure states and cultures have a much more complex relationship to sex/gender assignments than is the case with the two-sex/gender system in the west. Usually western scholars, commenting on non-western acknowledgement of sex/gender diversity, have tended problematically to define those non-binary sexes/genders that do not fit into a binary configuration (Eckert, 2010, 2017), as a 'third' (Herdt, 1993) and sometimes a 'fourth' sex/gender (Lang, 1998) to house the diversity of human bodies, expressions and roles.

Cultural and legal acknowledgement that sex/gender cannot be divided into binary configurations, has been documented by many anthropologists across the world (Murray and Roscoe, 1998;

Blackwood and Wieringa, 1999; Croall et al, 1999; Mahalingam, 2003; Nwoko, 2012), but is too vast an area of research to explore in more depth here. Nonetheless, essentialists can be critiqued for insisting on the presence of male and female species classification because the singularities within each continuously disrupt such classification (Dillon and Lobo-Guerrero, 2009: 4). Suffice to say that the conflation of bodily morphology and the cultural practice of binary sex/gender assignment as a classificatory system is culturally bound and, because culture shifts and unfolds, warrants a less essentialist and more materialist understanding of sex/gender assignment. While I am not advocating that we define genders/sexes into a 'thousand tiny sexes', because this too would be unnecessary, I am suggesting that body morphologies provide us little by way of understanding the emergent capacities of all bodies because they are restricted by being binarized and then triaged – assorted according to their 'quality' – into arbitrary representations. These binarized and triaged bodies need to be understood through the ephemeral molar/molecular systems that they are momentarily situated in to know them as fully as we can. Bodies are not static but emerging entities (Deleuze, 2004).

Nonetheless, the present and future is not all negative. We can juxtapose the legal, medical, and pedagogical policies regarding sex/gender differentiation in some parts of the world that have been challenged and then developed to incorporate, to a degree, the 'messiness' and movement of sex/gender, to observe the reconfigurations and what they mean for our understanding of sex/gender more generally and sex/gender self-determination on a practical policy level.

The fact that sex/gender socialization can affect and sometimes obstruct our ability to express ourselves in multiple ways should be enough to raise the question: does the practice of sex/gender assignment alongside sexed/gendered socialization require rethinking in relation to the multiple possibilities and thousands of sexes that are produced in the many societies worldwide? What does sex/gender determination do and what purpose does it serve? If it is true that we can all 'self-determine' our sex/gender, then sex/gender assignment at birth is unreliable as a social technology. Absolute dimorphism, according to Blackless et al (2000), is a Platonic ideal that medical and psychological science has incorporated to secure a single developmental pathway for 'two sexes'. This two-sex model is used to generate data for producing baseline indicators of 'normality' and to infer what is pathological. However, it is clear from numerous studies of common diseases that there is substantial heterogeneity in, for example, survival among 'singular-sex' patients, and it has continuously proven difficult to predict survival time based on the 'healthy' and 'pathological' indicators used. While these data ranges are the 'best' we have based on binary 'sex/gender differences' at the moment, there is a movement in medicine towards more personalized medicine that is attempting to improve biomolecular screening and increase the plethora of biomarkers with better characterized implications. Surely, in relation to patients (as singularities) then, it ought only be the materiality of body parts and their functioning that needs to be explored for the most beneficial diagnostic results and prognoses for more predictable health outcomes. All this renders the assignment of sex/gender at birth relatively arbitrary. The first glance at the aesthetic surface of the body can tell the attending doctor nothing about the internal materiality of the molecular body. As Karina Karkazis (2019: 1899) notes in the *Lancet*:

> If we are concerned with certain cancers, for example, knowing whether someone has a prostate or ovaries is what's important, not their 'sex' per se. If reproduction is the interest, what matters is whether one produces sperm or eggs, whether one has a uterus, a vaginal opening, and so on. For those arenas where it's not clear what purpose sex designation serves, we might question whether we need it at all. Doing so could lead to better science and health care, and, crucially, less harm.

Similarly, Bettcher suggests that while there are material biological truths, 'such truths can be expressed without the notion of sex' (cited in Freeman and Ayala López, 2018: 243). Moreover, the use of female or male as distinct categories will inevitably overlook the complexity and variety of material bodies, which runs the very real danger of causing more harms, increasing poor health care, oversimplifying assessments and over-pathologizing through sexist stereotypes.

Foucault (2003), in *The birth of the clinic*, showed us the ways that physicians started to explore beneath the surface of the skin, at the molecular level, and how they began to address the question of why some people developed some diseases, conditions and illness and others developed different ones. To understand this analysis in more detail consider Birke and Best's (1980: 98) argument that we are trained to believe in the fallacious idea of the constant sex/gender differentiated 'human male' and the imbalanced 'human female'. They show us that:

> [t]here are many changes in the body's functions, as well as in the behavior that occur during the [menstrual] cycle.

Brain waves (as measured by the electroencephalogram) are affected by the cycle, so that epileptic fits are least likely between ovulation and premenstruum, and most likely just before a period. Various other functions change, such as carbohydrate metabolism (the rate at which sugars are used by the body), thyroid function, mineral and water balance, resting temperature, and sensitivity to smells.

Birke and Best are not arguing that metabolism and thyroid functioning are the same for everyone who menstruates, but suggesting that bodily processes affect multiple aspects of the body in more complex ways. They suggest that there are multiple metabolic and what I will call bioemergent functions being produced that are internal but not essentially manifested. They emerge in ways that, according to some biologists, have gone beyond (sexual) organs at birth (Freeman and Ayala López, 2018). Similarly, new materialism has moved us towards an understanding of the material body as a complex open system subject to emergent properties (Hird, 2004). It is not the sex/gender assignment that is important but the forces and impact of bodily material processes.[10] As such, the surface of a body tells us nothing of these molecular processes nor would looking at the surface of trans, sex/gender expansive, or intersex people's bodies be able to tell us anything.[11]

Moreover, sex/gender assignments will not be able to tell us about their rates of metabolism, or functions or other material factors impacting behaviours, thoughts and desires. This is, for example, because hormones:

> that are concerned with sexual phenomena are also qualitatively the same in both sexes. They are produced and released by the following scheme: the pineal gland, which regulates the hypothalamus; the hypothalamus secretes hormones that regulate the rate of pituitary hormone secretion; the anterior lobe of the pituitary gland secretes hormones that control the gonads and mammary glands; the gonads in turn secrete sex hormones in response to stimulation by pituitary hormones called gonadotropins; the adrenal cortex or cortices secrete sex hormones in response to stimulation by another of the pituitary hormones, ACTH or the adrenocorticotropic hormones. (Briscoe, 1978: 33)

These do not manifest in the same way in all cis people, all trans people, all sex/gender expansive people or all intersex people.

Within second-wave feminist approaches to biology, accounts are overflowing with biological processes (Ahmed, 2008). Now, while we can assume that women (or men, sex/gender expansive and intersex people) who are menstruating may function biologically in similar ways to each other, and that we may discern this from observing the body, we cannot assume that the measurements, the risks or the functioning of each component part of a woman's (man's, trans, sex/gender expansive or intersex person's) body will be the same in each aggregated category. To suggest that they function in the same way as each other, that is, to have a truth, will be useless in trying to understand any of the diverse biological contributors to what constitutes health or illness. The affective intensities of multiple processes will manifest differently. This will only be able to be understood in a particular way, for instance by modern health technologies measuring different biological effects of bodies as singularities which attempt to understand the (internal) workings of the healthy, dis-eased and ill body (Webster, 2007). Webster (2007) suggests that the technologies have indeed shifted the way physicians (and other healthcare professionals) are trained. They no longer only rely on the physical bodies but learn to read the data that are produced through numerous types of technologies (non-human bodies). These data are then deployed beyond the body to understand the possible outcomes, prognoses and whether the person is 'ill' or 'stable'. However, because the materiality of desire – remembering that a Deleuzian desire needs to be understood in terms of anything's immanent capabilities or power – is unruly and induces intensities of attachment beyond these machines, they are outside of this calculation. It makes no sense then to suggest the assignment of birth sex makes you into anything other than a potential representation, rather than a configuration, of a material body that may or may not be able to be constrained within the parameters of that designation (Fausto-Sterling, 2000; Freeman and Ayala López, 2018). This is probably most starkly observed in the sex assignment of intersex people, when (social and scientific) technologies are deployed (in part) to determine the 'nearest' or 'best' option for sex/gender assignment.

I have previously demonstrated (Davy, 2011b) that the 'best' option model was developed, and its utilization was made more popular, by John Money and the paediatric endocrine group at Johns Hopkins hospital in the US. This group of sexologists, endocrinologists and surgeons in the 1950s started to assign children born with ambiguous genitals an 'Optimal Gender' as noted earlier. Money et al (1955) argued that newborns with an intersex condition (known then as hermaphroditism and pseudo-hermaphroditism) are psychosexually neutral and could be raised as a particular sex/gender, following (surgical, hormonal and cultural) interventions, without any problems. Parents were also often told not to disclose to the child that they were born with genital ambiguity or about the interventions that they may have received.[12] Rather than allowing the child to grow up and decide for themselves, physicians and parents acted by proxy in the determination of the child's sex/gender for social and legal reasons.

I have just suggested that in contemporary policy, academic and lay literature much is drawn both implicitly and explicitly from biological and legal fields to offer the proffered accounts of 'sex' an air of truth, and that 'gender' is often conflated with sex and vice versa depending on the truth effect that is required. Nonetheless, there have been policy movements across the world in which a broader understanding of sex/gender self-determination is being produced as a viable way to be recognized as a 'citizen'. In the UK, however, there has been a recent stumbling block. In 2020, the Conservative government considered (and subsequently rejected) new ways for citizens to self-determine their sex/genders within the binary system and beyond it.[13] A review, organized by the Gender Equality Office started in 2017, called for evidence on how best to update the Gender Recognition Act 2004 to make registration of a self-declared sex/gender status easier, and for commentaries about inclusion of sex/gender expansive people. However, Liz Truss the Minister for Women and Equalities, on 22 April 2020, addressing the Women and Equalities Select Committee, argued that any amendments should prioritize the protection of single-sex spaces, ensure that 'proper checks and balances' are in place and that children will be 'protected' from making decisions about medical interventions that they may later regret. Sex assignment at birth is given more weight as an anchor upon which gender is overlaid and rendered as a choice. Here, gender choices are understood to be potentially regrettable, and it is asserted that people may want to return to the original 'correctly' assigned sex. This speech undermines an autonomous self-determination approach, implying, as Pearce et al (2020) suggest, a continuation of some form of gatekeeping, with checks and balances to avert these potential regrets. However, Truss's declaration raises serious concerns, not only for young trans, sex/gender expansive and intersex people, but for all young people being able to access medical care in light of these proposals. For instance, some young people may be denied emergency contraception, on the grounds that they may regret not going through with a potential pregnancy, or an abortion.

To summarize, due to all the issues highlighted in this section, I will be reconfiguring sex and gender to sex/gender, so that I too do not fall into the same quagmire of separating sex and gender within binary semiotic, social and material systems. I will bind them together within several assemblages and on several planes of immanence throughout the book. I will now turn to the more than human notion of sex/gender.

Sex/gender self-determination in neoliberal times

Foucault (1994a) delivered his influential study of governmentality in a lecture at the Collège de France and published it in 1978. In it he argued that from the 16th to the 18th century in the west, issues were raised by commentators about 'how to be ruled, how strictly, by whom, to what end, by what methods' (Foucault, 1994a: 222), resulting in a departure from decisive sovereign power and disciplinary regimes, and an increase in governmental administrations at home and within the colonies. The questioning of sovereign power emanated from the developing philosophies of liberalism and liberal democracy, and was eventually fought out in several revolutions in the 19th century (Laclau and Mouffe, 1985). Numerous texts, according to Foucault (1986), develop ideas around the population, political economy and security through emergent complex knowledges [*savoirs*]. Knowledges underpinning these three key aspects – population, political economy and security – were the sciences, statistics, demography, legal contracts, including birth registrations and so on. They are constituted in what Dillon and Lobo-Guerrero (2009: 9) call 'a complex cultural and epistemic apparatus'. These knowledges all started to intersect at various points to support the de jure state apparatuses and governing parties to develop the effect of a social contract. The appreciation of the social contract between the de jure state and the population is ensured by people acknowledging and working towards the political principles of consumption, profitability, efficiency and social order in connection with their own and others' value and utility (Foucault, 1986). These knowledges also encourage the population to look inwards at the relationship they will develop between themselves and their social contract. The de jure state in return would facilitate a range of techniques and capacities to help citizens achieve the social contract and particularly contribute to the interconnected socioeconomic and legal systems. The social contract encouraged by the de jure state supports the development of social taxonomies through the production of 'truths' so that the population can 'police' their own social standing. Foucault (1986: 266) succinctly states: 'A normalizing society is the historical outcome of a technology of power centered on life.' As such, the techniques of neoliberal forms of government focus on what Foucault (1990) sees as developing 'technologies of the self', where governance mechanisms are in place to give the impression of freedom to work on one's sense of self as a citizen subject. Citizens are encouraged to forge a symmetry between the governance of population, political economy and security that de jure states aspire to. Everyone is encouraged to appreciate these governmental processes and norms as rational tactics of life. However, Dillon and Lobo-Guerrero (2009: 9) also note that these complex cultural and epistemic apparatuses also retain a profoundly ambiguous status; on the one hand they are autonomous founts of knowledge, and on the other they are fields that can be transformed through active intervention informed by knowledge of how it all operates.

Rose (1990a: 10) suggests that, through the choices people make 'about family life, work leisure, lifestyle and personality and its expression' through which the subject's life emerges, and through their own self-determination and volition, people *feel* that they are indeed controlling their own destiny rather than being coerced by the de jure state. Health is similarly conceived, shifting from a problem of illness and dysfunction towards a dynamic and political process of optimization (Rose, 2001). Optimization is the appeal from the epistemic apparatus, urging the modern individual to maximize their 'biological destiny' (Rose, 2001: 17). New developments in biotechnological advances are being produced to 'optimize' the cellular aspects of bodies, and as a result the emphasis now is arguably less focused on macro processes of biopower – although still connected – and moving more towards the molecular processes in order to enhance and thus extract the surplus biovalue of bodies (Waldby, 2002). Biovalue, according to Waldby (2002: 308): 'refers to the yield of vitality produced by the biotechnical reformulation of living processes. Biotechnology tries to gain traction in living processes, to induce them to increase or change their productivity along specified lines, intensify their self-reproducing and self-maintaining capacities.' These biotechnologies are engineered in the laboratory and are, as Rabinow argues, an: 'exploitable reservoir of molecular and biochemical products and events' (cited in Waldby, 2002: 308) that we as humans are meant to access. When people do not have the same capacity to choose enhancing products *vis-à-vis* others in the population this is often understood to be a result of wrong decisions made by the individual, a lack of educational attainment and/or them being part of the 'dependency culture' created by the welfare state. This, Monica Greco (2004) asserts, certainly invites normative judgements regarding the character of the ideal (healthy) body and normativizes the goals, values and practices with which such a body must concur.

Dillon and Lobo-Guerrero (2009: 10) argue that: 'Such governing through contingency is increasingly also governing through emergency, since the complex adaptive emergence of the contemporary understanding of what it is to be a living thing is the emergency of its continuous emergence.' Dillon and Lobo-Guerrero are using the concept of emergency to both understand the state of things that unexpectedly arise and demand urgent or immediate action, and the delivering of a thing from concealment or confinement. State governing through contingency necessarily operates through insecurity, in which the biopolitical powers of transactional freedoms of a people are continuously evolving with the powers of (self-)surveillance. There is a similar theme of social emergence in the work of du Guy (1996) and Burchell (1996), who both situate subjects in relation to enterprise in neoliberal systems, where people are required to have a commitment to become self-fulfilled contributors and accomplish their social contract within their society. To self-determine ourselves, then, is to make the 'correct' (or 'incorrect') choices arising from our deference to expertise, education, law, science and other policy domains, and by working on biovalued emerging self.

Biopolitics, bioethics and policy

According to Foucault (1986), the right to kill or let live gave way to more lateral forms of power. Foucault argued that this development can be clearly witnessed in archival records in which the body started to be conceived through its capabilities, utility and value within economic (capitalist) systems, all safeguarded by the so-called knowledges surrounding it, which he termed the 'anatamo-politics of the human body' (Foucault, 1986: 262). Foucault (1986: 262) notes that: 'this bipolar technology – anatomic and biological, individualizing and specifying were all directed toward the performances of the body, with attention to the processes of life [and] characterized a power whose highest function was perhaps no longer to kill, but to invest life through and through'. All this was attempted by administrating bodies. Dillon and Lobo-Guerrero (2009: 8) describe the administration as: 'when the discourse of species "life" becomes the referent object of politics, and politics becomes equated with the rule of species-being'. Rose (1999: 48) too suggests that the effectiveness of neoliberal rule lies in the administration's ability to align the 'objective of authorities wishing to govern and the personal projects of those organizations, groups and individuals who are the subjects of government'. Rose is suggesting that alignments need to be fostered by which the promotion of enterprise in all its formulations – in work, family, health, leisure and so on – is functioning for the benefit of the political economy, the health and security of the population, unimpeded, as much as possible, by conflict and anomie. Anomie is characterized by normlessness (Durkheim, 1951). Durkheim (1951) suggests that those who have not been sufficiently incorporated into society's norms are more likely to die by suicide. Considering the polity's anxiety about the public not promoting and contributing to neoliberal capitalist ideals, Foucault (1986) suggests that suicide is perhaps the most powerful act against the administration of the body. Perhaps this is why the practice of suicide has long been a social and religious taboo and, until relatively recently, illegal in many countries.[14]

We often draw boundaries around what constitutes good/ bad, worthy/unworthy, intelligible/unintelligible life (and death), particularly when somebody alters their bodies in some way. Dieting to lose 30 pounds and stomach stapling for some fat people are often regarded as good ways of restoring a 'normal' or 'natural state' of wholeness. Moreover, those clinicians wanting to reshape intersex infants' genitals and those patients wanting chest reduction or gonad removal in light of potential health problems or disease, respectively, are worthy, whereas those wanting to remove a 'healthy' limb, and trans people wishing to reshape their genitals are deemed, by many, to be in a delusional psychological state, especially in psychoanalytical and psychosexological opinion (Millot, 1990; Chiland, 2000, 2005). Others have linked the body modifications to a sexually motivated fetish (Freund and Blanchard, 1993; Lawrence, 2006). These pathologizing opinions start from the premise that even to consider transforming the materiality of the body there must be something pathological going on. This is in spite of the fact that the procedures are materially and technically speaking similar to others that are not deemed to be pathological, such as intersex interventions. As such, the reasons underlying the various bodily interventions are understood within different bioethical assemblages, based on historically situated and valuable bodies. It is clear, however, that in the valuing of particular family, health, and leisure practices, some people have recourse to their morphological self-determination and some do not. Those who do not are denied their autonomy, bodily integrity and self-determination (see Hughes, 2006).

An example may be useful here: endocrinologists have admin- istered what in lay terms have been called puberty blockers (gonadotropin-releasing hormone analogues [GnRHas])[15] to many cis sex/gender and intersex people, cancer patients and to children who experience 'precocious puberty' and this is deemed ethical and medically just and safe (Giordano, 2008; Houk and Lee, 2011). However, when trans adolescents request them, with the agreement of their parent(s) and the attending medical team, some commentators – media, academics and representatives from various (medical) organizations[16] – vehemently oppose them attacking these adolescents' autonomy, bodily integrity and self-determination. Those cis sex/gender and intersex children taking the same drugs or the parent(s) advocating for them do not have the same vitriol aimed at them. One main argument that is levelled against trans and sex/gender expansive children already taking or wanting to take GnRHas is the potential for them to change their minds about their sex/gender identification in the future. Another key argument against the intervention is the potential and as yet unknown risks to their fertility and brain development. While it is widely accepted, as Rose (2005) has suggested, that mental health legislation, psychiatric and, I would add, general medicine is dominated by risk-thinking that produces a context of checks and balances, it seems strange to 'worry' more about the fertilities and potential changes in neurodevelopment of one group of children than of another such group. This suggests that the concern is not about the dangers of the drugs themselves but something else entirely.

The challengers reject the belief that trans and sex/gender expansive adolescents can understand the consequences of ingesting the drugs and, as a result, cannot provide fully informed consent. Moreover, the critics suggest that the parents are (ignorantly) pushing their children down a wrong route. This denies any validity to either the child's self-determination or the proxy determination of the parent(s), and whether they ought to be the co-causal agents in these life choices when it comes to sex/gender transitions. The opponents, in effect, would like to see a tiered system of healthcare provision, in which the negotiations between physicians and patients are restricted for some children but not for others. What we can deduce from this is that some biopolitical arguments, at least from the critics highlighted, prize personal responsibility through autonomy, bodily integrity and self-determination for some sexed/gendered bodies while denying it to others.

The boundary between more and less valuable lives, which impact people's self-determination, has been a key motif through time. Foucault demonstrates that in Greek antiquity a good life was one of moral imperatives. These moral boundaries are now often supplemented with some (pseudo?) scientific knowledge. With each passing decade, new scientific discoveries and technological developments, such as DNA profiling, NMRI scans, medical testing and reformed classifications in the medical and psychiatric manuals, such as the *Diagnostic and statistical manual of psychiatric disorders* and *International classification of diseases* (*ICD*) are incorporated into debates, and increasingly utilized and deliberated on both globally and locally, which enables people to (re)formulate and craft justifications for or oppositions to, and to approve or disapprove of legal, medical and lay organizing of self-determined, sexed/gendered, liveable lives through the lens of bodily integrity and autonomy.

Autonomy

The concept of an autonomous liveable life helps us to start to think about how to question the production of biopolitical and bioethical lives of sexed/gendered humans *vis-à-vis* other bodies (both human and non-human), and the importance of social recognition, which paradoxically is at the heart of self-determining life (Butler, 2004a; 2015). Implicated in any reformulations is a person's autonomy in choosing what happens to their body. However, there are multiple supportive and opposing forces entwined. On the one hand there are technologies of an individual's desire and on the other hand technologies of 'experts', non-experts and de jure state functionaries, all vying for the power of positioning representations of the living individual, and groups or 'types' of people. According to Dillon and Lobo-Guerrero (2009: 10), autonomous 'freedom is an artefact of liberal regimes of power, it has ineluctably also become linked in biopolitics to the prevailing cultural and scientific expression of what it is to be a living thing'. They suggest that it is in these assemblages that mingle on multiple planes that we can begin think through what happens to regimes of governance as well as the discursive and material affectivities of human autonomy and desire. As such, I will be exploring autonomous self-determination in more depth throughout the rest of the book on varying planes of immanence, and how it is connected to bodily integrity and self-determination.

Bodily integrity

Bodily integrity can mean several things. First, bodily integrity can mean the inviolability of the physical body. This conceptualization emphasizes the importance of someone's personal autonomy and self-determination. People are no longer limited to the domain of reproduction and subordination to work, but increasingly have individual bodily integrity with some recourse through political organization (Hardt and Negri, 2000). An intrusive act against a person is a violation of their bodily integrity and is now generally understood as an unethical infringement, and in some instances can be criminal. In this case, the body is depicted as having an inherent integrity that can be marred by someone or some policy. The person may or may not have the means to rectify the wrongdoing against their bodily integrity and thus relies on having well-regulated liberties, which in turn rest on complex national and international infrastructures that may support the resilience required by those living such infringed lives (Dillon and Lobo-Guerrero, 2009).

As we have seen, the desire to modify the body is biopolitical and is particularly related to bodily integrity debates. This is the case when the body is deemed by some to be 'marred' though there is no 'viable' reason to modify it (Schramme, 2008). Of course, this argument requires knowing what constitutes being marred, and thus must be situated in a transcendental morality framework. What transcendental morality theories do, according to Deleuze (2004), is stop the human (body) deploying its capacities. In his reading of Deleuze, Daniel Smith (2007: 67) suggests that 'the fundamental question of ethics is not "What must I do?" (which is a question of morality) but rather "What can I do, what am I capable of doing?" (which is the proper question of ethics without morality) [...] How can I go to the limit of what I can do?' For Deleuze, then, moralistic transcendentalism actually prevents ethics from taking place. The desires of supranational institutions, nation states, social movements and individuals about self-determined body modification are feeding into notions of bodily integrity and autonomy in some areas of social life. In many European societies, bodily integrity, underpinned by autonomous self-determination, requires rights-based support to transform healthcare based on informed consent (Kapp, 2007) and the capability approach in educational contexts (Walker and Unterhalter, 2007). These approaches are the main ways that will help to provide more neutral grounds upon which choices and provision of self-determined medical interventions (Schramme, 2008) and educational services can take place (Wehmeyer et al, 2003; Wehmeyer, 2014).

Alongside this molecular approach, the Lisbon Treaty has made respecting human rights – incorporating bodily integrity, autonomy and self-determination – a core set of values and objectives for all European Union (EU) actions and policies. In recent decades, these values and objectives have supported social and cultural transformations surrounding bioethics, bio-law and human principles in relation to biomedical developments (Muller, 1994; Whittle, 1999, 2002; Rendtorff and Kemp, 2000; Rendtorff, 2002; Shildrick, 2004; Halpern, 2005; Schramme, 2008; Waites, 2009; Gordon, 2012; Ivanović et al, 2013). Although there have been significant changes to the possibilities of autonomy, bodily integrity and sex/gender self-determination, there are also many evolving obstacles. These forces have impacted the norms and values around biological and biopolitical interventions and have evolved, in some cases, to factor in personal, interpersonal and interdependent understandings about bodily integrity. These extend human rights frameworks beyond the humanistic to a recognition of the co-productivity of patients' and clinicians', and teachers' and students' choices in clinical and pedagogical service provision respectively.

First, in medicine, the literature on the ethics of the body (Shildrick and Mykitiuk, 2005) inevitably has highlighted some key concerns in relation to sex/gender. It offers significant analytical insights into the complexity of rights-based claims of the patient and, to a lesser degree, the medical practitioner, the activist and the lawyer. According to Shildrick (2005), analyses of the ethics of the body tend to be fixed within normative templates that often assume people in varying bioethical and medico-legal relationships have relatively stable standards of judgement, underpinned by a determinable calculus of harms and benefits made by the rational and impartial professional. This hinders the human (body) from deploying its full capacities. Shildrick develops this area of work by including a Deleuzian and Merleau-Pontian approach to bodily integrity. Following many challenges about who gets to decide what and when treatment is appropriate, the medical relationship generates forces more in favour of the patient when the legitimacy of intervention is not in question. However, medicine and, to a certain degree, wider social institutions that use authoritative medical assertions that view physical attributes as the basis of sex/gender determination and the subsequent right to something, such as citizenship rights, contain contractionary tendencies that affect the right to self-identification of one's sex/gender. Nonetheless, this is a contested area of biopower, biopolitics and bioethics where multiple actors assume that they have the right to determine another's sex/gender. This gives rise to multiple implications for the biopolitical management of populations (Rabinow and Rose, 2006) and a requirement to understand this complexity in contemporary society.

The right to choose one's sex/gender

There is no universal idea or transcendental consensus about European and national bodily integrity human rights (Rendtorff, 2002) and thus such rights have been dependent on, in our case, (emergent moral) law and medical interventions that lawyers, activists, patients and clinicians wish to claim, employ and utilize. Different actors utilize the edicts within socio-legal contexts that facilitate or constrain different bodily integrity narratives. Each country's bioethics, bio-law and medico-legal frameworks inevitably function through various cultural, medical and legal assemblages in relation to various (human and non-human) bodies, ages, sex/genders, human rights and cultural frameworks. Edicts assemble and fold into structures of power as well as co-produce bodily becomings. As such, to be able to understand how activists and lawyers merge and separate out issues surrounding bodily integrity for the patient and for the physician, and in order to pursue understanding of the 'everyday' management of bodies within medico-legal frameworks, requires a place-by-place, time-by-time analysis, which we look at in the next chapter.

Concluding remarks

In this chapter, the aim was to outline the rights-based theory of bodily integrity justice and the ethical debates taking place around sex/gender self-determination. Sex/gender assignment and its reverberations through the life-course is key to self-determination. That is, the enfolding of power within multiple assemblages that impact bodily integrity and self-determination, is territorialized through sex/gender assignment. Nonetheless, through the demands of supranational institutions, nation states, social movements and individuals, the notion of sex/gender self-determination is emerging.

2

The desire for (political) self-determination

Introduction

The concept of 'self-determination' in social work, medicine, education, human rights and political theory functions on both molecular and molar planes of immanence. The term, however, is often treated as a transcendental phenomenon unconnected to the physical matter of the human drives (desire) to become. Deleuze and Guattari (2004) understand the molecular as the micro affective intensities, which can be produced in relation to macro communities and beyond, but this is complicated with the idea that communities can also become the molecular when talking about, for example, larger bureaucratic agencies, such as government, the United Nations or the NHS, technology, the environment and so on. DeleuzoGuattarian thinking provides an ontological basis for the analysis of multiple governance networks and allows for imaginative modes of non–representative democratic governance because of its refusal to homogenize the affective intensities into binary structure/agency arguments without denying either. DeLanda (2006, 2016) proposes that social complexity connected to governance networks can be thought through assemblage theory and is a valuable basis to conceptualize the heterogeneity of key affect, affecting and being affected by humans.

Each assemblage consists of molecular and molar configurations and exists as a collection of bodies, communities, organizations, technologies and de jure states. As I have argued elsewhere (Davy, 2019), the notion of an assemblage is helpful to understand human connections and relations with other humans, animals, objects, institutions and cultural artefacts. Moreover, an assemblage does not privilege the human (body) as the site where sex/gender and sexual desire is always located. Desire is produced at the interstices beyond the human body. The assemblage disrupts the notion of a unified sex/gender. This is a different approach from that of those who suggest that the quest for self-determination often implies an isolated 'self' with aspirations for absolute freedom to interact with others (Ronen, 1979).

Even in the case of group formation in the work of Ronen (1979), for example, the 'self' is often understood as a unified monad within that group, forging a crucial alliance to produce new communities that will strive against perceived oppressions created by the de jure state. Ronen (1979: 62) argued that as a 'self,' and to satisfy our own social needs, we create our own self-determination by developing social groups to form a functional or conscious aggregation of demands to fulfil our desires *vis-à-vis* the '(nation-) state'. He suggests that the '(nation-) state' is a mere backdrop, a stage upon many stages that are affective in our quests for self-determination. I wish to offer a different 'self', by drawing on Shildrick's recent work. Shildrick (2015) agrees that we should be offering a different approach to the 'self', The 'self' for her and for me is connected and fluid, and assumes that humans consist of a hybridity of connections within assemblages that are all different, while concomitantly attending to the plasticity and unfolding meanings about sex/gender embodiment beyond the self. This approach to the 'self' enables us to look epistemologically at the points at which the connections collide.

Self-determining sex/gender is complicated by the fact that our thoughts and desires seem to be, on the one hand, part of our interiority that philosophers such as Kant and Descartes expound. Thoughts as interiority – the distinction of a thought as originally existing in itself – are quasi-sedentary insofar as one 'finds' the *cogito* within, rather than seeing it produced through a multiplicity of competing drives and connections. On the other hand, a thought's destiny, because of reason and the reasonable human, is often wedded to the de jure state (Deleuze, 2004). Individuals generally see the de jure state and its apparatus as rational and reasoned, which helps to form an identification with it while concurrently conceptualizing their own reasoned (national) identification. Deleuze and Guattari (2004: 414) argue that we often do this because we assume that: 'The more you obey, the more you will be the master, for you will only be obeying pure reason, in other words, yourself.' As a result, a continually transformed nationalism emerges, as people imagine a common rational, political and ethical citizenship within a specific nation state. The ever-transforming nationalism, with its characteristic modes of political activity, invokes the idea of a people collectively determining its own destiny.

We also look to those with reasoned arguments – that are elevated by and/or have manoeuvred themselves into the role of a functionary of the de jure state – to understand what our bodies can reasonably do in relation to other people and the de jure state apparatus. As such, we curb our desires and thoughts and allow norm entrepreneurs – the poet, the philosopher, the professor, the physician, the sociologist and so on – to operate in the role of functionaries of the de jure state, affecting our thoughts within our own echo chamber (Deleuze and Guattari, 2004). There are now, according to Deleuze and Guattari, many more 'pretenders' to the functionary roles, which produce new human and non-human bodies. In this chapter I will consider educators, scientists, physicians and psychiatrists among other lay 'norm entrepreneurs' who are all desiring to become willing functionaries of the de jure state and to whom we often look for answers.[1]

This chapter will develop an analysis about how the concept of 'self-determination' has been connected to the rational, reasonable interior self. I will suggest, though, that these connections can and should be seen through numerous assemblages that connect molar and molecular entities into other assemblages. I will also show how exteriority is 'contained' and reduced to interiority through ritualized biopolitical assemblages that can be sources of limit-situations (Freire, 2000). According to Davy and Cordoba's (2020: 350) reading of Freire's limit-situations, they are produced:

> at the interface at which a person meets micro and macro structural limits, and at which time people think and reflect on their situation, ontologically considering it, but experiencing it as limiting. Limit-situations are (consciously and unconsciously) [co-] created by people. These limit-situations support particular social structural inequalities [but] can be challenged and changed.

For example, a community can administer norms, organizations can enforce rules and de jure states can attempt to block 'self-determination,' by asserting constraints on humans and other non-human components that are part of particular assemblages. According to Butler (2015: 169) self-determination is all bound up with the future and desires that are yet to be lived through. This desire for self-determination, as a people, is a performative act. A form of political self-determination. DeLanda (2016) also suggests that communities are emergent and, in spite of the constraints, the affect emanating to and from them can provide resources to their members when it comes to political mobilization and team work through which processes of deterritorialization emerge and help detach members from habitual ideas. To focus attention exclusively on people's metaphysical vision of subjectivity, and not on the assemblage of which they are constitutive, undermines understanding of the complexity of experiences. This further fixes individuals in a solipsistic space without any logical justification to claim a remedy. Braidotti (1994) makes a similar point about us needing a philosophy of (animate and inanimate) life that does not fall into solipsistic language games that are endlessly or ritually repeated. Considering this, I will attempt to demonstrate that self-determination is a misleading way to represent issues about the sovereign-self's agency if we accede to understanding assemblages in their complexity and in their continuous movements. These continuous movements have been conceptualized by Deleuze (1988: 49) as 'affectus' which accounts for subjective modulation in particular contexts and accounts for the materiality of change: 'the passage from one state to another'. The analysis will come to a point, as many have done before, where the question is raised: if people are limited by biopolitical assemblages, administered norms, and norm entrepreneurs of the de jure state, can the affectus be called self-determination at all?

Self-determination: a legacy from revolution

Many have written about 'self-determination'. Weitz (2015: 462) argues that 'no phrase has had greater political resonance in the last one hundred years than self-determination'. Notions of the state and citizenship in swathes of political theory, derived from liberal and then socialist idealizations, from the 17th century on portrays citizens as having the right to be free from coercion. Citizens ought to be able to self-determine their future within the bounds of legal and social structures that exist to preserve their liberty[2] (Brilmayer, 1991; Gilbert, 1998; Yack, 2012).

Post-feudal nation states, however, produced the idea of self-determination at the same time as norm entrepreneurs were exerting powers over territorial spaces by developing *their* signs and laws that work towards harmonizing, indeed territorializing (Deleuze and Guattari, 2004), a people and the nation's territorial integrity. These signs and law are what Sara Ahmed (2006: 562) calls 'straightening devices', which attempt to make bodies, both human and non-human, line up or be corrected. As an example, we can describe the binary sex/gender assignment system, sex/gender normativity and heteronormativity as 'straightening devices' that link us to citizenship. Both Ronen (1979) and Sureda (1973) argued similarly about self-determination not being about forces of light prevailing over forces of darkness to free human bodies and overcome any bad faith in government and nationality, in order to develop a new world order. The term 'self-determination' is closely associated with the history of the popular sovereignty principle proclaimed by the French Revolution, for example (Ronen, 1979). Sureda (1973: 17, emphasis added) illustrated that revolutionaries decreed that 'government should be based on the will of the people, not on that of the monarch, and people not content with the government of the country to which they *belong* should be able to secede and organise themselves as they wish'. However, national and now international law does not provide a clear right of secession for an ethnic, tribal or separatist group or minority so that they may set up a new de facto and de jure state; nor are they entitled to any territorial sovereignty within any recognized sovereign state. The United Nations' attempts to uphold territorial sovereignty, and this was affirmed in 1970 by the UN Secretary General U Thant (cited in Moore, 1997: 902) who stated:

> So, as far as the question of secession of a particular section of a Member State is concerned, the United Nations' attitude is unequivocable [*sic*]. As an international organization, the United Nations has never accepted and does not accept and I do not believe it will ever accept the principle of secession of a part of its Member State.

This is despite the rhetoric surrounding people politically self-determining their lives.

The principal reason for the space between any anticipation and realization of self-determination on this molar plane of immanence is the universal propensity of governments to take decisions with a goal of preserving the nation-state as a political unity. Part of the goal of any political unity, and any claim to the right of self-determination at this molar level, warrants governments stamping out any rebellion in order to prevent secession (Connor, 1967). Also, national laws globally do not allow for unlimited dissent from de jure state authority and block the way for anarchy. A person 'enters' the de jure state as a citizen through their connection to the (capitalist) democratic polity and the territory it governs through birth or birth right, or through other means such as migration or refugee status. At these entry points, contractual relations are developed and from these an inferred consent is assumed by the polity to provide governance and act in the interests of all citizens. Self-determination in this assemblage then assumes a moral imperative of the de jure state and a general will of the people (Qvortrup, 2014).

From the late 19th century there was a rise in anti-colonial movements. Since the Second World War – supported by United

Nations' instruments – anti-colonial movements began to specifically adopt self-determination principles, which were particularly important for decolonizing within already demarcated national boundaries. For example, the United Nations' General Assembly Resolution 1514 states: 'All peoples have the right to self-determination; by virtue of that right they freely determine their political status and freely pursue their economic, social and cultural development' (United Nations General Assembly, 1960: 67). This resolution was adopted a little later (with minor grammatical changes) in the United Nations International Covenant on Civil and Political Rights 1966 (United Nations, 1966). But as Margaret Moore (1997: 902) states:

> Elaboration of the right to self-determination by a whole series of resolutions passed by sovereign states, concerned about the potentially destructive effect (for them) of this principle, makes it clear that the 'peoples' in question are not national groups [within a state], but, rather, peoples within territorial states; and it could only be invoked by people under colonial rule or people living under alien and racist regimes (Palestinians under Israeli occupation, blacks under apartheid in South Africa, respectively).

The participation of the citizen in the development of the postcolonial de jure state was the expression of the highest ideal regarding a person's freedom in state rhetoric. This meant that the territorial element of colonial predominance was lost in favour of the personal element where postcolonized people were conceived as active citizens and not mere serfs (Sureda, 1973; see also Brilmayer, 1991). Implicated in all this is a social contract between a (new) sovereign state and its citizens.

Social cont(r)act

The social contract is premised on the idea that government is consented to by the people and in return the de jure state will provide security.[3] The contract however does not allow anyone to opt out if they remain in the territory. The contract connects people to a political framework and its regulatory bodies that allows them to have some electoral influence. Agamben (1998: 5) notes that Foucault, in 'Society must be defended' (Foucault, 1994b), argues that modern western states have incorporated numerous individualizing techniques to an unprecedented degree, alongside durable and powerful juridical, medico-pathological and educational systems that produce a political double bind. Integrative and regulative operations function through the idea of self-determination but deter dissent through the double bind. The de jure state apparatus:

> performs a D [deterritorialization]; but one immediately overlaid by [different] reterritorializations on property, work, and money [...] Among regimes of signs, the *signifying regime* certainly attains a high level of D; but because it sets up a whole system of reterritorializations on the signified, and on the signifier itself, it blocks the line of flight. (Deleuze and Guattari, 2004: 560, emphasis in original)

That is, the de jure state apparatus affects and is affected by our desire through signifying regimes while moving our thoughts away from the territory and towards the fantasy of an 'interior self'. Successive governments, regardless of their political proclivities, attempt to dissuade thinkers from having exterior thoughts about self-determination. Deleuze and Guattari, (2004: 417) suggest that we are persuaded to have thoughts that appeal 'to a people instead of taking [it] for a government ministry' (Deleuze and Guattari, 2004: 417). At the same time, people are required to accept the term of office, even if they disagree with the decisions and processes that transpire from government.[4]

Self-determination is both a principle and practice. At the macro level of international relations, self-determination over the last hundred years was related to, among other areas, postcolonial state sovereignty and politics. Hannum (1996: 27) concluded that '[p]erhaps no contemporary norm of international law has been so vigorously promoted or so widely accepted as the right of all peoples to self-determination'. The declaration came at a time when post-Soviet and socialist states were all vying for self-ruling independent autonomy. However, there were obvious problems with the term prior to these developments, as the lawyer Sir Ivor Jennings (1956: 56) argued: 'On the surface it seemed reasonable: let the people decide. It was in fact ridiculous, because the people cannot decide until someone decides who are the people.' Jennings was referring to the fact that it was those politicians and policy makers 'representing' the populace who were producing statehood and coordinating 'self-determination' through biopolitical forces rather than the people self-determining themselves. This theorization infers that the populace was being affectively co-produced.

The polity retains the term 'self-determination' but alters its meaning from a source of threat into a resource for containing it. This recourse by the polity assemblage territorializes the material – capitalist – flows by linking them to trade routes, tariffs and trade laws, while supporting de jure state functionaries to guide citizens' thoughts about the good life, and by attempting to connect each of them to predetermined meanings about the good, reasoned and responsible 'self'. The polity is well aware of revolutions and contagious riots. Successive polities attempt to manage the connections we have as a community, while continuing to hope that we do not have revolutionary nomadic thoughts. Nomadic thinking is thinking at the limit of freedom and turns the nomadic thinker into a 'war machine'. This is because nomadic thoughts are on a direct collision course with the static, institutionalized thought that Deleuze and Guattari associate with, among other things, the de jure state apparatus. For Deleuze and Guattari, the de jure state apparatus marks out borders, erects boundaries, and creates spaces of interiority, sovereignty and control. In contrast, the nomadic war machine has principles of exteriority, it becomes indifferent to the boundaries laid down by the de jure state apparatus. Nomadic thinking creates movement and becoming beyond being a 'self'.

As noted earlier, the population is encouraged to curb nomadic thoughts and look inwards at the relationship it will develop with the de jure state. The power to develop this relationship can be held by any individual and can be transferred or alienated through a juridical act or an act that introduces a right. The state 'in return' develops a range of techniques and capacities to 'help' people achieve the social contract with the state, such as supporting the development of social taxonomies through the production of 'truths' so that a people can monitor their own social position, health, education and so on.

The concept of self-determination, nonetheless, travels to the connected realms of meso- and micro-politics and social demands as principles and a practices. Self-determining sex/gender is something that we all attempt to do whether we are trans, sex/gender expansive, intersex or cis sex/gender, that is, if we understand sex/gender as masculine, feminine and androgynous forms of presentation, roles and bodily aesthetics. We must recognize, however, that these characteristics are affected by a shifting sense of becoming a man/masculine, man/feminine, woman/feminine, woman/masculine or intersex and expansive forms of sex/gendered becoming(s). For example, as children we do not present or feel our sex/gender the same way as when we are older, regardless of the social positioning of one's sexed/gendered 'self'. Of course, whether we are recognized as boys, girls, men, women, expansive or intersex is partly constituted and affected by others' ontological recognition of us, and thus we are affected by the performative registers – birth certificates, laws, physician notes, passports, school registration and many other documents – relating to, among other things, our bodies, other bodies, clothing, civil status in law, medicine and policy (but not always), and the wherewithal of others' many judgements and values. Therefore, we may see ourselves in many I/Thou relationships in different fields and as someone constituted, at least in part, through our own desire and through other people's attitudes. Another set of factors, and what I will call social technologies following Foucault, such as birth certificates and the declarations of physicians that affect the self-determining of our sex/ gender may or may not be in line with how we would like to become, with appropriate pronouns and salutations for example. In short, the idea of any micro- or meso-level self-determination, relating to sex/ gender, is both personalized, intersubjective and interdependent on human and non-human bodies beyond the 'self'.

The establishment of mutual recognition of the self and of the other nonetheless engenders a shift from conceptualizing the self as isolated, self-contained and coherent, and situates sex/gender identification within a productive realm. Rather than having an inner stable core identity, which modernist sociologists such as Mead and Simmel have been accused of clinging to (see Burkitt, 1999), there needs to be an understanding that an inner self-identity has been overstated. Similarly, there is an overstated set of claims about core identities in psychology and cognitive social psychology, in which we are often told that good and normal development is when we align our core selves with pre-ordained developmental goals and other normative courses of action (Nicolson, 2014; Money, 2016). Nonetheless, some research in social psychology from the 1990s started to explore and acknowledge the multiplicity of selves 'in' the mind that can be represented *vis-à-vis* several social spaces, with each space corresponding to a distinct social structure (age, sex/gender, class, race and so on) (Nowak et al, 2000). For example, Sheldon, Williams and Joiner (2003: 11) suggest that it:

> seems that each of us is populated by a veritable society of selves with different goals and self-perceptions. These different mental self-models and patterns of executive functioning typically alternate over time in the amount of control they exert over momentary behavior. In an important sense, then, we are not necessarily the same person today as we were yesterday.

They further add that: 'from this perspective, the health- or growth-seeking self that desires medical or psychological treatment is likely to be only one of many partially autonomous selves, grappling for ascendancy within the psyche' (Sheldon et al, 2003: 11). This, I would argue, is only partly correct. In new materialism, an approach I am advocating for throughout the book, we are always in a process of becoming through affective forces (Braidotti, 2002, 2006b; Deleuze and Guattari, 2004). In recent work, the concept of the 'self' has been produced as complex, personalized, intersubjective and interdependent assemblages of ongoing, variously intensifying affects impacting, for example, the sex/gender that one is attempting to determine. However, for Deleuze and Guattari, and in much DeleuzoGuattarian influenced work, an autonomous self-identity cannot be articulated in terms of 'selfhood' in a metaphysical sense. The human body is a proactive disposition from which one, as the affected and affective agent in one's life, does not simply manifest through one's freely chosen goals. As Lahti (2020: 130) states:

> actual bodies have a limited set of traits, habits, movements and affects. However, actual bodies also have a virtual dimension: a body without organs is a process of production, through which desire spreads over and across: it is an accumulation of potential features, connections, affects, intensities and movements.

We are produced, indeed, in an ongoing way, not as fragmented multiple selves, but in a singularity produced by many intensities of human and non-human bodies. As such, 'self-identity' may be better understood as self-identification and identification with what I will call a *productive category* within a relational assemblage. For self-determination to be actualized then, other human and non-human affects are also integral to co-empower one to become in one's life. As an example, Foucault (1980a) has argued that it was agreed civilly in the Middle Ages in France that the people then named hermaphrodites (intersex people) were understood to have a mixture of two sexes/genders. In several texts analysed by Foucault, and notwithstanding the many executions and infanticides that also took place, sex designation of the intersex child was first the role of the father or godfather. These patriarchs were able to choose which one of the two sexes/genders should be legally and socially retained. Interestingly, it was when the intersex person reached sexual maturity and the time to get married that they themselves could choose their own sex/gender designation. 'Self-determination' was often based upon one's dominant sexual object choice, desire and heterosexual trajectory. Once the sex/gender was decided upon, however, and to avoid accusations of sodomy, this self-determined sexed/gendered body would have to be 'lived' until death, as too would the direction of one's desire towards non-sodomite practices. The point is, as we will see throughout the rest of the book, that 'self-determination' is co-produced among different intensive (human and non-human) forces at different junctures, and functions in leaky, nomadic ways affecting autonomy and bodily integrity.

Structure/agency

Many have argued in numerous fields, from political theory, science and technology studies to sociology, that there was a great divide between de jure state democracies and public or civil society participation in pursuit of a (democratic) social contract. In much of the literature, according to Laclau and Mouffe (1985) and Giddens (1982), this has allowed a residual essentialism to set in. In the representations of the 'state' and 'the public' there are two vying positions commonly conceptualized as structure/agency that, they argue, lacks adequate theorization. This position assumes an amplified totalitarian power working against a class-based civil society, such as in the analyses surrounding the student risings of 1968, the class wars (1970s and 1980s), and in much work in post-Marxist postmodernist theory. Theorists were trying to understand the state as a 'rational, transparent order' (Laclau and Mouffe, 1985: 2) and civil society, in this binary configuration, was trying to break down the machinery of the de jure state. Giddens (1982: 165), commenting on the field of sociology, suggests that:

> One of the most prevalent tendencies of much sociological writing in the 1960s was to suppose that the main forces of change in a society – or even in a generic type of society – were 'built in' to that society. This I would call an 'unfolding' conception of social change; it imagines that there is something like a natural evolutionary tendency contained within societies which propels them along predicted paths of development. What the stance ignores, among other things, is something Max Weber drew attention to rather forcibly many years ago: the contingent character of major processes of change.

Despite this theoretical development, newer theories of governance and the populace tend to dissolve this division between the de jure state and civil society. Feminist theorist Ruth A. Miller (2016) illustrates a nuanced argument about how biopolitics functions contingently in relation to women's sexuality, particularly in relation to abortion rights, adultery and rape in different Christian and Islamic cultures. 'Woman citizen' (Miller, 2016), a concept that is useful for us to understand, is used to represent the contingent production of women's aggregated position in civil society, which replaced that of being a possession of a man in some societies. However, this production of 'woman citizen' cannot be understood as only a women's fight against the de jure state machinery, with unified desires emerging through the nomadic thoughts of women. 'Woman citizen' produces the polity in multiple ways at many events. Similarly, the contestations from lesbian, gay, bisexual, trans, intersex and queer people, environmentalists, the peace movement, disabled people and people of colour activists who have tried and continually try to radically change the standards of living *vis-à-vis* the de jure state apparatus and 'majority' populations, cannot be situated solely within a set of dichotomous state/minority contentions. While the de jure state machinery has much to do with the plane of consistency, power and affect is dispersed through civil society, through de jure state functionaries, and through the people themselves. While the state, law, religion and de jure state functionaries continue to affect powers and develop limit-situations, restricting women, men, lesbian, gay, bisexual, trans, intersex and queer people, environmentalists, disabled people and people of colour, for example, through the threat of death, unfolding and often unknowable contingent events have got us to where we are now. This was not a pre-empted road; it is what it is and where it is precisely because of contingent factors. Nonetheless, one of the contingent factors that is required is that an individual needs to be 'known', to exist in public, political and autonomous spaces in order for legal, political and social contracts to be remade and new interactions pursued. When the de jure state, democratic participation and the public are reduced to specific entities and represented by others as having pre-given unchanging characteristics, however, the 'autonomous' individual is reduced to a simulacrum.

The simulacrum reduces the power that somebody can hold. While many philosophers and social scientists have used the categories 'woman', 'man', 'person of colour', 'working class' to refer to a collective of subjects, the links between each person in each category are not necessarily an a priori, nor are they essential to their particular participation with the de jure state's social contract, nor do they predefine their connections with it (Mouffe, 1992). Evaluation-focused work that has explored capitalist democratic practice and participation tends to import predefined, homogenized and fixed categories into evaluations of past, and in the design of future democratic participatory practices through, for example, epidemiology in healthcare, which can only really take hold of some aspects and not others.

Other examples of a simulacrum have come from feminists, such as Pateman (1970), who offered a very early insight into patriarchal, political relations and suggests that patriarchy has declared the political subject in the image of what men are capable of at the expense and devaluation of the particularities that women have to offer, namely carrying children and motherhood. This capacity of women and their contribution to the nation state, she suggests, ought to have equal political weight as the willingness of men to sacrifice themselves at war for their country. This position has been easy to dismiss in many ways and, in particular, on the grounds of binary sex differentiation – the 'men' and 'women' in each one of the binary differentiations function through the same homogenized masculine or feminine principles/values/desires as each other respectively – it is a position that would be impossible to sustain in relation to a meaningful set of value characteristics that would do justice to all women, men and others.

One objection to this form of de jure state-feminist agenda and political participation was developed by Mouffe (1992) on the foundations of what she refers to as a 'radical democratic' citizenship. Mouffe challenges Pateman's thesis because it cannot develop into exercising one's citizenship within the ethico-political principles of modern capitalist democracy, through which we can observe many forms of citizenship while emphasizing numerous social relations in which domination of particular groups exists. To put this another way, if feminists are committed to ideals of sex/gender freedom, all ought to be able to pursue claims to living free from the constraints of dominating sexed/gendered positions, while pursuing self-determination. It is this domination that must be challenged, rather than attempting to arbitrarily strengthen a particular group's assumed characteristics within an already developed system. Foregrounding the characteristics of a class of people would only elevate some 'good' women, 'good' black people or 'good' working-class people and so on over others. The only way to democratic life is through a revolution, as a 'subversive force that can be spread throughout the social in the form of an infinite series of contingent recitations' (Smith, 1998: 5), and the recognition of differences. As one trans woman Tweeter eloquently states:

'Someone accused me today of trying to render the word "woman" meaningless. But I'd suggest that woman is a term that bears too ★much★ meaning, at least as far as trying to trace its borders goes. Woman is a term that is remarkably accretionary. That is, if we imagine words as things that hurtle through time and cultural space like meteors, then woman is one that has passed through several debris fields along the way, so that it is so laden with history, importance, biology, legality and values that it is all but shapeless. And much like a meteor in motion, drawing a line around all the edges of "woman" is an impossible task. It's a term that leaves behind it a vibrant trail of meaning and value that is nevertheless hopelessly ragged at its farthest edges. We can never ★trace★ "woman," merely draw a big circle around the space it occupies and say "there it is, more or less".'[5]

Mouffe's challenge of undoing domination, she asserts, would not eliminate the group 'women' for example but democratize it. According to Mouffe (1992: 379) the role of social group collectives, such as women, would be articulated through a principle of 'democratic equivalence', rather than characteristic sameness, which:

views the common good as a 'vanishing point,' something to which we must constantly refer when we are acting as citizens, but that can never be reached. The common good functions on the one hand, as a 'social imaginary': that is, as that for which the very impossibility of achieving full representation gives to it the role of an horizon [and] a 'grammar of conduct' that coincides with the allegiance to the constitutive ethico-politico principles of modern democracy: liberty and equality for all.

Similarly, community networks have developed alongside changes in social organization. What Mouffe is referring to here is similar to Ronen's (1979: 62) assertions surrounding self-determination. People, Ronen (1979: 62) argues, activate one (or more) of their identities to achieve their aims and aspirations; however, it is not the identity that achieves the revolution but the quest, which produces the forces towards new quests for self-determination and social imaginaries and, if the assemblage collides in favourable ways, then a mini revolution is produced. This is in stark contrast to arguments provided by Simmel's (1955) theoretical framework, about how individual interest groups have taken the place of preordained religious dogma, providing more rational ideas and freedoms while, at the same time, generating more tensions and thus more precarious relations within their networks. Interest groups have always been produced alongside religious desire within assemblages. All that changes is the relative affective and affecting nature of the connections. Network boundaries are and have always been too difficult to contain (physically and conceptually), and why would we want to? Mouffe (1992) suggests that because social groups' and networks' principles are open to many competing interpretations, one must acknowledge that a fully inclusive political community can never be realized with aplomb. There will always be a 'constitutive out-side', an exterior to the community that is the very slippery and leaky condition of its existence.

Nietzsche's insight of the human as incomplete, adapting in the face of desire, which Mouffe draws on, has fuelled a comprehension nonetheless of 'potentiality' in that life is in a constant state of struggle. Similarly, Mouffe (1994: 108) suggests that we must accept that hybridity creates us as separate entities, it affirms and upholds the nomadic character of identifications. Mouffe's understanding of the nomadic character of people is close to the ideas of both Deleuze and Guattari, and Braidotti, about nomadic subjectivity. Braidotti (2006b):

> The nomad [...] stands for the relinquishing and the deconstruction of any sense of fixed identity [...] The nomadic style is about transitions and passages without predetermined destinations or lost homelands. Thus, nomadism refers to the kind of critical consciousness that resists settling into socially coded modes of thought and behaviour. It is the subversion of set conventions that defines the nomadic state, not the literal act of travelling.

There is one glaring difference, however, in that Mouffe suggests that agency is inherent in the 'self', which is the core of generating nomadic changes, whereas Deleuze and Guattari and Braidotti would suggest that potentialities emerge on planes of immanence. It is not the agency of a self as an organic monad that is the driving force, but the flows of energy that bring together material (human and non-human bodies) that enable us to imagine and create surprising new potentialities within assemblages. What these potentialities also attend to is the possibility that we can, as humans, be given value or not, by ourselves, by others and by cultural systems, establishing the value-direction of human flesh (Miller, 2016).

A critique of value

Nietzsche (1997) suggests that the will to systematize humans and non-humans through values shows a lack of integrity on the part of the evaluator of life. This is because: 'One would have to occupy a position outside life, and on the other hand to know it as well as one, as many, as all who have lived it, in order to be allowed even to touch upon the problem of the value of life' (Nietzsche, 1997: 28). It is at this nexus that all human concepts, ideas, beliefs and values that are uttered are at the expense of other possibilities. As such, life as we 'know' it is never without objective meaning, purpose, or value to us, but we have to be mindful of other possibilities.

As such, there is no 'we' without 'them': 'we' without those human and non-human bodies within an assemblage. By being acutely aware of the absurdity of a pure self-determination, the impossibility of reaching a firm representation of things and the acceptance of an unfolding nomadic existence will affirm the 'freedom' from 'self-determination' as it has been previously theorized. As mentioned in Chapter 1, the de jure state's and civil society's administration of what form of 'self-determination' should be pursued for the populace is made easier when it has the biopolitical parameters enfolded and has formed governance mechanisms that give the impression of a person's 'freedom' to work on their 'sense of self' as a 'good' citizen.

Being a 'good citizen' means to continue despite any hardship, to not give up. We can perhaps see the anxiety of successive governments of 'their' people giving up in their allusions to suicide rates. There is ample evidence from the polity to account for the fears of (economically) productive people's death by suicide producing 'depopulation anxiety' (Miller, 2016: 17), especially surrounding some 'important' groupings of people. Beauchamp and Childress's (2001) bioethical claim is nonetheless notable for its consideration of, and call for, physician-assisted suicide. There are a few nation-states across the world that allow physician-assisted suicide (assisted death).[6] For example, in the US there are five de jure states that allow assisted suicide, Oregon, Washington, Vermont, New Mexico and Montana. However, the legal frameworks dictate that physicians are not obligated to assist but are permitted to do so if certain criteria are met. These criteria are: voluntary request by a competent patient; an ongoing physician–patient relationship; mutual and informed decision making by a patient and physician; a supportive yet critical and probing environment for decision making; a considered rejection of alternatives; a structured consultation with other parties in medicine; a patient's stable expression of a preference for death;

unacceptable suffering by patient; and the use of a means of death that is as painless and comfortable as possible. Despite these 'maverick' de jure states in the US administering death by assisted suicide they do require the person desiring death to convince a physician to facilitate it. Nonetheless, the antipathy surrounding suicide is widespread, which creates limit-situations concerning the ultimate self-determination, by reterritorializing 'the value of life' through particular limitations.[7] As such, and with this in mind, I will now look at some of the de jure state biopolitical forces that affect the micro and macro planes of immanence in relation to self-determination.

Political and ethical self-determination and biopolitics

There are numerous empirically driven scholarly contributions in the area of contemporary self-determination. In particular, a number of these contributions have been situated within human rights debates that are produced beyond the confines of colonialist war, torture, murder and the harming of bodies as a set of issues related to autonomy, bodily integrity and self-determination. These rather abstracted molar visions of the free person and their relationship or contract with the de jure state as a citizen with rights awarded to them, misses many key points when looking at molecular political 'self-determination' theory. Mistakenly, the individual is often considered a monad even within a social group or network: an indivisible individual who has the same rights as anyone else and acts *vis-à-vis* the same *dispositifs* as others (see Foucault, 1980b). Therefore, the many ways that human bodies can possibly transform, and the ways that non-humans transform each body, in co-productive[8] sets of relations, is rarely considered. In this section, consideration is given to a range of co-productive practices of temporal transformation that includes socially 'acceptable' as well as 'unacceptable' types of people. For instance, some 'elective' surgeries that the physician, psychiatrist, patient, law and regulation attend to are considered viable options while others are deemed illegitimate. It is not enough for someone to argue, for example, that a wished for bodily aesthetic ought to suffice for receiving the services of a physician to facilitate them. Foucault famously described the increasing personal and political investment in (human and non-human) bodies resulting from the development in biocapitalism (Rose, 2001; Venkatesan and Peters, 2010). Rose (2001: 9) argues that Foucault's notion of 'governmentality', combined with the 'care of the self' (Foucault, 1990), was developed as a theory about both collectivizing and individualizing de jure state power over society, pastorally functioning as the guardian of 'their' 'flock' in a way that verges on eugenics. Rose (2001) questions the biopolitical parameters of the de jure state more in line with Deleuze and Guattari, and suggests that biopower is developed and produced within contested fields with many affective intensities, such as the regulative framework of medicine, law and economics, where ethical considerations are pursued by self-help organization representatives, all of which can co-produce particular bodies that may or may not be transformed in ways that people desire. As Duff (2014: 44) observes, this may: 'disrupt or decompose the body's relations in that it involves a diminution or immobilising[, which] tends to diminish a body's power of acting in its own right, yet it also entails a very distinctive occupation of this power'. Each (human and non-human) body is 'constantly in processes of becoming through its proximity and movement with and through other bodies, artefacts, institutions and so on' (Davy, 2019: 90) despite the diminution. Because the human body is in constant movement, Deleuze and Guattari (1984: 85 emphasis added) state that:

> the full body does not *represent* anything at all [...] cultures designate regions on this body – that is, zones of intensities, fields of potentials. Phenomena of individualization and sexualization are produced within these fields. We pass from one field to another by crossing thresholds: we never stop migrating, we become other individuals as well as other sexes[/genders].

In the context of reproduction and what Ruth A. Miller (2016: 3) calls 'collisions between law and sexuality, [which] produce not only the flesh bound political subject, but also [de jure states, which are] in a constant process of redefinition', this production and reproduction is, as Miller argues, productive of 'a distinctly flesh bound rather than law bound political subject'. Drawing on Agamben's thesis, Miller (2016) asserts that the nation state, by centring the biological in contemporary understanding of the rights of citizens, leads us to assume a biopolitical model of rights and citizenship.

At a different political level many societies that 'work' on the basis of liberal individualism have developed the notion of autonomy; that is, bodily integrity underpinned by populations requiring self-determination, through the changing of, for example, the landscape of medical regulatory bodies, to have rights-based support to transform their healthcare towards a patient-led relationship and help provide 'neutral grounds' upon which choices and provision surrounding self-determined medical interventions can take place (Schramme, 2008).[9] The locus of causality is perceived to be internal in relation to the decision to take action. People distinguish their behaviours as originating from the 'self', rather than from external control or coercion. This has been called *intrinsic motivation* in psychology, in which people work on an interesting activity, regardless of whether it is rewarding or unrewarding (Deci, 1971, 1975). But this theorization also turns the self in on itself, as most of the psy disciplines do. These types of theorizations result in yet more (unwitting) de jure state functionaries attempting to maintain the neoliberal subject's focus on its interiority (Binkley, 2011). Rose (1988, 1990b, 1996, 1998) has been a prolific investigator into the role of psychiatry and psychology and their connection to neoliberal power relations, which he concludes are principally instruments of social governance. Rose (1990b) demonstrated in such studies as *Governing the soul: The shaping of the private self*, the ways in which processes of subjectification are affected through the problem of assimilating large numbers of individuals into institutional forms of governance aimed at such de jure state concerns as 'military, readiness, worker productivity, civic responsibility, public order, family and childhood' (Binkley, 2011: 84). Binkley (2011), however, critiques the neatness of Rose's articulation about the way power is manifest from the many de jure state functionaries and the way the population are subjected to this assumed power, which I tend to agree with. Binkley notes that it would take a whole army of functionaries to agree on each of the mechanisms and implement them unilaterally in order to subjectify those deemed in need of control. One issue is the possibility that articulations require representations of universal identities in order to function for total subjectification. However, in their quests for self-determination, people can switch from one identification to another, insofar as all identifications can be used as possible modes in pursuit of self-determination. Binkley (2011), following Foucault, sees Rose's theorization as a skilful history of the mechanisms that the de jure state, and its functionaries in the psy practices and sciences, articulate at this particular time in relation to the UK's welfare state, whose effect was the disciplinary production of subjectivity, but that now we have to understand – as we have seen from Deleuze – that the de jure state and its functionaries travel through time with newer emerging tasks and forms of governance in light of new forms of identification and subjectification that transpire from earlier subjectifications on an ongoing basis. Binkley (2011: 87–88) suggests that subjectification is a:

> transformative task applied to an object outside of itself, [it] cannot be an effect 'read off' from the rationalities of any given *dispositif*, nor from an imperative voice that silently insinuates itself from the discourse on the government of others to the thoughts one carries in one's own head about the government of oneself. It is a project, a task, focused on specific durable objects. Importantly, the time of this task is not given as a neat package contained in the form of the *dispositif* itself, or the governmental rationality that disposes the individual to act upon such objects. To be disposed to the task of de-subjectification is to be inclined to the undoing of those older subject formations, residues of historical techniques, habits and embodied dispositions left over from earlier processes of subjectification.

For example, the shift in 'sick role' subjectification and the emerging policies surrounding informed consent are premised on patient autonomy over competing values, including the value of good medical care (Dworkin, 1992). This has been developed through the work of a number of de jure state functionaries and patients in which people have the right to a detailed explanation of the pros and cons of healthcare interventions by physicians and medical teams, whether one is forthcoming or not. This temporally significant manifestation in UK healthcare, which I am using as an example, builds on an undoing of traditional subject positions that patients have habitually embodied and built into their understanding of welfare state health *provision*. Now more controversial and problematic than ever is the sustainability of welfare states (Esping-Andersen, 2000). Following reforms in the UK that imposed a quasi-market on state-administered health care systems, a shift to the widespread appreciation that taxes pay for, and that workers pay tax into modern welfare states, has transformed patients into quasi-consumers of healthcare. This example can be made more explicit by comparing the subjectification of UK and US patients. Due to historical differences, patients' subjectification is affectively different, because the majority of the population in the US receive health insurance from employers and private healthcare is the standard. Public health programmes are limited to relatively few people (Giaimo and Manow, 1999). As such, in the US the healthcare consumer form of subjectification has long been the norm.

Informed consent is another such context where each (human and non-human) body is 'constantly in processes of becoming through its proximity and movement with and through other human and non-human bodies' (Davy, 2019: 90), which brings about a number of political, legal and ethical dilemmas in cases where the person is deemed unable to offer or deny consent. Liberal individualism, in these cases, becomes a rhetorical fiction and may require the individual to surrender their right to consent to someone else's principles. For example, a major (ongoing) debate about early medical interventions on intersex children is often polarized as: should parents be able to consent to physicians performing procedures to normalize the child's genitals or is it more appropriate to delay the decision until the child is capable of making an informed choice about their own bodies? This dilemma may be further complicated if the interventions are of a bodily aesthetic nature or couched within a medical emergency framework, in which some cases indeed are placed (Murray, 2009). At this stage in their life they are incapable of consenting to medical treatment in the UK (until the age of 16) and even then it can be overruled in exceptional circumstances until the age of 18. Young people (aged 16 or 17) are presumed to have capacity to decide on their own medical treatment unless there is significant evidence to suggest otherwise.

Young people under the age of 16 can sometimes use the Gillick competency ruling for certain medical interventions, such as contraception and abortion (Grimwood, 2010). However, a ruling in *Bell v Tavistock and Portman* in 2020 concluded that GnRHa could not be prescribed to children under 16 years old because they could not have Gillick competence. While a person with parental responsibility can usually consent on behalf of a non-Gillick competent child, the court ruled that if medical opinion was that GnRHa should be prescribed and the child and parent agree, it is appropriate that the court should determine whether it is in the child's best interests. This ruling affects England and Wales. The health services for children in Scotland and Northern Ireland are not affected, which shows the lack of inherency in healthcare assemblages resulting in inequitable distribution of services in the UK. Moreover, it is unclear from the ruling whether cis children who want to take GnRHa for precocious puberty will be judged against the same standard and will also need to apply to the courts to determine if taking them is in their best interests. If this is not the case, cis children and trans, gender diverse and intersex children will be treated differently in relation to their citizenship rights. Due to their age, a medico-legal framework and a group of people who accept the inherency of chronological age as an important factor in trans, sex/

gender diverse people's human development, these children below the age of 16 are not considered competent. According to political and legal 'liberal individualist' standards the trans, sex/gender diverse and possibly intersex children (like all children) do not qualify for a fully formed social contract nor can they acquire full citizenship rights until the age of 18 and thus, when circumstances dictate, are required to pass over their autonomy, bodily integrity and self-determination rights to their parents or advocates. This context appeals to the sovereignty of the family relationship, which stands in for the child and, along with the physicians, co-produces 'choices' for them. This can sometimes be complicated, as Dworkin (1992: 729) has shown how, in the US legislation, the law can treat informed consent cases as negligence cases, even if the parent consents by proxy:

> That means the patient must show a physical injury in order to win. The loss of dignity, autonomy, free choice, and bodily integrity that is so exalted in the rhetoric of informed consent is worth nothing at judgment time. In order to avoid liability physicians must inform patients either of the risks and benefits that a reasonable physician would disclose, or of all material information, that is, what a reasonable patient, in considering whether to accept the proposed procedure, would need to know to make a reasoned decision. Neither standard has anything to do with patient autonomy. One is directed exclusively to the collective preferences of professionals; the other amalgamates patients into one standard of reasonableness. Honoring autonomy would require the adoption of a subjective standard of disclosure that recognized the patient's right to be unreasonable.

In the US, and in many other nations such as the UK, the law must reach a balance between individuals' right to parent their children and the de jure state's obligation to protect the health and welfare of children. Regardless of Dworkin's claims, in the case of an intersex child known as MC, whose adoption four months after recommended surgery was facilitated by South Carolina Department of Social Services, the adoptive parents brought a case about the lack of adequate information provided to the birth parent about what the adoptive parents saw as an unnecessary surgical intervention. It is unclear if the courts would have held that the consent provided by MC's birth parent had enough bearing on the decision to go ahead with the physician's recommended genital surgery, and that the South Carolina Department of Social Services was negligent in the facilitation. After four years of litigation the parties agreed that it was mutually beneficial to resolve the case amicably. This case recorded no admission of liability or wrongdoing on the part of the Medical University of South Carolina, South Carolina Department of Social Services, or any of the physicians and/or employees. The argument for either waiting or performing medical interventions in this assemblage is rather a superfluous one in many respects. It is not inconsequential, however, because of human and non-human affect involved in the consent issues surrounding 'self-determination' and the possibility not to pursue the case through the courts. The contingency of the decision to persist with or desist from the interventions is the outcome, and does not value the right of the child eventually to decide what happens with their body. The connection between molar and molecular lines of desire that produces the body of the intersex child at particular junctures eliminates the child by defining them as impotent and without legitimate choice-making authority. It is clear whose voices get heard and this will affect how the risks and benefits to other intersex children are understood and evaluated. This process may be based on a few people's opinions, which results in what Abraham and Lewis (2000: 25) call 'judgmental relativism'. The child's body is not produced purely within the self, but at the interstices of many human and non-human connections that are ephemerally situated, and will continue to be through time.

If we assume autonomy is the capacity to make an informed, non-coerced (by proxy) decision to consent to something that results in 'self-determination,' the subjective and represented characteristics of it become leaky, slippery forces that are always on the move. As such, the potential lines of flight (*lignes de fuite*) that can be produced on an ongoing basis render any representation of a reasonable physician and a reasonable patient unreasonable. Therefore, a reconfiguration of our understanding of self-determination seems desirable. Key to this is to consider the assemblages involving scientific developments, changing public values, the directions of medical law and ethics, and the biopolitical forces that can generate affect affecting self-determination in their singularities.

Embodying the widely acclaimed notions of autonomy, bodily integrity and 'self-determination', the Lisbon Treaty, for example, that was developed for EU countries, has sought to provide a framework for nations to follow that will affirm a citizen's enterprise as an autonomous self and as an agent within a field of opportunity. The treaty highlights how respecting and promoting human rights is a core value and objective for all EU actions and policies. These developments in human rights discourses in recent decades illustrate the significant social and cultural transformations surrounding bioethics, biolaw, and human and non-human (technology) principles in relation to, among other things, biomedical developments (Muller, 1994; Rendtorff and Kemp, 2000; Rendtorff, 2002; Shildrick, 2004; Halpern, 2005; Schramme, 2008; Gordon, 2012; Ivanović et al, 2013). It is to these that I now turn.

Personal self-determination

The Declaration of Principles on Equality developed by the Equal Rights Trust (2008) (an NGO based in London), through its advocacy work sets out principles for a unified conception of equality, provides legal definitions and interprets affirmative action. It also merges civil and political rights, and merges economic, social and cultural rights, as a means to ensure comprehensive consistency when dealing with discrimination. However, the provision of services is notoriously difficult to do equally and perhaps then we need to think about equity rather than equality in relation to service provision. Considering this, self-determination and equality or equity needs unpacking. We may ask what aspects of autonomy, bodily integrity and self-determination require equality? I want to suggest that equality is a problematic line of argumentation in relation to self-determination for trans, sex/gender expansive and intersex people because it clearly ignores the roles that physicians, as qualified and hopefully experienced professionals, have in providing the services. It also ignores conscientious and scientific objections, those paying for the service (tax payers in systems like the NHS or insurance companies in market-led systems), licensing and self-governance models, substituted judgements (transferred consent in cases of those unable to consent), all of which can reduce autonomy, bodily integrity and self-determination to an inequitable state of affairs for some rather than others. Many trans, sex/gender expansive and intersex people have struggled for self-determination since their existence is pathologized in particular biopolitical contexts (Hines, 2009). Pathologization impacts their ability to produce identifications as acts of living and acts of resistance. This is due to many sexed/gendered and sexualized projections being imposed on them on molar and molecular planes. Nonetheless, trans, sex/gender expansive and intersex people simultaneously co-produce the foundations for self-determination to an extent, which I will explore in more depth in Chapter 4. However, first I would like to explore the possibility that the equality position may be problematic, following Katrina Roen's

(2008) claims that too often we assume that sex/gender is fixed and knowable, and by accepting that this too can generate the foundations for reproducing and enforcing a binary sex/gender on all people at a molar level, through treatment protocols, legal frameworks and policies. As Dworkin (1992: 733) asserts:

> The liberal individualist model of autonomy is so obviously unsuited to the resolution of difficult problems of medical law and ethics and so clearly distanced from the real — as opposed to the rhetorical — law, that one is tempted to consider the possibility that a somewhat different view of autonomy may be more useful. Yet a more refined sense of autonomy seems no more in keeping with reality than liberal individualism and ultimately offers no more desirable guide to solving hard problems.

Suffice to say we must now turn to an ethical 'co-determination model' based on equity that everyone is committed to. hooks (2013) argues that a model of resistance against the forces preventing self-determination must be underpinned by an unlearning of dominating and dominators' scripts and systems, which will in turn pave the way for the 'love ethic' that combines the love of others with the love of the self and evoke new possibilities. In the case of trans, sex/gender expansive and intersex people, the key dominating scripts and systems are the binary biological and political frameworks in which we are born and interpolated into. Indeed the interpolation of trans, sex/gender and intersex people whose experiential, material and behavioural sexes/genders exceed the binary sex/gender categories, remind us that even medical science attempts to situate bodies akin to socially constructing them, rather than understanding them in their material complexity.

Ethical co-determination and bodily integrity

This section will explore self-determination against the backdrop of an ethical framework that incorporates bodily integrity and autonomy as a human rights issue in relation to clinical services as fields of potential. The medical interventions considered will highlight the importance of understanding: whose body is it to do with as one determines (Fabre, 2008)? While the themes of bodily integrity and self-determination have been explored in relation to trans, sex/gender expansive and intersex people, a deeper understanding about the inherent difficulties in 'claiming' bodily integrity and self-determination when faced with physicians, at some levels is frustrated by the regulatory and governance models that they work within, and the claims of one group of people to be able to, or not as the case may be, assert their autonomy and self-determination rights while disregarding others' claims. As such, autonomy and bodily integrity human rights and self-determination that have been considered within this ethical dilemma have been largely absent from scrutiny in the literature surrounding trans, sex/gender expansive and intersex people. There is, however, some understanding surrounding the complex relationships to medico-legal constraints, human rights advocacy and patients' demands from feminist, trans, sex/gender expansive and intersex people's perspectives, where medical interventions are mediated through people needing or rejecting interventions, and the need to take into consideration the restraints and freedoms placed on any interventions and assistance in healthcare domains.

Another issue concerning bodily integrity arises when carers in medical domains advocate on behalf of those who, due to their age, or perhaps when the patient's ability to consent is marred, for example, while unconscious or if they are deemed too unfit to consent for themselves. Focusing on the medico-legal frameworks then, has been important in these proxy consent contexts, to understand and investigate the ways in which human rights activists and human rights lawyers understand their roles in defining bodily integrity cases for those non-consenting patients and any interventions undertaken by clinicians. The primary aim of all health workers is their dedication to the patient as the starting point of any ethical engagement (Ivanović et al, 2013). As such, I will here in part reflect on medical 'judicial activism' (Jacobson, 1997), where (supra-national) legally sanctioned, culturally normative registers are produced and imposed.

As mentioned earlier, there is no universal idea or transcendental consensus about bodily integrity human rights (Rendtorff, 2002); so bodily integrity has been situated temporally and spatially depending on, in our case, (moral) law and medical interventions that lawyers, activist, patients and clinicians wish to claim, employ and utilize. In the socio-legal research that discusses facilitating or constraining models of bodily integrity, some studies have considered the 'ideal' and the 'practical', by understanding the phenomenology of embodied practices (Benner, 2000) within medico-legal systems. Benner draws on Merleau-Ponty's point that the 'world is inseparable from the subject, but from a subject which is nothing other than a project of the world; the subject is inseparable from the world' (Merleau-Ponty cited in Benner, 2000: 6). He uses this point to argue against the 'Kantian metaphors of the agent [...] the independent, autonomous, uncoerced actor who acts with clarity of thought, and mirrors the Socratic and Cartesian views of mind and body relationships' (Benner, 2000: 9). Benner sees the Socratic and Cartesian philosophical understanding as problematic when applied to market relationships and procedural ethics, when they are connected in the relationship of exchanging goods and services. Feminists such as Butler (1990) and Harding (1991) have long questioned the understanding of 'autonomy' that transpires when human bodies are culturally situated and clearly demonstrate how human possibilities are affected differently on sex/gender lines. These feminists and many queer theorists have argued that conceptualizing the person as acting autonomously may theoretically offer some respect for the idea that individuals choose or act independently and rationally, but then go on to show that there are inherent problems with this conceptualization insofar as it ultimately overlooks our human and non-human interdependence.

Considering these critiques, I would like to invoke a Deleuzian approach here, which conceives meaning making through a continuous oscillation between the subjective accounts of meaning and its wider collective interpretation (Durnová, 2018). These two dimensions are not in conflict but create meaning through their interdependence, which engenders a *pensée de la différence*. In Deleuzian terms, the notion of authentic difference is contrasted to inauthentic difference by suggesting that difference can only be understood between two distinct temporal modalities, that is entities are not located 'in' time *vis-à-vis* other entities, but understood as becoming through time: lines of flight unfold rhizomatically, opening and closing chaotically rather than in clear equally rational lines towards a particular goal or event. Effects are irregular and contingent material conditions that can both enable and constrain the provision and receiving of goods and services for example, and we continuously make meaning from the effects because of the different 'intensities' and different times bodies are moving through.

> In the first place, a body, however small it may be, is composed of an infinite number of particles; it is the relations of motion and rest, of speeds and slownesses between particles, that define a body, the individuality of a body. Secondly, a body affects other bodies, or is affected by other bodies; it is this capacity for affecting and being affected that also defines a body in its individuality. (Deleuze, 1988: 123)

Drawing on the philosophy of Spinoza, Deleuze suggests that (human and non-human) bodies are not forms, functions, substances or subjects – but modes, defined by the effects of which they are capable, by the set of affects that occupy a body at each moment.

> 'We do not yet know what a body can do,' which points at how there are things in the body that exceed our knowledge. We can never know in advance the affective capacities of a body, the affects of which it is capable, 'in a given encounter, a given arrangement, a given combination'. (Deleuze, 1988: 125)

In spite of the differences that 'intensities' can produce and the inherent difficulty in apprehending them coherently, resistance events via bodies 'colliding, mingling, separating', reconfiguring an 'intercorporeal materiality' (Foucault cited in Lash, 1984: 6) are possible. The bioethics, biolaw and medico-legal frameworks of countries inevitably function as bodies, and function through various cultural, medical and legal nuances in relation to various bodies, ages, genders, human rights and cultures. Understanding multiple connections can offer empirically based material to comprehend on what grounds professionals, activists and lawyers merge and separate out issues surrounding bodily integrity for the patient, clinician, educator, student and so on, so that we may understand the everyday 'management' of bodies being produced/presented within medico-legal and pedagogical assemblages. As Elizabeth Grosz (1994: 13) argues:

> human bodies have the wonderful ability, while striving for integration and cohesion, organic and physical wholeness, to also provide for and indeed produce fragmentations, fracturings, dislocations that orient bodies and body parts toward other bodies and body parts.

The question, then, is how can encounters between human and non-human bodies that hold these complexities be conceptualized? If this is the correct way of understanding bodies, as their capacities to affect and be affected, how can we account for the relational variation in intensity, power, and pace of bodies without becoming totalitarian in our relationship to bodily integrity and self-determination?

If the body is multiple, bodily integrity must also mean several things. Bodily integrity can mean the inviolability of the physical body. People are no longer limited to the domain of reproduction and subordination to work, but increasingly have individual autonomy surrounding their body with some recourse through political organization (Hardt and Negri, 2000). We may consider that an unethical infringement of, and an intrusive act against bodily integrity to be a violation of bodily integrity, which may be criminal (Miller, 2016). The body, from this perspective, is depicted as being negatively marred without a means to rectify the wrongdoing (see for example Agamben, 1998). Bodily integrity is complicated further when the body is deemed to be marred when there is no 'viable' reason to modify the body, as in some cases of medical body modification (Schramme, 2008). Schramme (2008: 8) introduces an interesting dilemma:

> Consider two cases: Ms A sees a doctor to get a breast amputated. She suffers from breast cancer. Her doctor has recommended the treatment and she has agreed. It is a straightforward case of a legitimate intervention into bodily integrity, because it is based on voluntary informed consent. Ms B also sees her doctor to get her breast amputated. She does not suffer from cancer but is a highly ambitious archer, who believes that her athletic abilities will be considerably enhanced by the amputation. She has read widely about the Amazons and therefore knows about the optimal preconditions of drawing a bow when the obstructing body part is removed. So in the case of Ms. B we can also identify an example of voluntary mutilation. But the proposed intervention nevertheless does not seem to be justified. Why?

He argues that, in liberal societies, any (medical) intervention that affects an individual's bodily integrity and self-determination needs the support of a good reason either to perform it or not as the case may be. And because of this we must understand what is and is not a good reason. In the cases he describes, the amputation of a body part is set against two scenarios, which will affect people in complex ways. However, whose decision is it and who gets to decide whether the reason is a good one or not? This conceptualization emphasizes the importance of the service user's personal autonomy and self-determination, more than that of the service provider. However, through supranational institutions', nation states', social movements' and individuals' demands, the notion of self-determination connected to bodily integrity in healthcare is emerging as a contested terrain of biopower and biopolitics, giving rise to multiple implications for the biopolitical management of populations (Rabinow and Rose, 2006) in light of contemporary healthcare practices. For instance, if we see affect as a desirous force, or form of power, that is located in either the bow/flat chest or the tumour/scalpel as a contact zone between the organic and the technical, we can bring forth an acknowledgement of the productive connections between the human and the non-human in dis-ease.[10] Whether that product is material or imaginary is irrelevant. As mentioned earlier, another possible scenario may be the decision for trans and sex/gender expansive people to ask physicians to intervene in modifying their bodies in a way that will promote the body and technological contact zone as a site of self-care and wellness. Or, when the physician asks the parent(s) of an intersex child to consider the same or similar interventions as a site of care and wellness. However, in all these cases the power is not equally distributed at these contact zones, but is produced by the ethical utterances of patient empowerment and utterances from regulatory functionaries about the potential risk of harm or benefits.

Literature on the 'ethics of the body' (Shildrick and Mykitiuk, 2005) offers significant analytical insights into the complexity of rights-based claims of the patient and, to a lesser degree, the practitioner. This work, however, tends to be fixed within normative templates that often assume people, in bioethical and medico-legal fields of possibilities, having relatively stable standards of judgement, underpinned by a determinable calculus of harms and benefits made by the rational and impartial person (Shildrick, 2005).

Recognition, diagnosis, ethics and healthcare practices are overlapping and intrinsic parts of how the de jure state and medicine assert a negotiated power over bodily integrity issues. Assertions by clinicians, lawyers and policy makers, through court rulings and healthcare practices, attempt to establish performative limits to the ways different bodies are experienced and treated. Concomitantly, modes of subjectification, in which individuals work on themselves in the name of health and wellness, are gradually incorporated into the negotiations through which bodily integrity takes on new meanings in healthcare systems. This is in part reflected in a 'massive increase in judicial activism' (Jacobson, 1997: 106). In such a context, it seems important to consider the mutual implications of bodily integrity and 'self-determination' by exploring the extent to which issues of recognition, choice and provision of healthcare are important considerations in human rights scholarship. Given this challenge we must move beyond Agamben's (1998) repressive dimensions of the de jure state and law by understanding that agency only dwells in human desire and moves (momentarily) through 'life politics' (McNay, 2000; Miller, 2016).

The struggle for recognition (and non-misrecognition) has been observed in various ways, from Hegel onwards. Axel Honneth and colleagues (Honneth, 1992, 1995; Honneth and Margalit, 2001) have refined the Hegelian concept of recognition, which I suggest is only partly useful for understanding healthcare provision. His work on recognition introduces a tripartite scheme of evolving recognition based on solidarity (Honneth and Margalit, 2001). The examples I will use exemplify the relationships between physicians, psychiatrists and surgeons and trans, sex/gender expansive and intersex people albeit not all in the same way. The examples are helpful to show that the 'recognition' and 'misrecognition' of bodies of trans, sex/gender expansive and intersex people by physicians are rarely in solidarity with them. Recognizing human bodies as purely human undermines the claims of those involved in transforming bodies to conceptualize bodily integrity and self-determination.

Social recognition is nonetheless an important lens through which the redistribution of rights and resources is understood through social struggles and conflict (Fraser and Honneth, 2003). Fraser and Honneth suggest that the experience of being without rights is typically coupled with a loss of self-respect and the inability to relate to oneself as a partner in any interactions. To inhabit our bodies, we desire being accepted and, to a certain degree, this needs to be confirmed and recognized by others. This is paramount in tax-funded healthcare scenarios in order to develop an equitable and sustainable approach to healthcare resource allocation. Hence the struggle for the recognition of a patient's bodily integrity seems to be an obvious goal for them to participate in medical relationships at the same level as others. With this recognition comes representations, which will always be contested.

McQueen (2016) has shown that someone is recognized when they are deemed authentic by telling an authentic story. Authenticity is incorporated into medical protocols, psychiatric diagnoses and the stories that patients tell to the norm entrepreneurs providing the services. The stories that patients tell may or may not be true, as I have shown elsewhere, and forms strategic productions of bodies (see for example Davy, 2010; Speer, 2013). The intersecting service provision encourages strategic production of bodies among marginalized populations as a necessary although disputed way of obtaining services. This can and does lead to a representational and atomistic account of sex/gender identification that, in turn, distorts the ethical issues involved in, for example, sex/gender transitions (McQueen, 2016).

Against this backdrop, we must still think through the ways that bodily integrity and self-determination is being recognized by other functionaries within the de jure state apparatus and how we can attend to the issues of responsibility and responsiveness, and how bodily integrity rights negotiations are situated in ethical, social and medical struggles for 'self-determination'.

Self-determination and the healthcare professions

Recently there has been a shift in clinical responsibility towards encouraging, guiding and assisting patients in making fully informed decisions about their healthcare. Arguably, this shift has moved from a moral obligation to an ethical obligation to support patients with their healthcare. Deleuze (1983) describes 'morality' as a constraining set of rules that attempts to judge intentions and actions within a transcendental framework and assumes a universality about what is good and bad and so on. What he calls 'ethics' is a set of facilitative processes in relation to the immanence of existence, without recourse to normative universals (Smith, 2007). In fact, this is the goal that courts, policies and regulatory frameworks have established, at least semantically, mandating physicians to solicit and respect the informed consent of their patients. The collaborative frame challenges health professionals' paternalism and encourages working towards supporting health interventions, by redressing service provision gatekeeping so that people can actualize their health interventions in the ways that they wish (Davy, 2015; Schulz, 2018). Some research has revealed, nonetheless, that individualized attempts to negotiate shared decision making in many healthcare domains is fraught with difficulties from the perspectives of both the patients (Frosch et al, 2012; Dewey, 2015; MacKinnon et al, 2020) and clinicians (Caldon et al, 2010). Health policy, however, continues to promote individual and collective patient rights as dominant values and goals (Newdick and Derrett, 2006). This emerging body of work has contributed greatly to our understanding about how to redress paternalism within healthcare provision.

This anti-paternalism is witnessed in contemporary medical ethics, which is founded on autonomy (of the patient), non-maleficence (do no harm), beneficence (benefit) and justice (for the society as a whole). Choice and self-determination within a finite system of healthcare makes an important contribution to these debates. As such, rhetoric about great gains in health outcomes and the benefits of a co-productive nature of – patient/clinician – healthcare provision and shared decision making is widespread. However, the notion of 'being informed by' is problematic. It gives the impression of patient autonomy and choice while obscuring the inherent issues that patients have in assessing the information and services. Moreover, it obscures the issue that physicians are willing to provide services to some but not others who request them, which has consequences for patients to determine their medical and health care needs. I will now turn to one key issue surrounding self-determined healthcare provision, that of physicians' conscientious objections.

Conscientious objection and clinicians' bodily integrity rights

Despite the push by the courts and other organizational functionaries mandating physicians to pursue and respect informed consent, there are some reactionary elements in medicine and healthcare. A case in point is those policies that uphold objections through conscientious objection clauses, restricting the choice-making role that patients have. Conscientious objections have mainly been considered within the abortion debate, the rights of the fetus and women (and now some men), and usually situated in the context of religious or 'moral' convictions under the maxim: 'right to life'. Pro-choice advocates counter this conviction with their own maxim: 'the right to choose'. This binary debate situates two different bodies as having the right to choose (one by proxy for the fetus).[11]

Similarly, some relevant research has shown that life-extending technologies and end-of-life palliative care are *regarded* differently for fetuses, neonates and older people by physicians, engendering a situation where life-extending technologies are conscientiously objected to because the interventions are viewed as causing more harm than good (Catlin et al, 2008). That is, technology unnaturally extends life. While I do not have the space to develop these arguments here and they are not strictly the focus of this book, there are some cross-overs in debates about trans, sex/gender expansive and intersex people insofar as the maxims are often argued about beyond the bodies that are being produced. For instance, conscientious objections particularly against hormonal interventions and surgical technologies for trans and sex/gender expansive people – intersex people are rarely brought into this natural/unnatural debate – seem to be based on trite notions of the natural/unnatural or God-given nature, which cannot be changed through technologies. Of course, counter-arguments are easy because if those critics of biotechnologies have nothing much else to reference than that they are unnatural, then we can point out that people have always changed nature, from growing crops in particular ways, animal husbandry and ingesting different foods to enhance our lives to developing medicines, travelling and numerous other aspects of technological life through the ages. As Düwell (2013) argues, the character of the argument against technological interventions as unnatural seems to be because they have gone 'too far'. This is a moral argument that attempts to advance a hierarchical understanding of what life is, can or should be. A potential interpretation of this moral argument is that people dislike seeing their familiar world threatened. This of course does not invalidate the critics' moral stance, it just means it is a stance that they have to argue with more gravitas if they wish to overhaul the relationship between, in our cases, the physicians and patients who find it morally acceptable to utilize technologies to enhance *their* lives.

There is little empirical knowledge about clinicians conscientiously objecting to trans, sex/gender expansive or intersex interventions.[12] There are a few studies, particularly from the US, however, that consider trans interventions within law, and which, in their recommendations, seem to want to provide a compromise between those who hold religious beliefs about not providing certain healthcare and those needing or desiring certain interventions. Farmer (2017) suggests that the religiously grounded exemptions in healthcare provision are beneficial in upholding religious liberty. For instance he states:

> The provisions of § 1557 are needed. But it and its implementing regulations should be specifically limited such that a health care provider with sincerely held religious objections will not be compelled to perform gender transition procedures, even if that provider performs similar procedures for purposes not related to gender transition. (Farmer, 2017: 231)

Similarly, the right to freedom of religion or belief is a fundamental human right recognized in many human rights treaties. Article 18 of the Universal Declaration of Human Rights adopted by the United Nations in 1948, Article 18(1) of the International Covenant on Civil and Political Rights 1966, and Article 9(1) of the European Convention for the Protection of Human Rights and Fundamental Freedoms 1950 all guarantee freedom of thought, conscience and religion. Numerous commentators have suggested that healthcare professionals' right to conscientiously refuse to carry out medical or healthcare interventions 'respects the moral agency of those who hold *reasonable* dissenting views' (Weinstock, 2014: 12, emphasis added). They also suggest that conscientious objection is central to a moral life, to the extent that if physicians are made to give it up, they are no longer acting as moral agents (Curlin et al, 2007a). Curlin et al (2007a), who suggest the latter argument, are drawing on the philosophical position of Rawls (1971) or Kymlicka (1990), who both suggest that a person ought not to be obliged to perform a public service because that obligation would curtail their self-determination. Curlin et al's (2007a) understanding of conscientious objections in healthcare is indeed an interesting one, if somewhat off the mark as I will explain later. For now, though, Curlin et al's (2007a) empirical findings suggest that there are indeed many healthcare providers who object to particular medical interventions on religious grounds. In a response to critics of their article 'Religion, conscience, and controversial clinical practices', Curlin et al (2007b: np, emphasis added) argued that:

> Of course, the profession of medicine cannot permit *all* purported judgments of conscience. For example, the profession cannot permit physicians to refuse treatment of the sick on the basis of a patient's ethnic background or sexual orientation. Such refusals undermine the primary goal of medicine, which is to restore the health of those who are sick. But the practices about which we surveyed physicians were not examples of treating sickness or restoring health. Unwanted pregnancy may have health risks associated with it, but it is not an illness. Terminal sedation is not the treatment of illness, unless the illness is consciousness itself. These practices are controversial precisely because there is disagreement about whether they are consistent with the goals of medicine.

They seem not to understand that non-illness services are provided and supported by the medical field. Indeed, the medical field is paid for the interventions that they carry out in these instances. Nonetheless, they suggest that in order to respect both the physician's and the patient's rights that patients who want information about and access to procedures may need to ask their physician if they would assist in their requests. While there are obvious issues here in relation to a patient's ability to know all the different options available or to understand the procedures in all their complexity, it seems that the power balance according to Curlin et al (2007a) ought to be in the physician's favour. These pro-religious conscience arguments also infer that these physicians' objections have *moral* underpinnings, although they do not provide a taxonomy of the morality of refusing the varying interventions that are objected to. This position thus falters on a fundamental question of what is universally moral and amoral, because this is not self-evident in relation to the many different 'religious convictions',[13] which may vary even within the same religious denomination, or indeed wider philosophical ideas.

This moral position also assumes that physicians either do act as moral agents rather than as providers of a service or intervention that is legally available, or that it is an intrinsic part of their profession's remit for them to do so. If more interventions were included in Curlin et al's (2007a) study, the findings and conclusions perhaps would have been much less clear. For instance, they do not consider one of the most common procedures practised on boys – that of circumcision – which does not often restore health and is generally done for both religious and cosmetic reasons. One interesting turn of events is the emergence of a number of physicians who object to providing circumcisions but may fall foul of the law on religious grounds in some US states. In these situations, which are on the increase, the advocacy group Doctors Against Circumcision suggests that:

> Circumcision violates all five principles of modern bioethics, and many human rights principles. Circumcision endangers healthy minors who are in no need of genital surgery. Circumcision is medically unnecessary since the claimed (and debatable) prophylaxis is easily provided by less intrusive, more conservative means. Circumcision is a culturally driven practice, not medically-indicated, therapeutic, evidence-based care. (Doctors Opposing Circumcision, 2016: np)[14]

Nonetheless, the advocacy group also warn that, no matter how recently acquired a claim of religious belief is, it is much easier to assert and sustain than one based in (bio)ethics, and the challenged physicians could then make their conscientious objection on the basis that:

> most religions have general principles that can be asserted in opposition to unnecessary, unwanted, non-therapeutic cutting of a child. Even if you are an atheist or agnostic, you may be able to assert your personal ethical beliefs, though this varies by state and by institution. (Doctors Opposing Circumcision, 2016: np)

Notwithstanding the fact that trans and sex/gender expansive patients being treated by physicians who were fundamentally opposed to providing them with health interventions would be potentially dangerous and not conducive to good healthcare provision, it seems that international and national law, and medical regulatory policy is written in such a way that objections on the basis of religion and 'morality' can always be upheld. I will explore this in more depth in the Chapter 3. Moreover, although discrimination cases could possibly be brought and won if the conscientious objector cannot prove their religiosity, it seem likely that only a few people would be able to bring forward such cases, due to the expense involved (Grant et al, 2010, 2011). Nonetheless, this dearth of understanding about other forms of 'conscientious objection', such as those not based on religious convictions, requires that we explore the clinician's experiences of conscientiously objecting and understand the implications of adopting patients' bodily integrity principles when they differ from those of the clinician. The centrality of whose rights matter and whose body matters in these debates marks this as a significant struggle for recognition, choice and provision in clinical settings.

Neal and Fovargue (2019: 221) pose the question: 'Is conscientious objection necessarily incompatible with the role and duties of a healthcare professional?' The complexities of conscientious objection as a self-determination and bodily integrity issue figure in patient negotiations and healthcare providers' obligations written within policy directives, organizational responses and law surrounding the provision of medical interventions. While Neal and Fovargue (2016) have previously recognized that there is a connection between conscience and moral integrity, their most recent discussion is with those who suggest there is an incompatibility between the provision of every healthcare practice and the personal integrity of the healthcare provider. The 'incompatibility' thesis, Neal and Fovargue (2016: 545) argue, is grounded 'either in claims of value neutrality or of an "internal morality of medicine"', but recognizing such a connection merely sets up a conflict. Wicclair (2000), for instance, has argued that an appeal to conscience has significant moral weight if the core values on which it is based correspond to core values in medicine. An example may be useful here: the ethical principle of beneficence and non-maleficence are writ large when delivering healthcare procedures, and if these are in danger of not being upheld then one can claim the moral high ground. The core values in medicine, according to Savulescu (2006), however, include ensuring the legal, equitable and efficient delivery of healthcare. This demonstrates the contested nature of the key principles, at least between these ethicists, on what healthcare is or should be. Nonetheless, if we understand that the core values include ensuring the legal, equitable and efficient delivery of healthcare, then it would seem that a doctor's moral conscience has no place in the provision of modern medical care and thus doctors should not refuse to provide healthcare on moral grounds (Savulescu, 2006). Therein lies a key problem for understanding self-determination, bodily integrity and autonomy. Both the physician's and (opposing) patient's views about certain medical interventions that only physicians can legally perform will always engender contested bodily integrity cases and self-determination issues.[15] As such, to request a medical or healthcare intervention in the case of trans and sex/gender diversity people, or to condemn such intervention in the case of intersex people, requires us to understand the potential social situation in relation to the health system that both the patient and physician are in.[16]

This socio-medical situation is particularly obvious in de jure states that have created a taxonomy of illnesses and the medical procedures and technologies that have been clinically accepted for treatment. When the boundaries of illness, healthcare and medical interventions are a little more medically vague – such as with regard to abortion, pregnancy, cosmetic surgery and interventions that may or may not alleviate psychological issues, such as trans, sex/gender expansive or intersex people's gender dysphoria for instance – objections to providing the services become an assemblage of human and non-human bodies vying for self-determination. To push this point a little further, I would like to consider how these objections have been used in the UK in relation to trans and sex/gender expansive children and adults. To date, little is known empirically about clinicians conscientiously objecting to trans, sex/gender expansive or intersex treatments, although we have some healthcare research evidence from trans adults which suggests that many physicians do object to healthcare interventions for them. For example, some physicians refuse to provide prescriptions for hormone therapies, will not refer them on to gender clinics for more specialized care or dismiss or laugh at what trans people say in medical consultations. Some of these reported obstacles or lack of engagement are due, it seems, to the lack of trans and intersex oriented training and health education for professionals, and when there is such training, it varies in its educational level (Davy et al. 2015). Physicians' sketchy knowledge often results in suboptimal healthcare delivery for trans, sex/gender expansive and intersex people (Association of American Medical Colleges, 2007; Ng et al, 2011; Obedin-Maliver et al, 2011; Davy et al, 2015; de Vries et al, 2020).

Another interesting set of objections to trans, sex/gender expansive and intersex people's healthcare interventions happens between physicians themselves, when one (group) disagrees with the practice of another (group). One well publicized example in the UK was the case of Russell Reid. Russell Reid was one of Britain's best-known and respected psychiatrists working with adult and adolescent trans and sex/gender expansive people, and was a member of the parliamentary forum on transsexualism. In 2006–7 he was investigated for serious professional misconduct by the General Medical Council (GMC), the regulatory body for doctors in the UK. Following complaints from four psychiatrists from the NHS gender clinic at Charing Cross hospital and five of his former patients, it was alleged that he breached international standards of care set at the time by the Harry Benjamin International Gender Dysphoria Association (HBIGDA, 2001). Reid had 'inappropriately' prescribed hormones and referred patients for sex/gender affirmation surgeries without adequate assessment. The regulatory case rested on the claims of five patients who said that they were not fully informed about the prescriptions and/or surgery that they were offered or referred for, respectively. Two of the patients told the inquiry they regretted changing sex/gender, while the other three, it seems, continued to live their lives without regret. The Fitness to Practice response from the GMC acknowledged that they had received and evaluated a large number of positive testimonials from other patients and professionals about Reid. Nonetheless, the panel found him guilty of serious professional misconduct for failing to communicate fully with the five patients and their general practitioners, and for the lack of sufficient documentation detailing the reasons for deviating from the guidelines (HBIGDA, 2001). The panel did state, however, that 'it would be in the public interest if he returned to practice albeit under strict conditions'.[17] This allowed Reid to return to work, subject to some restrictions on his practice and prescribing for the following 12 months, but he retired prior to the verdict, passing over his practice to Richard Curtis, who also became a well-known and respected physician in trans and sex/gender expansive healthcare. A few years later the *SOC 6* was amended by the World Professional Association for Transgender Health (WPATH, 2012). In *Standards of care 7* (*SOC 7*) they 'allowed' physicians much more flexibility with treatments, based on the patients' needs, which would have potentially saved Reid's own practice (Pearce, 2018). Nonetheless, the allegations over informed consent and intra-professional objections did not end there.

Richard Curtis, the physician who took over Reid's practice, was also reported to the GMC in 2011, which was allegedly provided with case notes from Charing Cross gender clinic – where some of the same physicians worked who had forwarded complaints on behalf of patients in the case with Russell Reid – about a patient who was seen by Curtis before they transferred to the clinic (Pearce, 2018). The case was brought against Curtis for providing similar services to those provided by Reid. After four years, however, the case was dropped. Curtis was reported as saying:

> In short the GMC have entirely dismissed the case. There was no Fitness to Practice hearing and no sanctions. The conditions which were imposed over three years ago, as it turns out, inappropriately, will be removed when the process for that to occur is administered by the GMC and should be a formality. I would like to express my heartfelt gratitude for all those who have given their support during this very difficult time. (Reid-Smith, 2015)

Pearce (2018: 165) notes that this demonstrates that: 'many complaints against Reid were historically contingent: they reflected an international clinical consensus that has since begun to shift as more practitioners aim to centre patients' informed consent in their approach to trans-specific healthcare'.

Another recent regulatory case, this time against a primary care practitioner in the UK, found that he was acting against the rights of an adult trans patient by refusing to provide services because of his Christian beliefs. In Wales, however, another primary care practitioner, Helen Webberley, who was providing private care to some trans and sex/gender expansive children by prescribing GnRHas,[18] had her licence to practice revoked. As a result of being removed from the NHS general practitioners list, and because of an earlier conviction for not being registered to prescribe from her private practice, she was suspended from acting as a physician in any capacity until these matters have been looked at by the Medical Practitioner's Tribunal Service (MPTS).[19] This revoking of her licence and conviction occurred despite the same drugs being used for a variety of medical purposes, including treating cis sex/gender children whose puberty had started early (central precocious puberty – CPP). These drugs are also prescribed for cis sex/gender children with idiopathic short stature and can increase their height in adulthood, and the intersex condition congenital adrenal hyperplasia (Roberts, 2015). Many of these children are treated before the age of 8 years (Watson et al, 2015) with parental consent, because studies have shown that there is little effect if taken at a later age. Despite the claims that there is little evidence to support their use, GnRHas are commonly prescribed for children without CPP in the hope of increasing height, where shortness in stature can be classed as an unwanted morphological characteristic. Parents consenting to these treatments for their children may also be interpreted as an attempt to optimize the bodies of these children and not for the treatment of illness and disease. Although evidence to support this type of prescribing is only just emerging in relation to trans and sex/gender expansive children, those who have been carefully administering them are clear about the benefits outweighing any potential harms (Kreukels and Cohen-Kettenis, 2011). Trans children and adolescents are prescribed GnRHas because the suspension of puberty provides adolescents the time needed to consider a complex situation, without the accompanying distress that is reportedly caused by the actual and imagined physical changes of the body. GnRHas stop the development of bodily features that the child often fears and which are experienced as psychologically harmful and cause them distress, thus providing the time to explore their sex/gender identities (Olson and Garofalo, 2014). GnRHas have the added advantage that, if the child subsequently discontinues using them and does not have other interventions, such as hormone therapy, there will be a continuation of puberty (de Vries and Cohen-Kettenis, 2012). Many physicians working with trans children believe that at the right age and time, GnRHas are a key intervention for some of them, before a more certain decision regarding (hormonal and/or surgical) sex/gender reassignment, if so desired, is made (Steensma et al, 2013)[20] despite many false claims that they are offered 'sex change' interventions. In cases of intersex children, however, surgery can be offered in adolescence. This is not stated in any policy, as this would be too prescriptive, due to the complex nature of varying psychological, medical and social factors intermingling (Maharaj et al, 2005). Opponents desire a tiered system of these types of intervention, which in effect positions trans and sex/gender expansive adolescents differently to intersex adolescents, not only in relation to their informed consent, but in relation to their parents' decisions.

The reasons for prescribing have long been discussed and debated among many (cis) sex/gender specialists. While trans and sex/gender expansive children have been trying to access medical services for many years, the relatively recent increase in numbers accessing gender clinics across the world has been reported (Olson-Kennedy et al, 2016) and more are seeking care at younger ages (Bonifacio and Rosenthal, 2015). This has generated a media storm in the UK and elsewhere. Numerous medical and non-medical critics have publicly condemned the practice of administering GnRHas to trans and sex/gender expansive children. Some of these claims are underpinned by scaremongering tactics, such as the allegations that trans and sex/gender expansive children are receiving surgery – double mastectomies, breast enlargements, and genital surgeries – or 'irreversible' hormonal treatments. All these do not reflect the reality of medical practice or the fact that the GnRHa interventions are reversible (Endocrine Society, 2019).[21]

In light of all this, at this time in the UK, the religious and moral conscience objection clause is not officially available; as we will see in the next chapter, however, official recognition is not required due to particular assemblages being produced within the healthcare system. Healthcare options are provided and regulators collaborate with trans, sex/gender expansive and intersex people contingently regarding their healthcare. However, who gets to provide trans healthcare is firmly guarded by the NHS gender clinics, as it seems that those in private practice can find themselves in intra-professional objection battles with the GMC, physicians and sometimes their regretful patients. With regard to all this, the way medicine has set up the self-regulatory models of physicians' work, which demarcates many parameters surrounding legal, ethical and equitable frameworks that allow or disallow physicians to practise, and the regulatory organizations that ultimately judge any cases in question, need to be evaluated.

Concluding remarks

Theories of self-determination have been problematized in this chapter. While 'self-determination' is widely used to account for someone's desire to become, it has variously been represented as emerging from an inner core personality and manifested as a monadic battle against the polity, law, medicine and opponents. This sets up a false dichotomy of structure/agency in which the quest for and outcome of self-determination struggles miss the molecular and molar events that contingently manifest through biopolitical and bioethical assemblages. Suffice to say for now that 'self-determination' is always co-produced within multiple assemblages on many planes of immanence. In Chapter 3 I look at medical self-governed institutions, the elevated professional and social position of physicians, and the UK's development of a patient-centred approach to healthcare to demonstrate the context in which sex/gender self-determination is negotiated and produced.

3

Medical governance and governing the healthcare assemblage

Introduction

In the last chapter I suggested that self-determination theory is a widely researched and an empirically evidenced theory of human needs fulfilment and motivation and offers a potentially valuable conceptual framework for understanding why the current policy environment has not led to the anticipated improvement in equity, quality and safety of clinical care with trans, sex/gender expansive and intersex people. I also looked towards a more sustained move towards patient-centred self-determination models of healthcare provision, regardless of whether that provision is privately or state funded.

In this chapter, I will look at how self-determination is affected by and affects medical self-governed institutions, the elevated professional and social position of physicians, and the UK's development of a patient-centred approach to healthcare. This will not be an extensive genealogy of the UK system as that is too vast a subject to do justice to in a single chapter. Margaret Stacey (1992) has written an excellent detailed analysis of the importance of the role of the GMC in the UK in relation to the protection of both physicians and patients. Although Stacey's book is almost thirty years old, it still holds much relevance in the ways that medical registering and physicians' appraisals and revalidations have been and continue to be evaluated, and to some extent how the role of the patient/consumer functions (see also Quick, 2018; Gladstone, 2000). I will draw on some areas of contention that allow us to see some of the biopolitical assemblages that generate key forces in everyone's self-determination efforts related to health (Irving, 2008).

One key question I will address in this chapter is on what grounds are physicians given the role of arbiters of sex/gender declarations at birth?[1] The General Register Office started to register births, deaths and marriages in 1837 in England and Wales. Previously, baptisms, marriages and burials were recorded in poorly kept parish registers, which were maintained by Church of England clergy. With the establishment of a civil system it was hoped that improved registration of what were seen as vital events by the polity would help in the organization of voting, planning, taxation and defence, and protect property rights through the more accurate recording of lines of descent. Although this was relatively successful, there were several events that were still not being registered, resulting in a stricter law in 1874 that required births to be registered within a six-week period. Included in these rules was the need to register a child's sex. It seems that it became the purview of physicians, nurses or midwives attending the newborn, to inspect the genitalia and provide a sex/gender assignment. The rationale for sex/gender assignment and consequent registration appears to have been little questioned, along with who could provide this assignment for national registration processes.

The declaration is part of the biopolitical assemblage affecting trans, sex/gender expansive and intersex people's self-determination differently to that of cis sex/gender people. It is, however, productive in particular ways, in a Deleuzian sense, for everyone. I will show that trans, sex/gender expansive and intersex biopolitics are folded into medical self-governing structures of power as well as producing nomadic movements. That is, the affective intensities unfold in different ways, at different speeds and, importantly, in unknown ways. For example, if it transpires that amendments to the birth certificate are required, in cases where it is important in order for some trans, sex/gender expansive and intersex people to become healthy and economically viable citizens, it is often the role of a different set of physicians to those who assigned the sex/gender to diagnose gender dysphoria, transsexualism, gender incongruence or an intersex condition, and/or to detail any somatic interventions deemed to be sex/gender transitioning healthcare.[2] As such, different affective intensities are manifested surrounding sex registration at birth, colliding with trans, sex/gender expansive and intersex people's bodies and the regulations governing those who can judge bodies. Subsidiary questions to this are: is it necessary for the de jure state to retain the medico-legal process of sex registration? And what purposes does it serve, since birth certificates can be amended based on different (genitalia) criteria to those upon which it was registered in the first place?

We must remember, however, that in DeleuzoGuattarian terms, micro-politics develops in transversal relational fields because of bodies, materiality and ideas connecting (Deleuze, 2004). As such, Aizura (2006) notes that trans, sex/gender expansive and intersex people's bodies are dominated by medicine's and law's potential to facilitate productive citizens:

The affects are produced in relation to citizenship [which] here means fading into the population (and exercising the rights of populist democracy) but also the imperative to be 'proper' in the eyes of the state [functionaries]: to reproduce, to find proper employment; to reorient one's different body into the flow of the nationalized aspiration for possessions, property, wealth. (Aizura, 2006: 295–296)

In effect, people pursue self-determination within the bounds of the national social contract. A major part of these constraints is sex registration at birth. However, I will suggest that sex registration at birth seems not to serve any substantive medical purpose to my knowledge, nor does it impact positively on the competence of physicians' practice. In fact, it has been shown to hinder practice through creating stereotypes and unhelpful assumptions about sexed/gendered bodies. Thus I argue that it seems odd that physicians are the arbiters of this biopower (see for example McDonald and Gary Bridge, 1991; Andersson et al, 2013).

This chapter will start however by providing a brief history of the development of medical governance particularly in the UK, and the (self-)governance of the health professions, which has elevated medicine's social position, in order to demonstrate that self-determination is affected in different ways according to whether someone is trans, sex/gender expansive, intersex or cis sex/gender. We need to take this important detour in order to understand whether the relational fields or planes of immanence, and all the relevant parts implicated in the medical-patient-policy assemblage, continue to be fit for purpose in assigning a sex/gender at birth, whether sex/gender assignments have a medical purpose, and what challenges can be levelled at the practice in light of human rights declarations surrounding the rights of people[3] to their bodily integrity, autonomy and 'self-determination.'

The general focus in this chapter then will be on how the medical professions have continued to retain their elite position. While I cannot categorically state that the profession as a whole desires the power awarded it in interpolating and affecting everyone's sex/gender, I will suggest that because of the profession's elite status, this is an inevitable, but unnecessary biopower awarded to it. This all contributes to what Jutel (2019: 290) calls 'epistemic posturing' that in turn strengthens the power of medical knowledge contributing to their medical authority. In order to explore this in relation to the concept of self-determination I will demonstrate through analysis of intersecting policy, university degrees and scientific research, that they all contribute to the biopolitical epistemic posturing, while obscuring the fact that physicians habitually determine sex/gender without asking, or knowing why, or even for what purpose.

A brief history of medical self-governance

In the west, according to King (2001), the development of self-governing values relating to medical practices was advanced by Hippocrates. New physicians[4] would swear an oath to uphold specific ethical standards. Accordingly, Hippocrates advocated that medicine should be practised by a trained elite who would abide by rules and norms then pass on their skills and standards to others through an apprenticeship model. This type of programmatic declaration about the self-regulating physician contributed to solving several philosophical questions about the purpose of medicine, and the role that physicians would undertake and rules they would adhere to. As such, the pedagogue-physicians were forging the context for regulating themselves and their trainees by declaring values for the profession.

From the late medieval to the Renaissance period in Europe, training was provided by physicians in some of the earliest established universities and this is generally understood to have engendered a more formalized prestige hierarchy for the profession. In the modern period (from the 16th century on), with the advent of a more urban and commercial economy and the expanding sovereign courts across Europe, boundaries were set up between the learned, licit medical men holding academic credentials, and the illicit charlatans who did not (Wallis, 2010). University-educated physicians were sanctioned to deliver 'humoral medicine' (Lindemann, 2010). Physician trainees, who were also of the same 'gentleman' class as the upper echelons of society, the same 'sex/gender' and from the same types of families as the physician trainers, were deemed to be of appropriate social standing to care for those of the same or higher classes, such as the aristocracy and royalty. It was an offence, by royal decree in the reign of Henry VIII in England to practise 'physic' without a university degree (initially from Oxford or Cambridge) or a licence issued by a bishop (Chamberlain, 2009), all resulting in more territorialized steps towards elite professional norms.

Medical practitioners were eventually divided into physicians, learned surgeons, craft surgeons, apothecaries and midwives. These divisions were made with a certain amount of manipulation on the part of the elite physicians. The physicians were solicited by the aristocracy and upper classes, through personal contacts, and this awarded them in return the power and influence to manoeuvre politically and professionally, and keep their profession at the top of the medical hierarchy and assert their legally established professional positions. In effect they co-determined their own position within the hierarchy of healthcare provision with the support and patronage of high-ranking others (Chamberlain, 2009).

A sequel to this professional groundwork was the establishment of different measures for the recruitment, training and skill sets required for students. This seems to have been planned so that particular literati classes and their elite patients could access the profession. In England, after studying for six years and some extra time learning about the ancient medical texts, it was only those sexed as men who had passed the physician exams in English universities who could be awarded membership of the Royal College of Physicians, founded in 1518. Gaining this 'physic' education was also expensive, reducing the possibility for those with less social status and money to enter the profession. Surgery and apothecary training were much cheaper (Axtell, 1970). Physicians were 'gentlemen' and thus did not engage in the trade of supplying medicinal compounds but nonetheless reserved the power to prescribe. Nor did they partake in the manual labour of surgery (Jewson, 1974; Chamberlain, 2009). Thus, they represented a systemic way of producing social stratifications in relation to the range of medical practitioners.

Even so, surgery has been practised for millennia, in various cultures. The patients were richer men, due to them being able to afford the interventions (Holliday and Sanchez Taylor, 2006). One commonplace surgical intervention was that of circumcision, practised as a cultural marker of the initiated, who could access ancient mysteries central to godliness, for example, in Egyptian religion. Circumcision was also incorporated into the monotheistic religions of Islam and Judaism. Claudius Galen (AD c.130–c.200), was perhaps the best-known Roman surgeon. He was celebrated for surgically reconstructing gladiatorial wounds as well as for the removal of fatty deposits from men's breast tissue and correcting droopy eyelids (Holliday and Sanchez Taylor, 2006). According to Gilman (1999), through the Renaissance surgeons began speaking of both reconstructive and aesthetic surgeries. One famous French surgeon, Guy de Chauliac (d. 1368), defined the role of the surgeon in three ways: separating the fused, connecting the divided and removing the extraneous (Gilman, 1999). Gaspare Tagliacozzi (1554–99), a surgeon based at Bologna University, developed surgical techniques for skin grafting and the reconstruction of syphilitic noses. There is evidence that dissection was practised in 13th-century Italy and across Europe. Although the University of Padua played a leading role in autopsies and exploring the inner workings of the body through the Renaissance period, it must also be noted that at the same time these practices were deemed to be a violation of the body and God's will (Pouchelle, 1990). As such, the practice of surgery throughout Europe has been defined by many challenges. Its rise from crude butchery to being understood as an independent craft and a key discipline within the art of medicine has been genealogically different to 'physic' albeit not detached (see Schlich, 2018). In England, surgery's first institutional sign of professional standing came when prominent surgeons set up the Barber-Surgeon Company in 1540, but it was not until 1800 that the Royal College of Surgeons was formed. Jewson (1974) notes that, in England, there was a common distaste for experimental and scientific study of physiology and anatomy for which dissection was required, even though surgery had had a relatively long and prestigious history elsewhere across the world. Amputations and aesthetic surgeries, in varying degrees, were still generally seen as manual work and were left to the surgeon 'tradesmen' to carry out.

The apothecaries were similarly later than physicians in attaining a professional status and were granted a Royal Charter in 1617, which allowed them to dispense remedies that the physicians were prescribing. In 1703 they were legally entitled to attend patients, prescribe and charge for the drugs that they supplied (Jewson, 1974). Throughout Europe this hierarchical model dominated the medical provision landscape and was upheld in the various universities sanctioned by decree to provide medical education. The role of the physician was maintained in a relatively high position in society and only learned men from select academic institutions were able to practise.[5]

Registering and licensing physicians

Jewson (1974) argues that to begin with the physician was accorded respect based on an authority founded in his occupational role rather than because of his individually proven worth. In the UK, the Medical Act 1858 established the General Council of Medical Education and Registration of the United Kingdom (now called the General Medical Council – GMC). Stacey (1992) suggests that the GMC started off as a gentleman's club, with which all doctors must be registered; and doctors had to hold a licence recognized by the institute in order to practise medicine. Physicians and other medical staff throughout the world are now connected to national legally underwritten registers of qualified practitioners (Chamberlain, 2009).

As noted, the different specialisms were divided, and this functioned to control recruitment and training strategies and to establish skill sets that were deemed important, scientifically supported and discipline bound. History of medicine scholars and sociologists have tried to understand how these developments affected the medical profession's standing and privilege as more people began entering university to study medicine. Drawing first on Weber, several sociologists (Berlant, 1992; Parry and Parry, 2018) have looked at the 'monopolization' of the profession. These studies drew on theories of political economy to demonstrate that medical professionals were strategizing to monopolize the marketplace and control the supply and demand of healthcare provision and services. Concerned with how monopolization was facilitated, Chamberlain suggests that: 'by engaging in collective social mobility [...] occupational groups [...] obtain privileges from the political community, to become what Weber [...] calls a legally privileged group, ensuring the closure of social and economic opportunities to outsiders' (Chamberlain, 2009: 52). In his seminal work, Freidson (1970) argued that the upshot of this privileging awarded by the political elites was the development of unaccountable, self-governing institutions surrounding the professions. This structural, collective self-determination continues into the 20th and 21st centuries, albeit within much more complex healthcare assemblages of government funding, governing institutions, educational standards, revalidation processes, de jure state agencies and the more recent development of including patients' voices.

Professional prestige and the connection to health science

History has shown that doctors' ascent to powerful positions in society has been evolving for a long time. For example, from archived materials from 1844 to the early 1960s, Jutel (2019: 292) documents how physicians manoeuvred in such a way that they produced the discursive frame to shape 'the moral content of the clinical relationship', instil them 'with a "God-like" authority' and control 'the "facts" of disease'. Nonetheless, Chamberlain (2009) suggests that the profession's golden age in the UK started just before the creation of the NHS. The expert standing of doctors is demonstrated in a statement in the 1944 White Paper introducing the NHS, which stated: 'The doctors taking part must *remain free* to direct their clinical knowledge and personal skills for the benefit of their patients *in the way that they feel best*' (Ministry of Health and Department of Health for Scotland, 1944: 28, emphasis added). This statement suggests that tacit knowledge and expertise is key to the physicians' work and that they ought to be free to practise their art because they know best. Physicians' cultural authority (Elston, 1991) rests on the public's belief that medical definitions and judgements are generally valid, true and ethical, a belief that to this day holds considerable weight. In many parts of the world, the profession still holds the reins regarding the types of education and knowledge production in academe are conveyed to new recruits – which is, of course, not surprising. All this is in spite of some aspects of the medical profession's prestige and power being questioned. According to medical sociologists Gabe, Kelleher and Williams (2006: xiv): 'the corporate power of medicine has been increasingly challenged [and physicians] have become increasingly embattled as their position as experts has been challenged from inside and outside the health care arena'.

Critics suggest numerous factors have undermined physicians' prestige, such as incompetence, in the form of sexist, classist, homophobic, transphobic, racist and ableist traditions (Wilkerson, 1998). It is clear that physicians' work is never conducted in a social or economic vacuum, which inevitably affects their cultural competence in one way or another, and their ability to comprehend each and every one of their patients. Nonetheless, great strides have been made more recently where cultural competence has been included as a key feature in physician training (Bassett et al, 2002; Grove, 2009; Wilkerson et al, 2011) alongside the growth in evidence-based medicine.

In spite of this turn to cultural competence in physician training, one important factor rarely considered is the newer epistemological approaches that affect patient–physician interactions, such as positivism through experimentation, which was supposed to improve on the more subjective and tacit elements of medical and health service provision. Positivist approaches assumed that they could explain the science behind illness, medicine and healthcare rationally and through reason. While positivist experiments were being conducted, Le Fanu (2011) explains that the rise in medicine's privileged position in society was due to a mix of already established legal and professional credentials, as explored earlier, and numerous serendipitous curative 'findings'. These 'findings' included using newly formulated drugs and technologies, and discovering how they could be used to treat other medical conditions. Many of these findings were based on clinical observations of results that were not being tested for in the first place. Le Fanu (2011: 270) argues that physicians and psychiatrists:

just happened to be around at the crucial moment when it became possible to exploit the therapeutic potential [...] without having to create them in the first place or even know how they worked. The chance discovery and exploitation of these 'mysteries of biology' is the bedrock of the rise of modern medicine.

These serendipitous findings were of course underpinned by some intellectual contributions; Le Fanu (2011) claims, however, that the natural history of many diseases and conditions remains unknown, but that the fact that these opportune (bio) technological discoveries and interventions were not of physicians' and psychiatrists' making did not deter them, under the umbrella banner of 'medicine', from claiming credit for their role in the enhancement of people's lives and increased longevity.

The increase in positivist approaches to experimentation was extensively incorporated into healthcare research and practice, which also improved the social standing of healthcare as a scientifically driven field, enabling it to be marketed as providing evidence-based medicine. However, according to Le Fanu (2011) and Weatherall (1996), these experimental influences have only offered expensive technological investigations with relatively limited treatments, so much so, that modern medicine has, they say, become a 'failure'. What it has also done is reductively focus on healthcare to the detriment of understanding the cultural and material diversity of the human population in its treating practices, resulting in a crisis of knowledge, care and compassion alongside increased costs.

Other wider social factors too began chipping away at medicine's claims to scientific greatness. In fact, through postmodern thought, the reaction in academe attempted to demolish claims of evidence-based, universal and unilateral truths. These postmodern critiques were accompanied with calls for the disintegration of objective knowledge, political and social life, and of mass market economics. They challenged the healthcare system to try to employ a postmodern outlook towards its healthcare consumers. According to Muir Gray (1999), postmodern healthcare would have to maintain and improve on the achievements of the modern era of medicine while responding to the priorities of postmodern societies, namely: concern about diverse human values, fragmented evidence, and the rise of the well-informed patient who perhaps lives through other truths.

Medical and healthcare research now tends to emerge from different paradigms ontologically, epistemologically, theoretically and ideologically. Research concerned with understanding diagnoses, best practice and new avenues for progress in healthcare services emerges from a wider range of perspectives now. This research has become central in deciphering the complexity of what works and what seems to be less successful. For example, since the 1980s, evaluation procedures have filtered through the royal colleges that award qualifications and revalidations to physicians so that they are legally able to practise generalist and specialist medicine. What became prevalent was peer auditing of practice. It was assumed that auditing physicians' performance, and providing peer feedback, would make it possible to demonstrate where they are working well and where they are failing, and which areas needed improvement. Lord and Littlejohns (1997) note, however, that when there are high levels of complexity, uncertainty and conflict about the most reliable approaches to healthcare, it is often impossible to agree on goals or to identify the best mechanisms for achieving the stated goals – or how to usefully measure them. In a review of 140 audits and feedback studies by Ivers et al (2012: 2), they found that the effect of audit and feedback on professional behaviour and improved patient outcomes ranges from little effect to a substantial effect. While audit can indeed capture failure, this is only gauged against a pre-established protocol, and works better for easily defined specialist procedures. Audit can stultify any efforts to improve and can only sustain the meagre standards of the audit. An improvement plan should not rely on these easy victories but must include the way the whole system should behave in the future.

Because audit relies on a settled protocol, it rests on the assumption that whatever is being audited is already the best way to do things. Any evidenced-based improvement to a protocol is rarely integrated into the audit's methodology, which thus must be understood only as a current baseline benchmark. Moreover, audit is less able to measure or even inform the general practitioner (or indeed others) about complex healthcare practices, because it is not methodologically robust enough to capture more complex cases, co-morbidity and the system within which they are contextualized. For example, audit often does not consider diverse material realities, cultural factors, patients' desire, institutional factors and so on. The 'patient variable' cannot be firmly placed as an 'average' within the audit that will always act or recover in the same way due to not having a truly equivalent control group (Lord and Littlejohns, 1997). To recap, audit can only capture what rates go up or down within a finite set of procedures; it has been argued that audit stultifies, rather than encouraging better healthcare practice and procedures. Bowie et al (2012) have suggested that audits are often untried and untested prior to their implementation, which is not generally regarded as good scientific practice and, as such, there was little evidence that simple audit would improve patient care or management (see also Sellu, 1996).

A more pernicious effect of audit, however, is that it creates extra workload. Despite the longevity of audits, there is growing evidence that they may fuel low motivation and disillusionment in the profession (Bowie et al, 2012). By using audit protocols, physicians are restricted to routine practices that may not be fully relevant to their complex cases when choosing the best ways to treat patients. Allsop and Mulcahy (1996) have suggested that audit culture in healthcare undermines the ethos of professional 'craft knowledge' with which physicians can practise in more fluid ways. Through a Deleuzian empiricism lens we can suggest that complexity is not an audit's strong point, because desiring machines are unruly and induce intensities outside of calculation. They make threats to established modes of being. Audit does not lend itself to any production of new desires. One particular interest in relation to self-determination is that audits and evaluation of health services have little to say about augmenting more nomadic and relational responses to revitalize the human and non-human dimensions of healthcare practice. As Fisher and Tronto (1990) argue, the web of caring has no beginning or endpoint but is a moving set of assemblages of bodies (human and non-human) that need to be acknowledged (see also Tronto, 2013).

Crafting knowledge

While different medical specialisms will rely on different scientific evidence trends in the literature, non-propositional knowledge still forms part of professional 'craft knowledge' (Howells, 1996). Polanyi (2009) understood craft knowledge as being connected to tacit knowledge in three ways. One of the main critiques of the scientific approach is that tacit knowledge has implications for claims to a depersonalized knowledge base, where science is claimed to work from. This has negative implications for the objectivity claims that can be pursued with the move in medicine from an being an 'art' to becoming a science. Polanyi argues for the impossibility of depersonalized knowledge, in contradistinction to positivists' assertions of being able to pursue detached verification and falsification within their work in order to claim the reliability of their science. In Polanyian approaches, the scientific knowledge of health professionals is linked to their personal knowledge, learning and practice, and is thus intrinsically developed from their life experience, enabling them to make prognoses, diagnostic decisions and treatment plans (Higgs and Jones, 2000). Rycroft-Malone et al (2004: 83) argue that: 'unlike research-based knowledge, professional craft knowledge is not usually concerned with transferability beyond the case or particular setting'. They go on to argue that craft knowledge can potentially become academic knowledge once it has been 'researched', then peer reviewed and verified through wider academic community practices, published and then taught as a scientifically valid formal knowledge. I will develop this point further in Chapter 4 in relation to how the diagnosis of gender dysphoria is reified – considering or representing (something abstract) as a material universal thing – through tacit knowledge rather than scientific evidence. Suffice to say now, that since the 1960s, the work of Becker et al (1960), which has provided an extensive ethnography looking at medical education; Bosk's (2003) work, which addresses surgical failures; and numerous critiques of psychiatric practice (Szasz, 2009; Davy et al, 2018) have all suggested that the medical practitioner is generally more reliant on tacit knowledge, 'the authority of his own sense, independently of the general authority of tradition or science', and 'if his own activity seems to get results, or at least no untoward results, he is resistant to changing [his art/practice] on the basis of statistical or abstract consideration' (Freidson, 1970: 170). To intervene in this way, however, gives rise to intuitions derived from the physician's own practice, rather than fostering the self-determination of the patient. Moreover, tacit practices are not generally regarded as good scientific approaches to medicine.

Ironically, it was the suspicion of the validity of science that lies at the core of the social critiques of medicine and the regulatory forces surrounding it, alongside strong feminist analyses (Oakley, 1993). The main idea behind these critiques is the socially constructed nature of life as we know it. In postmodernism and the postmodern approach to life, the critique of universal grand narratives of religion, sovereignty and science, were once and, in the latter case continue to be, held widely to be true. For instance, postmodern accounts of the scientific method claim that a powerful textuality, and thus tacit thought, is rife in medicine to this day. Postmodernist thinkers have widely asserted that the natural world as described by scientists and physicians is nothing but a human artifact, often produced for economic gain and/or prestige, which wittingly or unwittingly feeds into the de jure state machine. Jameson (1991), in particular, has produced this type of critique of the sciences as an art.

Deconstructionists have also contributed to this debate. Deconstruction is a method of interpreting artifacts to expose the limitations or inconsistencies of any particular set of conceptual claims and any research priorities observed that claim to be objective. The most critical deconstructionists often show how the artifact attempts to maintain the (capitalist) de jure state system. However, deconstructionism undermines the very principles of its own operation. In relation to Derrida, who is arguably the most famous deconstructionist, Jane Caplan (1989: 268) states that his:

> rhetoric takes a form that constantly acknowledges the provisional nature of his own readings [...] that subverts his own authority as a reader, and offers his body to those that follow (in that sense, the poststructuralist can never have 'the last word').

Constructionist/deconstructive frameworks that are connected to postmodern thought, then, are less productive and arguably less able to challenge the power relations than has been claimed. If we take the reading of texts in its widest sense, including research interviews, artifacts and perhaps even critiques of statistical analyses, deconstructionists tend to try to show the social constructedness of the texts and deconstruct them out of existence, or banish them as mere social constructions, waiting to be replaced by more social constructions and so on. Deconstructive work on universal truths has its own set of forces that have helped to fragment existing paradigms and to generate an attack on medical hegemony (Illich, 1977). However, this has had little effect in terms of overhauling the powerbase. Nonetheless, deconstructionism, in our case here, can illustrate that the self-image of the medical profession as being scientifically based, value-free, patient-centred and based on evidence, may be far from the universal reality it is often believed to be.

Modern medical knowledge and expertise, like that of other professions analysed by the social sciences, has been understood as produced in particular ways that benefit those who hold the means of production, such as physicians, educators, researchers and law makers, under the auspices of modern liberal government regimes. At one level of the debate, the linguistic conventions used to understand medicine and professionalism, and the way that medical judgements are seen as valid and true, underpinned by so called 'objectivity' and 'neutrality' developed through the scientific method, are in of themselves mere social constructions laden with clandestine power relations. Medical professionals, researched through a Marxist lens for example, were seen as agents of classification, in which their bourgeois status was unaffected by claims to liberal meritocratic rights. Medical elites were analysed as both producing well bodies for the production lines, and sexed bodies so that women can become unpaid carers to enable an efficient workforce to generate more capital and thus profit. Also, according to Navarro (1980), discussing the writings of the philosophers Mills, Locke and Spencer among others, medical professionals reinforced ideas of the naturalness of the class and sex/gender status quo, the biological and mental inadequacies of the proletariat to govern the means of production and, more importantly, how bourgeois ideology appears and is reproduced in medical knowledge.

Others have suggested that while social constructionist thought via postmodernism can show how these producers of knowledge and professional practitioners can emit influential affects that underpin what has widely become to be known as the clinical gaze (see Foucault, 1995, 2003, 2006), there seem to be aspects of medicine that have a material biological dimension, and cannot be dismissed as a purely linguistic power games (Turner, 1995). Multiple material factors have contributed the status of medicine, and the ongoing:

> establishment of state-sanctioned jurisdictions for emergent professions such as medicine over surveillance, classification and care of rich-poor, sick-health and mad-sane subjects, was not solely the result of successful occupational strategies of advancement based upon claims to possess esoteric expertise and an altruistic code of conduct. Rather class and gender inequalities influenced the 'club rule' form that professional self-regulatory institutions such as the GMC took […] the outcome of programmes and policies [at the same time shaped and enhanced] the self-regulating capabilities. (Chamberlain, 2009: 67)

Chamberlain mentions two forms of forces: class and gender. How we can understand this is worth noting. Since the 1980s, feminists have claimed that there was increasing pressure within their movement to make healthcare research, services and policy sex/gender sensitive (Doyal, 2006). The need to develop research and healthcare services that are sex/gender specific, they argued, was long overdue and attributable to the empirical binary differences of both biological disease and illness, and also socially acquired disease and illness, and the ways in which some physicians make assumptions about sexed/ gendered bodies and wellbeing. Research represented many sexed/ gendered patterns of disease and illness – made more obscure by class, ethnicity, geography and healthcare accessibility – that should be accounted for in the quest for the development of an optimized healthcare service (Annandale and Hunt, 1990, 2000; Doyal, 2006). Witnessing multiple interactions in complex systems has turned the tide of postmodern critique as a deconstructive action, due to its failure to attempt to reconstruct medical materialities in meaningful ways. In what has come to be known as the 'affective turn', researchers have begun the task of understanding the material realities of complex health systems, human and non-human interaction, molecular and molar assemblages with an acknowledgement of their emergent properties. By understanding that small changes can have affective intensities that produce large effects, and that large changes, such as national healthcare strategies, can produce small effects on the health of patients, I will suggest that sex/gender is affective, but not in the binary way that research and healthcare strategies have assumed. This has been highlighted in other areas of scholarship, such as feminist biology (Longino and Doell, 1983; Fausto-Sterling, 1993, 2000) and social studies of science, which have provided a sustained critique by continually questioning physicians' relative lack of understanding of the mysteries of biology. In relation to a contemporary example, parents and their intersex children are routinely misinformed, kept in the dark about the actualities of biological processes and medical procedures, and thus denied appropriate support, both during and following consultations (Bauer et al, 2016). One UK health policy is revealing in this sense. In an information sheet from Norfolk and Norwich University Hospitals NHS Foundation Trust and the Ipswich Hospital NHS Trust (2019: np) in the UK, detailing one relatively common intersex difference named hypospadias it states that:

> The cause is unknown. It occurs because the penis has not developed normally in the womb. Sometimes there is a family history, so a father and son may be affected. If left untreated, your son may suffer with the following issues: 1. Downward spray of urine (instead of forward), and so difficulty with passing urine whilst standing 2. Embarrassed by curvature of the penis as it will look different from that of other boys 3. Difficulty with sexual intercourse when older if the hypospadias is severe. The surgery will aim to correct

these problems and make the penis look more normal or circumcised look. We prefer to perform the operation at about 12 months of age or above.

Because the cause is unknown, this statement seems to be implying blame, particularly towards the parents, such as it is happening in the womb or that it is (maybe) genetic. This linguistic force is submerged within a language of normalcy and medical emergency when 'preference' for early intervention is favoured. While within the policy there are statements that parents can ask questions prior to signing any consent for interventions, many excerpts and testimonies from parents and some older children (see for example Kessler, 1998; Preves, 2005; Siedlberg, 2006) suggest that there is a lack of information given to parents, that physicians pressure parents to adhere to surgical emergency recommendations, and that parents are often bewildered by the technical jargon that physicians use.

There is convincing evidence provided by critics about the widespread lack of understanding about 'sex differences'. This warrants one of the questions I wish to pose in the book: Why then do doctors have the right to determine sex/gender? I am not the first to question this, particularly in relation to intersex people. Lena Eckert (2017) argues that, despite bioethicists and some feminist biologists understanding that sex/gender figure in complex and multidimensional spaces, there is still an unwarranted assertion of binary forms of masculinity and femininity in their analyses. For example, Eckert critiques McCullough's assertion that a child will form a *particular* gender presumably within the binary system, and Fausto-Sterling's contention that there are 'levels of masculinity and femininity in almost every permutation [of intersexual embodiment]' (cited in Eckert, 2017: 120). This, Eckert asserts, drawing on a DeleuzoGuattarian framework, falls back into the binary system of masculinity and femininity rather than understanding that the binary system provides us with nothing more than poorly evidenced and explained ideas about sexes/genders that cannot cope analytically with the unlimited configurations of *n sexes*.

Biological and psychological processes are still far from being understood beyond basic binarized chromosomal, autosomal and endocrinological bodily morphology in medicine, creating (political) social divisions based on cultural beliefs about, for example, masculinity and femininity and men and women which are all couched in much metaphor (Haraway, 1976; Martin, 2002; Roberts, 2002). Cultural femininity and masculinity are interpreted alongside the physiological findings of scientists working on the processes of genes and hormones, and then binary sex/gender differences – which many assume, but do not *actually* know exist – are actively transformed by the scientific work. From their 'findings' scientific advancement stories are amplified in their research reports with an air of authority. For example, initially, 'female' sex hormones were thought to exist only in women, causing femininity, and 'male' sex hormones only in men, causing masculinity. Sex hormones were once seen as chemical messengers of masculinity and femininity (Oudshoorn, 2003). However, only a brief time later Roberts showed that 'estrogen and testosterone are chemically very similar, and that testosterone is sometimes converted into estrogen in the body' (Roberts, 2002: 14). The lay stories about male and female hormones persist, resulting in perceptions about their affective forces upon our psyche. A quick foray into some early science underpinning 'hormonal sex differences' shows the myriad social processes that have territorialized binary sexes on molar and molecular planes. While these critiques are important and allow us to question any scientific credentials and the body of science that they are built upon, they do not answer the question: on what authority, in the first place, do physicians and midwives have the right to assign a sex on a birth certificate, or indeed another group of physicians to provide the evidence to give another sex when somebody wants to change it, in cases of trans, sex/gender expansive and intersex people. I intend to question this because it is not a mere quirk of medical discourse. Indeed, it has more wide-reaching implications for, for example, social division, and has limiting and prescriptive effects on people's lives, or on which bodies can do what. We must ask: What purpose does it serve? And is it in the interest of their patients' health and healthcare that a sex is 'known' despite the fledgling state of knowledge about the development of both physiological and psychological disease in relation to binary sexes/genders? I will take these questions up later in the book. We can suggest for now though that, as Foucault (1995) documented, the medical complex uses diagnoses to define and, thereby, socially and institutionally constrain certain behaviours, and that these knowledges are compounded with economic, epistemic and biologic 'folds of finitude' which are derived from previous 'elite' conceptual frameworks assembling and connecting with each other. The folds of finitude are represented as having an *assumed* origin, rather than being what Deleuze (2006) calls 'branches of organizing' and, thus, elements are being folded in particular ways through biopolitical surveillance.

Medical surveillance

Foucault's extensive work has been influential in our understanding of the unfolding of medical power and governance (Foucault, 1996, 2003, 2006). Foucault has revealed to us that over the last five hundred years a multiplicity of factors have been produced and assembled in relatively random ways; however, surveillance of the body through legally sanctioned clinics has increased self-surveillance. Foucault's work is, in many respects, a critique of the Marxist tradition, in which it was claimed that those who own the means of production oppress others for the benefit of the capitalist system, of which the medical fraternity were key norm entrepreneurs. While the medical fraternity have indeed produced norms, Foucault's work instead shows how multiple compounding forces point to non-human-forms and illustrates how the economic, epistemic and biological territorialize for a fleeting time, only to be reconfigured again and again, by everyone, in the ever-changing assemblages. Indeed, the three areas of conduct need to continually refold and refold, to retain their power. As Deleuze argues: systemic conduct, in its broadest use, 'continuously loses itself in infinity; as Michel Serres says, it loses all centre and territory, agonizes over its attempts to fix the place of the finite in the midst of all the infinities, and tries to establish an order within infinity' (Deleuze, 2006: 103). The infinity of ideas refolds into the system which forms the condition of new desire. While still predominantly in the domain of expert witnesses coming from the field of medicine, physicians must successively contend with incorporating the multiple forces of the profession, science, economics and, ever more so now, the voices of the public.

The high costs of health technologies, medical techniques and new types of medical care, and physicians' greater ability to intervene to sustain and improve life, have been the reasons for the penetration of regulatory agencies, to audit performance and monitor health service provision day to day (Allsop and Mulcahy, 1996). Also, patients seem to have become more important in the assemblages, in which human rights and consumer choice, alongside higher expectations of healthcare for them and members of their family, have contributed to producing an audit of performance culture, and allowed administrators to take action against doctors whose performance appears not to match those of their colleagues. This is all in spite of the issues surrounding patients, providers, and commissioners defining the quality of healthcare services differently, which translates into different expectations from the healthcare system and thus differing evaluations of its quality on the part of professional and lay people (McGlynn, 1997).

Although successive academic developments in the UK, alongside legal reforms, have helped to refine the various roles of the GMC, the royal colleges and universities in regulating the conduct and training of new and qualified practitioners, the medical professionals' ongoing freedom to practise as they see fit in the consultation room can still unequally permeate the relationship between patent and practitioner. This point I will take up again in more detail later. Nonetheless, there have been several challenges to the ways that the quality of health services have been internally evaluated by successive governments. Some social science critiques of the medical profession have argued that many de jure state interventions have curbed the privileges based on professional role status and increased the importance of individually proven worth. Allsop and Mulcahy (1996) have claimed that, across the spectrum of healthcare institutions, the regulatory web has expanded. So too has the potential for regulatory bodies to introduce and continuously change and scrutinize clinical and managerial practices within the health system. Internationally, medical governance is perhaps much more easily applied in those countries that provide universal healthcare to their citizens through healthcare budgets derived from taxes than, for example, in insurance-based systems such as the US. As Jordan Cohen suggests, in the foreword of Stern's (2006: viii) book, *Measuring medical professionalism*:

> [w]hether by intent or otherwise, our country [US] has chosen to rely on the commercial marketplace in an effort to control the escalating costs of health care. As a consequence, medicine is increasingly being viewed by policy makers and others as no different from any other commercial entity. In their view, medicine is just another business. Witness the terminology that has crept into common usage: doctors are commonly referred to as providers; patients, as consumers; health care services, as commodities.

This is an important reminder of the fundamental differences between commercialism and professionalism seen in different medical systems. Cohen goes on to say that self-interest is the dominant paradigm of the marketplace and that this is the very antithesis of self-sacrifice called for by medicine's commitment to patients' interest. While it is unclear what Cohen means by this, it is clear in this critique that attitudes to the material networks in play between practitioners, patients, institutions, and policy and professional expectations, seem to be different when you pay for your healthcare through insurance-based cover rather than publicly through a universal tax system. From this perspective, it is assumed that, as institutional reforms become more bedded in, and both practitioners and patients are more exposed to ever more competitive market forces in the UK's NHS, we may see a change in the attitudes towards each other of practitioners/providers and patients/consumers in the future. The effects of public spending reforms, support for government deregulation and the development of new public management principles through public self-regulatory agencies are matters of concern and have resulted in a number of policy changes by (particularly Conservative) governments in the UK (Allsop and Mulcahy, 1996), and all undoubtedly affect the healthcare assemblage.

In the NHS, changes have started to occur through a number of social factors, such as identifying malpractice, and the rise of conservatism and neoliberal market forces, which have put the GMC in the UK under pressure to reform, for example by introducing professional performance indicators. Successive Conservative administrations from the 1980s onwards, in which greater managerial control over hospital information systems and clinical budgets was taken up by the de jure state, enabled market forces to seep in (see Department of Health, 1989). Similarly, the intrusion of market language and market models of healthcare delivery has put medicine in danger of abandoning, or at least marginalizing, the profession's central values and public duties in the NHS. Nonetheless, these material factors are unsettling and transforming the historical protectionism installed at the macro-institutional and micro-patient relational levels in the NHS. These Conservative policy initiatives, successive governments have claimed, were to ensure cost efficiencies and increase service quality. One other outcome of these programmes, however, was the changing relationship of power within the self-governance model in most medical fields.

Allsop and Mulcahy (1996) argue that medical autonomy in the NHS was being actively challenged by government's 'interventionist' systems. These changes started to infringe on the clinical freedoms awarded through the development of the royal colleges and GMC, which until then had relatively free rein to put their own members' interests above those of the public (Chamberlain, 2009). Despite training and education reform, the disciplines were left largely unchallenged in relation to what was researched and what was then taught to new recruits. Nonetheless, a 1993 publication from the GMC called *Tomorrow's doctors* (General Medical Council, 1993), which has been updated a few times since (General Medical Council, 2003, 2009) highlights the need for doctors, including psychiatrists, to become more patient-centred and interdisciplinary focused.

The changing role of the patient

The traditional characterization of the doctor–patient relationship places the patient in a passive, compliant role (Brody, 1980: 718). However, more recently, patients' experiential knowledge and expertise in healthcare has been incorporated into policies by policy makers, altering the relationship. Early commentators on the role of patients in medical and health research, such as Veatch (1987), outlined the ethical processes that treat participants as subjects rather than objects to be experimented upon. Veatch describes the implementation of dialogical I–Thou relationships between patients and researchers that began to change the method of research that impacted healthcare. The I–Thou relationship is meant to create intellectual abstractions from the research results in order to help create patient-centred outcomes. This approach allows two different subjects to meet to name the world in order to transform it. Veatch (1991) in his sequel to *The patient as partner* (1987), extends his argument about patient-centredness to the setting of clinical care. He posits that there has been a significant paradigm shift in the doctor–patient relationship and explains its cause. These physician–patient encounters are telling with regard to how patient-centred medicine is implicated in contemporary bioethical constraints on who has the right to do what to a human and non-human body.

The involvement of patients, carers, the public and their expectations in health decision making, accordingly, was the mantra at the core of the modernization of the NHS in the UK and in much of the developed world. In the UK, rising public expectations, according to the Blair government in 1997, should be channelled into 'shaping services to make them more responsive to the needs and preferences of the people who use them' (Department of Health, 1997: para. 1.19). In a series of consultations and research projects, the public were encouraged to talk about where and by whom and in what form healthcare ought to be provided (Farrell, 2004). In another example, the GMC now consists of equal numbers of lay members alongside professionals. In spite of this reform, both Stacey (1992) and Chamberlain (2009) suggest that policy has still left flawed aspects in place, holding that clinical autonomy is largely left unregulated, while relying on those physicians who take pride in their practice to promote egalitarian ways of working with the public to achieve good health outcomes. As such, tensions remain on all sides about how all these changes affect patients, professionals and related professions, such as law makers, educationalists and researchers.

Physicians repeatedly make claims about how they aid patient participation in clinical decision making. However, as Hardwig (1985) points out, the patient remains relatively inferior to the expert in matters in which the expert is expert, resulting in patients refusing to think for themselves, which affects the need to, in our case, trust and depend on practitioners, not only as authorities but also as collaborators in their patients' medical inquiries and desires. On this view, the patient's only obligation is to seek competent help and to cooperate with the physician's expertise. Nonetheless, physicians also respond to patients' demands in tacit and subjective ways, which are laden with values, when requests for treatments either coincide with or differ from their own decisions as to what to offer them (Brody, 1980). Nonetheless, the patient–centred collaborative frame challenges health professionals' paternalism and encourages working towards supporting health interventions, by redressing service provision gatekeeping so that people can realize their health interventions in the ways that they wish. Arguably, then, there is a widespread need to understand better those health matters and the mattering of health, through a debate concerning the rights of patients versus the responsibilities of physicians, and the ramifications of this for the linkages between citizens, healthcare practitioners and health governance, and its pedagogical underpinning.

Education and policy for improving the safety and quality of care

Policy developments for medical, health and social care increasingly rely on standardization and control models. However, this has not had the expected impact on improving the quality and safety of clinical care. For example, the Royal College of Psychiatrists (RCP) is conducting an extensive revision of all psychiatric training curricula, to be completed by the end of 2020. This will meet the new standards set by the GMC, and make sure that the training programme is in line with the principles in the *Shape of training* review.[6] The new requirements signal a departure from supplying lists of low-level competences and working up to areas of greater capability. Emphasis, it is claimed, will be on knowledge, skills and attitudes that can be applied to a wide range of circumstances. However, currently much empirical work shows that trans, sex/gender diversity and intersex competences in the curricula are rare. Redfern and Sinclair (2014: 31) have suggested that: 'Not surprisingly, professionals or trainees with less knowledge about transgender persons tended to have higher anti-trans sentiments and behaviors whereas those who had attended a gender and sexuality class exhibited lower levels of anti-trans attitudes and behaviors.' Education for mental health providers may then be a key component in favourably affecting the provider/transgender patient dynamic. Similarly, participants in inter-professional workshops I conducted about trans and sex/gender diversity (for professionals and those in training) were saying that they lack the skills to support trans, sex/gender expansive and intersex people. In addition to this, there is resistance to learning about sex/ gender and sexuality from some educators and students that may impede future clinical relationships (Davy et al, 2015), which suggests that training should be made a priority if not mandatory.

Psychiatry and sexology, a becoming discipline

In 2007, the Department of Health in the United Kingdom declared that the NHS would improve the availability and distribution of more evidenced-based psychological treatments by providing the necessary funding, training and infrastructure. The Department of Health committed a total of £300 million from 2007 to 2010, with plans to fund beyond that time. The model was developed collaboratively by Department of Health, stakeholders and healthcare experts to provide treatment recommendations, and service choice and provision, consistent with the National Institute for Health Care and Excellence (NICE) guidelines (McHugh and Barlow, 2010). While allusions to egalitarian approaches are now widespread in sex/gender clinical literature, a hierarchy of importance remains between the different disciplines treating trans, sex/gender expansive or intersex people.

The RCP in the UK is accountable for representing psychiatrists. Moreover, the RCP provides advice to those training and certifying psychiatrists in the UK. Annual appraisals take place, however, there is little knowledge (except among those who undertake them), about the depth of review, the ability to identify underperforming psychiatrists, or whether follow-ups are done to ensure appraisal outcomes have a positive impact on clinical performance or service delivery. Indeed, this was also found to be the case by Chamberlain (2009) in general and surgical medicine. The institute that regulates who can and cannot legally practise medicine in the UK is the GMC. However, on a day-to-day basis the RCP is key in assessing psychiatrists' fitness to practise. Nonetheless, annual appraisals for psychiatrists have not to my knowledge been researched or evaluated for their efficacy. What is known is that Personal Development Plans (PDPs) are meant to be used as an element of the appraisal process and are understood to be a key tool by which practitioners identify their training plans, to support them in keeping up to date and enabling them to understand new skills and knowledge required to meet the changing requirements of their patients and the organizations within which they work (Newby, 2003). However, it remains unclear whether these appraisal systems work for psychiatry due to the potential hold of paradigmatic influences regarding mental health conditions and treatments on professionals, based on their epistemological and ideological approaches.[7] Nonetheless, we may be able to infer the utility of such appraisals from wider organization studies, which generally suggest that appraisals are poor at improving individual and organizational effectiveness, productivity, efficiency or accountability (de Bruijn, 2007) and any follow-up work that is required due to many impacting factors such as lack of resources, job satisfaction, known expectations.

As I will explore in more detail later, this epistemological boundary work can work against the principles of doing no harm to patients while maintaining the gatekeeping powers of psychiatrists over trans, sex/gender expansive and intersex bodies (Davy, 2015; Davy et al, 2018; Schulz, 2018). In the case of trans and sex/gender expansive people, it is the psychiatrist who diagnoses the patient with gender dysphoria (APA, 2013) or gender incongruence (WHO, 2018) through a form of symptomatic judgement, rather than through a diagnostic measurement of a disease. Once the diagnosis is made, this can then lead on to other clinical interventions, if these are sought by the patient, such as hormone treatments, voice therapy and surgery. That is, the distress (if present) can be alleviated following the process of assessment and hormonal and surgical therapies, and multidisciplinary teams support these medical interventions on the recommendation of one or more psychiatrists who have deemed the patient trans enough (see Pearce, 2018).

In the case of intersex infants, who may be displaying morphological variance, the gynaecologist, andrologist, surgical teams and endocrinologists would be called in to assess the genital morphology of the infant and, in many cases, their chromosomes and gonadal structures, in order to advise parents about their prognosis and offer an opinion about the 'best' course of action for intervening medically, the infant's psychosocialization and consequently assigning their child a 'true' sex. This begs the question of where this knowledge was derived from. For psychiatric decisions to be legitimate, valid and reliable, the knowledge base needs to be transparent and sustained over time. While the professional policies of psychiatry maintain that its present impetus is towards closer integration of education, research and practice, as enshrined in what has come to be termed evidence-based medicine (Royal College of Psychiatrists, 2018), the process of knowledge acquisition and creation must be seen to be beyond reproach (Salter, 2000). A number of challenges have been levelled at sex/gender healthcare self-regulatory processes in psychiatry, even from within its own ranks, in the form of contestations over ethical practice and unscientific approaches to therapy (West, 2004; Giordano, 2008; Whittle et al, 2008; James et al, 2016; Davy et al, 2018; Ashley, 2019a). In the UK, the Gender Identity Healthcare Practice workforce and the University of London have recently developed a nationally recognized training programme for transgender healthcare, but up until this there were apprenticeship training models in the few specialist gender identity clinics. It was unclear what these models looked like or, in fact, whether they were fit for practice; we never knew who monitored or evaluated them, or whether they were updated in line with contemporary research and best practice models.

There have been a few debates about the best approach for treating a wide range of sex/gender expansive patients (Singh, 2016), which I will unpack later in this chapter. I will continue with the critique in Chapter 4, in which I will develop an analysis about the politics surrounding sex/gender healthcare, diagnosis and healthcare outcome evaluations that challenge the apprenticeship training models that clinicians are working from. I will point to other models that increase patient autonomy, bodily integrity and self-determination that is generally wanted by trans, non-binary and intersex people, in line with other (medicalized) conditions. Suffice to say here that sex/gender affirmation healthcare whether it is for trans, sex/gender expansive or intersex people, requires a public health framework with better quality health systems and access to healthcare practitioners who are cognizant of quality health and (social) science data developed through effective partnerships with local trans, non-binary and intersex communities, in order to ensure the cultural specificity and competence in any healthcare programming (Reisner et al, 2016; Winter et al, 2016). This is not to say that current sex/gender healthcare, diagnoses and outcome evaluations are outside of culture but, to paraphrase Bruno Latour (1988: 38, emphasis in original), if there is one thing the physicians, psychiatrists, surgeons and endocrinologists 'do not do [it] is [to] *reflect* their existing culture; this does not mean that they escape the confines of the collective, but that they are building a *different* collective[, they] revolutionize the very concept of society and of what it comprises' in relation to sex/gender.

In relation to trans, sex/gender expansive or intersex people's healthcare, the scope of training or education is not visible or clear on the RCP website (Royal College of Psychiatrists, 2018). Nonetheless, some guidance has been provided that claims to try to improve standards and quality through a range of measures, including quality improvement and evidence-based research for sex/gender minorities (Wylie et al, 2014). This push towards evidence is worthy but, as sociologists and epistemologists from functionalists to postmodernists have debated extensively in the methodological literature, claims that are regarded as reliable, value-neutral and ultimately universal always stand on contested ground, especially when clinicians are attempting to elevate the value of their particular medical profession (see Saks, 1983).

Some education policies nonetheless do apply some candour to the requirements of exposing psychiatry students to how health is affected within diverse sex/gender communities. Psychiatrists are meant to receive a broad curriculum, which covers many mental health issues, however given the so-called specialist nature of trans, sex/gender diversity and intersex medicine (in the UK and elsewhere throughout the world) and their clinics within the range of psychiatric services, urological and other specialist teams, planning provision is complex. Policy does not automatically translate into practice, and a lack of knowledge and understanding, and sometimes prejudice surrounding trans, sex/gender expansive and intersex patients on the part of both educators and students, continue to be major obstacles to inclusive medical and healthcare practice. For instance, the colleges leave decisions about the inclusion and interpretation of trans, gender diversity and intersex curricula content open to negation by educators who may be unable or unwilling to include it in useful ways in their courses (Davy et al, 2015). Obstacles to sex/gender-based curricula content cannot be overcome through changes to the policies alone and greater attention to curriculum reform is needed (Davy et al, 2015). Therefore, it seems strange that early degree level and ongoing specialist training is not offered to those who may work in gender clinics.

Medico-governing of citizenship

What is more curious, and de jure state-sanctioned, is that citizenship rights relating to sex/gender assignment are also inadvertently or purposely, depending on which side of the debate one sits, awarded through the questionably valid scientific diagnosis of gender dysphoria (Davy and Toze, 2018). Although this is currently being discussed through public consultation and wider government-led research (discussed further later), Pearce (2018: 27) notes that the production of:

gender identity disorders has worked to construct a professional class of gender identity *experts*, who may act as gatekeepers for trans-specific healthcare. Psychiatrists are responsible for assessing and managing patients seeking physical transition, discussing quantitative research and case studies in the clinical literatures, preparing protocols and care pathways for patients and peer reviewing these studies, protocols and care pathways.

It is clear that psychiatrists do pursue particular knowledge then develop regulations surrounding their own and their colleagues' work as a self-regulating, gatekeeping service.

This diagnostic-research-governance-patient assemblage has enabled those involved to hold forms of power over the typology of (viable) sex/gender identities and the medical processes that manage them (Davy, 2015). More importantly for this book, however, is the territorializing affect of the assemblage within legal and citizenship mechanisms, such as in the UK's Gender Recognition Act 2004, where the diagnosis of gender dysphoria and/or physical interventions such as hormone or surgical treatments are required to be evaluated by a Gender Recognition Panel that decides on whether a person can be recognized in law as a sex/gender 'opposite' to that assigned at birth (Davy, 2010). Similarly, although the assemblage is different, the powers to manage intersex people are affective, whether through surgical intervention or what Eckert (2017) calls 'intersexualization' when the (team of) physicians produce medical forces, by indicating to parents that their child is a casualty of nature gone wrong. In this assemblage, citizenship mechanisms affect and are affected by the attending physicians; and the consequences of privileging some corporeal and psychological assumptions over others in consultations with parents. The assemblage will influence the legal standing of the person in question on the basis of a negotiation in the consultation rather than based on the materiality of the body. For example, in the UK, chromosomes are now irrelevant in law for some intersex people with regard to sex/gender assignment, as the Office of National Statistics has stated that an intersex child who had XY chromosomes, and who had had genital surgery on the basis of medical recommendations, could have her birth certificate changed to female (Finn, 1998). Medical assemblages are nonetheless affective for many others in different ways, and have lines of connection to people's legal lives, which are related to types of matter connecting to the environment, and to producing a citizen body (Duff, 2014). This legislative role, I argue, ought not to be the purview of medical practitioners and psychiatrists because of the questionably valid scientific base that they work from and the tacit underpinning of their art.

Concluding remarks

In this chapter, I explored a number of collective structural self-determination desires that led to the rise in prominence of medical and healthcare institutions. I demonstrated how self-determination is affected by and affects medical self-governed institutions, and how the elevated professional and social position of physicians, particularly in the UK, holds much relevance in the ways that medical registrations, physicians' appraisals and revalidations have been and continue to be evaluated, and to some extent how the role of the patient/consumer functions. These social forces come together in healthcare assemblages that give rise to particular norms within societies, but they are not determinative of human desire. The assemblages shift and change through time and through space. Given the ever changing relationship between doctors and patients, I asked why it is that we still accept sex assignment at birth as part of the governing network affecting our citizen lives. If my argument about biological truths and the inability of medicine to test for a truly universal human sexed body, and that any attempt to do so results in naïve aggregations on so many biological, social, legal, epistemological and policy levels, then it makes sense to come to the conclusion that sex/gender is uncontainable in the parameters set forth within the medico–legal framework. The fact that the binary sex/gender system does not precisely describe the reality of a range of human bodies, and nor do non-human bodies equally affect human bodies despite common assertions within policy, led me in this chapter to question the uses of sex/gender categorization in healthcare.

Additionally, I drew on some areas of contention that allowed us to see that healthcare assemblages generate key forces in everyone's self-determination efforts related to health. In the next chapter, I continue to discuss self-determination efforts through biopolitical assemblages of trans, sex/gender expansive and intersex healthcare and activism, in order to explore how trying to universalize sex/gender without acknowledging different lived experiences through time and space, and the roles, and the desires that are produced in an ongoing way within healthcare relationships, obscures the constant movements of human and non-human bodies. This is especially so when human and non-human bodies challenge the territorializing overcoding of the social field through deterritorializations and nomadic lines of flight that proliferate and produce multiple rhizomic connections in our communities and beyond.

4

(Self-)determining trans, sex/gender expansive and intersex people

Introduction

In this introduction to the chapter, I would first like to contextualize some aspects of the diagnostic assemblage that trans, sex/gender expansive and intersex people are affected by in the UK. According to UK-based psychiatrists (Richards et al, 2015) working in a large gender identity clinic, the funding systems for sex/gender healthcare are arranged in such a way as to make it effectively impossible to assist trans people with hormones and surgeries if they do not have a psychiatric diagnosis which relates to their sex/gender. However, the clinicians accept that this should not necessarily be the case and write:

> Is diagnosis a useful frame within which to conceptualise trans experience? We submit that it is not. Diagnosis is still necessary for funding and sundry bureaucratic matters, but it is a poor method of understanding the complex interplay of biology, psychology, personal and social influences which form this complex topic; and especially the complex interplay of such elements in any given trans person. Our clinical experience is that understanding and assisting with these elements and the interplay within them is of far more use than the rather procrustean approach of 'fitting' a given trans person within a diagnostic box and potentially *dismissing the elements which do not comfortably fit* ... We will, of course use diagnosis for pragmatic ends to assist the trans people who see us, but, to help, not to label, and given the long history of pathologisation, and longer history of diversity, never as a de facto understanding that trans people are disordered. (Richards et al, 2015: 311)

The guest editorial from which this quotation comes has, potentially, a self-determination message and a patient-centring message, which would, if developed, produce new reconfigurations of trans, sex/gender expansive and intersex people's healthcare provision. The representation of this healthcare assemblage by these clinicians shifts from diagnosing trans as pathology to providing a facilitative process so that trans healthcare interventions can be supported. Richards et al (2015) suggest that diagnosing is strategic, and that they do not really think of trans and non-binary people as disordered. They have less to say about intersex people in spite of them now also being assumed to suffer from gender dysphoria in the *DSM-5* (APA, 2013), which I will come to later in the chapter.

Jutel (2011) has argued that diagnosis changes the practice of medicine from a purely biomedical process to a medico-social practice, with intersecting social, political, technological, cultural and economic forces connecting. Similarly, the reason for a psychiatric diagnosis, claimed by Richards et al (2015) is that adult trans and sex/gender expansive people's hormonal and surgical healthcare, if so sought, is connected to medico-economic forces and relational fields within which they 'must' work, but which are not of their making. This is the same in the US and elsewhere. For example, the authors of *DSM-5*'s (APA, 2013: 453) chapter on gender dysphoria argued that they needed to incorporate a 'post-transition specifier' that would allow psychiatrists to apply a code for health insurance reimbursement for those trans and intersex people who require ongoing treatments but have no (more) signs of gender dysphoria.[1] Strategic diagnosing, it seems, is political and economic rather than medical in these cases. Frank (2016), however, suggests that a diagnosis must not support any secondary gains, which is what Richards et al's (2015) 'pragmatic ends' and the *DSM*'s 'post-transition specifier' are.

Secondary gains from a psychiatrist for trans and sex/gender expansive people can be varied, including supplying referrals to surgeons for surgery, or providing evidence for amendments to the person's civil status on identity cards or birth certificates. In many countries across the world, the connection between medicine for trans and intersex people and their civil status has been made the responsibility of physicians by means of a specific diagnosis and/or other documented medical interventions, such as sterilization, genital reformulation or hormone treatments (Davy et al, 2018). However, this 'healthcare' service produces citizenship status inequitably because these services affect citizen bodies differently. In this sense, psychiatric diagnostics are personal-political-economic matters that at this level masquerade as medical measures (Szasz, 2009). This is the lesson we should carry forward in any understanding of the role of psychiatry and the power allocated to psychiatrists in relation to trans, sex/gender expansive and intersex patients and the law.

The concerns of psychiatrists, I contend, should be what is considered medically necessary. If the psychiatric diagnosis is not supplied by psychiatrists they fear that patients' obtaining elective medical interventions (hormones, surgery, hair removal and so on) may be more easily contested by health trusts or insurance companies, and that civil status relating to sex/gender will be denied. In UK policy, a number of hurdles have to be overcome prior to receiving a ('valid') diagnosis and being referred for 'elective' interventions, as we saw with those 'maverick' physicians – Russell Reid, Richard Curtis, Helen Webberley – who have paid a price for not complying with the 'consensus' in the UK's psychiatric 'community'. In the US and elsewhere, many are even more sceptical about psychiatric diagnosis leading on to medical interventions, due to trans and sex/gender expansive, rather than intersex, exclusions in the health insurance policies. The diagnosis itself, then, in the former cases is an extra barrier to rather than an enabler of medical interventions (Ansara and Hegarty, 2012). As such, the representation by Richards et al (2015) at the start of this chapter has political and economic dimensions, and is not just reducible to medically necessary interventions. Despite the epistemic posturing, the system in which a diagnosis is required for trans, sex/gender expansive and intersex people, is not entirely out of psychiatrists' control and a rethink is required in light of self-determination demands.

If medical self-governance and evidence-based service provision form the bedrock of physicians' ability to provide good, effective, safe care, and of good quality health services, as outlined in the previous chapter, then physicians must also be able to lay the groundwork for reconfiguring the system differently in the interests of their patients, if this is really what the aspire to do. For example, cis sex/gender people do not face the same burden of verifying their commitment to treatment, nor are they required to demonstrate dysphoria for a prolonged period of time, resulting in what many trans and sex/gender expansive people see as abusive and demeaning treatment (Drescher, 2010). As such, Pearce (2018: 47) suggests that the 'trans-affirming healthcare provision presented by Christina Richards and colleagues is somewhat misleading'. I too think that it is somewhat misleading. It was not so long ago that her co-author, the lead clinician at the Charing Cross gender identity clinic,[2] James Barrett (2007) published an edited collection entitled: *Transsexual and other disorders of gender identity* indicating that he actually does think that trans and sex/

gender expansive people have a sex/gender disorder. This in itself is not surprising, if we acknowledge the contemporaneous diagnostic manuals, such as the *DSM* (APA, 1994, 1995, 2000), the *ICD* (WHO, 1975, 1993) and *SOC 6* (HBIGDA, 1990, 2001), which represent trans, sex/gender expansive and intersex people as disordered and more than likely will have affected his psychiatric practice.

In the same year as the Richards et al (2015) commentary, however, at the inaugural European Professional Association for Transgender Health conference, during a workshop about sex/gender expansive (non-binary) people, James Barrett quipped that the rise in non-binary people's presentations to *his* gender clinic was because they had all taken a degree in gender studies and that he really did not know what to do with them. By learning in gender studies programmes how to question sex/gender binary thinking, his sex/gender expansive patients were challenging the system that has been co-produced and developed by the clinicians themselves, or at least those work groups that contribute to the development of diagnoses and service provision in this area. It seems that sex/gender expansive people's presenting at the clinic made little sense to him or why they were taking up his time. This is despite the emerging scientific literature (Callis, 2014; Ansara, 2015; Knutson and Goldbach, 2019; Pryor and Vickroy, 2019; Weinhardt et al, 2019; Cordoba, 2020) producing new knowledge in relation to trans, sex/gender expansive (non-binary) and intersex people, and surprisingly some of which is written by his colleague Christina Richards (Barker and Richards, 2015; Richards et al, 2016). This seems to suggest that either James Barrett is not the sex/gender expert that the NHS system positions him in as lead clinician at the Gender Identity Clinic[3] – or that he does not practice patient-centred healthcare and believes that such people are non-viable candidates for transitioning healthcare. The principle of binary sex/gender healthcare must give way then to the principle of difference, which will affect the way that each body is approached in the clinic.

While it is possible for clinicians to change their minds and learn from new evidence and new diagnostic contexts (becoming nomadic), and this is in fact mandated in the revalidation process detailed in Chapter 3, one ought not to ignore the act that both the clinicians' and the wider profession's discursive processes and politics within relational policy fields have elevated clinical expertise over those of their trans, gender expansive and intersex patients. As such, it is unprincipled of Barrett and his colleagues not to accept some critique for the way that (their) policies and their use of these policies affect their patients. The American Psychological Association (APA, 2008: para. 11) has long acknowledged this and states that: 'psychologists are in a position to influence policies and practices in institutional settings'. And the APA also acknowledges those epistemic forces which they develop during their academic and publishing activities and in their consultations.

The problem for Barrett, it seems, is consultations with patients who have attended gender studies courses and learned to question the authority of medical opinion and the biological and sex/gender ideologies underpinning the pathologization of trans, gender expansive and intersex people. These patients are perhaps able to strip back and reveal the social forces and discursive practices that are utilized in the clinics to create a cis sex/gender binary as an actuality rather than just another 'competing universality' (Butler et al, 2000: 136–181). Education and collective activist responses in this sense aid patients to question the territorializing assemblages that are produced when a person meets micro and macro limits, and at which time people think about and act on them. They attempt to force open any obvious gaps in clinical theories and start to question the epistemological basis upon which particular limits are produced (see Pearce, 2018). This produces new assemblages and forces new desires into clinical processes of becoming (trans, sex/gender expansively and intersexually) sexed/gendered.

In the previous chapter, I demonstrated the historical intensification of physicians' social power over patients' citizen bodies. I drew on the ways in which physicians demarcated the (epistemological and economic) boundaries between different medical professions, and how this served professional colleges to monopolize the diagnostic standards, ethical frameworks and medical education at both molar and molecular levels. This chapter will attend to the clinical and political authority of psychiatrists and physicians who develop the diagnostic standards for trans, sex/gender expansive and intersex people. Many of the physicians and psychiatrists produce wider academic and 'trade journal' commentaries and literature emanating from national and international collaborations. This literature points to the fact that many of them are at the forefront of developing policy, protocols and standards of care for trans, sex/gender expansive and intersex people's healthcare. Physicians and psychiatrists are not the only ones concerned with these issues, however; we are situated (momentarily) in a time when there are many (patient) critics of these processes, whose voices I will also touch on. As such, I will consider the relatively recent development of the informed consent model (Deutsch, 2012; Reisner et al, 2015), which points to developing a nomadic relational ethics in order to assess its potential for trans, sex/gender and intersex self-determination in healthcare.

The newly developed informed consent policies that I will discuss can certainly incorporate trans, sex/gender expansive and intersex people; however, the medical establishment in the UK needs, I will argue, a deeper understanding of equitable self-determination, bodily autonomy and integrity processes to improve the quality of healthcare services. The informed consent model can be seen through the lens of a nomadic ethics which, as I noted earlier, allows for nomadic wanderings beyond the established prescriptions of sexed/gendered identifications. Nomadic ethics enables the co-assembling of bodies, technologies, habits, affects and texts in ways that transform healthcare assemblages, reaffirm difference, and also destabilize the practice of being assigned a sex/gender at birth, which is a debate in itself and cannot be explored here.

A brief history of sex/gender variance in psychiatric clinics

In Europe and America, the medical profession has been assigned responsibility for the pathologization of sex/gender variance (Meyerowitz, 2002). In the 1920s and 1930s 'feminizing' and 'masculinizing' medical procedures, such as surgeries and hormonal therapies started to be experimented with as 'treatments' for specific forms of (pseudo) hermaphroditism[4] (see Preves, 2005). Sexologists managing the surgical, endocrinological and psychiatric treatment of intersex people were the forerunners of those managing the treatment of trans and sex/gender expansive people (Hausman, 1992). It was the assumed genetic and psychical connections between those people who were intersex that paved the way for transitioning procedures to be granted to trans people (see Heath, 2006). In 1949, the term 'transsexualist' appeared in the work of Cauldwell (1949). In his sexological work, Cauldwell detailed many of his thoughts about transvestism and gender variant lives. A few years earlier Hirschfeld had used the term *seelischer Transsexualismus* which can be translated as psychic transsexualism (Stryker and Whittle, 2006: 40). Cauldwell (2001), nonetheless, thought that trans people wanted to transition because of a genetically inherited disposition that was triggered by bad parenting. For him, to succumb to the pathological desires of trans people by co-facilitating transitioning interventions was contrary to the ethical standards of physicians. He stated that: 'it would be criminal to destroy healthy organs of any kind and just as criminally destructive to mar natural beauty and create in its stead a mutilation with its resultant scar' (Cauldwell, 2001: np). Soon after Cauldwell's

1949 genetico-environmental take on trans people was published, the medical diagnosis of 'transsexualism' appeared, instigating the formulation of regulations surrounding access to sex/gender affirming procedures for trans people, if these were desired.

University-based gender identity clinics (GICs) emerged during the 1960s and 1970s, most notably at Stanford in the United States (1968), in London in the UK in 1966 (the Charing Cross Gender Identity Clinic), and at the Vrije Universiteit Medical Centre in The Netherlands (1972). These clinics started to develop programmes to determine aetiology, diagnostic criteria and treatment protocols, although always against the backdrop of both insider and outsider critics. The institutionalization of protocols and sex/gender affirming procedures for medically assisted sex/gender transition were made available to a growing number of people who wanted them, which coincided with new forms of biopolitical control. In fact, it paved the way for the emergence of a normalized and binary pathway for sex/gender change that served transitioning demands while channelling multiple possibilities of sex/gender embodiment into a limited number of patterns that would preserve the stability of a binary sex/gender system (Spade, 2006; Davy, 2011b). Furthermore, the development of standardized protocols for medically aided 'gender transitions' was framed by a preoccupation with the creation of 'productive' and 'functional' citizens (Irving, 2008).

Trans 'diagnoses' and medical interventions became devices for (potential) subjection as well as the base for fulfilling the desire to transition. Psychiatrists, surgeons, endocrinologists and patients co-produced the affirmation of pathology as the dominant frame through which sex/gender diversity is read and reinforced, effectively helping to naturalize the sex/gender binary. For instance, Judith Butler (2004b: 91) suggests that the:

> only way to secure the means by which to start this transformation is by learning how to present yourself in a discourse that is not yours, a discourse that effaces you in the act of representing you, a discourse that denies the language you might want to use to describe who you are, how you got here, and what you want from this life.

Nonetheless, even though several scholars have described trans people as passive objects of medical power and discourse (Hausman, 1995; Billings and Urban, 1996), this is far from the case (Davy, 2011b). Transition-related medical procedures, along with the diagnosis that regulates the medical governance of sex/gender transitions (that is, gender identity disorder and gender dysphoria) (see Drescher, 2010; Drescher et al, 2012), have always been the object of both individual and collective negotiation and contestation. Indeed, medical knowledge and procedures have been and continue to be complex co-production sites; fields where individual desires and needs can potentially be met, but where these desires are always questioned. These have also been sites where collective praxis, healthcare social movements and the operations of institutional biopower interact, sometimes for and sometimes against the promotion of self-determination. However, these forces do not interact with equal intensities for each trans person, each sex/gender expansive person or each intersex person.

International (psychiatric) diagnostic developments

Over fifty years ago, patient-centredness, according to the case work consultant Enid Balint (1969) at the Tavistock Institute, was emerging as an accepted medical practice for *some* patients who required both general practice and psychological interventions. More recently, patient-centredness has taken on the mantle of being key in the ethical treatment and support of all patients, including trans, sex/gender expansive and intersex people, and numerous general health policy documents throughout the world have been produced (WPATH, 2012; WHO, 2015; WMA, 2015). In the UK's NHS, for example, the patient-centred approach emphasizes the need for clinicians to be trained before working with patients. It requires training from formal educational institutions, workshops and conferences, and from mentors within the specialism. In addition, the consensus statement from the WMA (2015: 1) declared 'that everyone has the right to determine one's own gender and recognises the diversity of possibilities in this respect. The WMA calls for physicians to uphold each individual's right to self-identification with regards to gender.' Introduced in the *World Medical Journal*, the policy states that there was a proposal from the German Medical Association, and that the committee was addressed about a document which was intended to highlight the need to consider patient–physician relations, urging better medical training to enable clinicians to increase their knowledge and sensitivity toward trans people. This approach is supposed to be applied in GICs. However, a focus on topics related to self-determination and autonomy in sex/gender affirming or intersex medicine is rare (MacKinnon et al, 2020).

A separate document was proposed for intersex people and was to be developed by the Royal Dutch Medical Association, which had volunteered to prepare the report to be sent to the Council for discussion at the WMA General Assembly for approval and potential adoption. Despite these calls to reform medico-legal systems to prevent self-determination rights violations at a national level, there is failure to protect intersex children in most states (Garland and Slokenburga, 2018; Monro et al, 2019).

Explicit in these documents is that the clinician treating trans and intersex people must examine the whole person in order to form an overall diagnosis. These holistic approaches towards a patient requires that the patient be understood as a unique human-being. While this task invites some innovation in the characterization of empirical factors that the patient may bring to the consultation, it keeps in place routine clinical inquiry. Finding clinicians who can compassionately provide self-determined trans, sex/gender expansive and intersex affirming medicine proves challenging. The clinical inquiry often holds in place a physician/patient duality; a patient defined by diagnostic terms rather than through an understanding of their self-determination rights. While these policies allude to a shift in ideas, they keep intact tacit medical thinking, which we can call illness-oriented medicine (Balint, 1969).

Still pervasive in sex/gender medicine in the UK and elsewhere, tacit medical processes take place despite a regulated symptomatology. Sex/gender transitioning processes and symptomatology have been included as mental disorders in the *ICD* since 1975 and in the *DSM* since 1980. The recent *DSM-5* has for the first time included intersex people under the diagnosis of gender dysphoria. This of course implicitly excludes sex/gender expansive people who wish for something more than the binary sex/gender system. Sex/gender expansive people could nonetheless be diagnosed with gender dysphoria within the vague conceptual framework of marked incongruence between the experienced/expressed and assigned sex/gender (APA, 2013: 452). This phenomenon of diagnosing gender dysphoria is somewhat inconsistent with normal psychiatric interventions in that transition-related medicine, such as puberty blockers, hormones and surgeries, can be recommended by psychiatrists to alleviate gender dysphoria (psychosocial distress), but are not generally considered to be psychiatric treatments resulting in trans, sex/gender expansive and intersex people being connected to different health assemblages with different virtualities.

In relation to trans, sex/gender expansivity and intersexuality the *DSM-5* (2013) has what Blashfield et al (2014) call 'a prototype-matching approach' to diagnosing, in which psychiatrists compare a patient's clinical presentation to a set of prototypes. Any diagnosis of this sort, suggesting that a person will have an invariant core and demonstrate inherent behaviours, relies on tacit medical processes that conceal the molecular and molar connections between the person and their world. There is much confusion about the extent to which gender dysphoria is actually present and indeed what it 'looks' like. This is witnessed in the usage of the term 'gender dysphoria' in the healthcare literature, where it appears sometimes as a diagnosis and sometimes an identity term (Davy and Toze, 2018). In wider academic literature there are claims of it being a specific diagnosis, a phenomenological experience of distress and a personal characteristic, and it is sometimes used interchangeably within a single piece of research (see Davy and Toze, 2018). If we combine this conceptual confusion with research about psychiatrists' diagnostic usage with other research that shows that psychiatrists were more likely to assign a diagnosis if the patient displayed symptoms that closely fitted with their own theoretical understanding of the condition (Kim and Ahn, 2002; Blashfield et al, 2014), we can assume that there are probably certain tacit applications being made about gender dysphoria in gender clinics. For instance, patients have suggested that if they reveal *too many symptoms of distress* (dysphoria) in the gender clinic they can encounter significant barriers to treatment (MacKinnon et al, 2020), such as physical interventions. In these cases, the distress witnessed signifies to psychiatrists that patients are not mentally 'ready' (MacKinnon et al, 2020). How physicians assess levels of gender dysphoria, and thus 'readiness', is not written into the diagnostic manuals nor have any studies been conducted on psychiatrists' understanding of readiness as far as I am aware; psychiatrists are assumed just to know.

Psychiatrists' intuition, in these cases, cannot be squared with two key aspects of contemporary medicine. First, it cannot be squared with the shift towards patient–centred medicine that the GMC (General Medical Council, 2020) suggests, insofar as psychiatrists must respect patients' right to reach decisions with them about their treatment and care, while improving and maintaining their (mental) health. This combines with international guidance that clearly states that psychiatrists must uphold each individual's right to self-identification with regard to sex/gender (WMA, 2015), even in cases where patients are desiring intensive irreversible surgical alterations. The second aspect of relying on psychiatrists' intuition is that it cannot be squared with contemporary medicine because tacit practice is unscientific and modern medicine relies on being seen as scientific to retain its contemporary hierarchical influence. The science surrounding sex/gender and sexuality was in fact what the Workgroup on Sexual and Gender Identity Disorders, chaired by Kenneth J. Zucker, was employed to consider when updating the *DSM-5*'s diagnoses for the APA.

In summary then, the mental readiness criterion discredits the psychiatric profession's claim that the diagnosis is of an adequate scientific standard, as Zucker (2013) has claimed, while also revealing a continuing paternalistic approach, which weakens co-productive decision-making processes of patients and clinicians, reducing self-determination and increasing pathologization (see Davy, 2015).

Consequences of pathologization

Pathologization can be defined as the psycho-medical, legal and cultural practice of representing a person, characteristics of a person, or a population as being inherently disordered. Several psychologists have critiqued the *DSM* authors' assumptions that link sex/gender to psychopathology (Marecek, 1993; Marecek et al, 2004; Hyde, 2005; Hyde et al, 2019). The use of 'masculinity' and 'femininity', for example, in all the *DSM*s, some say, is problematic because it really only invokes physicians' notions of what masculine and feminine (non)conformity is. Joseph et al (2013) suggest that this leads to inappropriate diagnosing and the increased pathologizing of femininity. Moreover, to pathologize nonconformity in relation to 'masculinity' and 'femininity' relies on fixed notions that must discount cross-cultural differences, temporal changes, and behaviours that are performed by all.

Trans, sex/gender expansive and intersex people are defined as inherently pathological, because of their trans sex/gender identifications, 'trans gender behaviours' and, in the case of intersex people, their not fitting the 'expected' morphological parameters laid out by physicians, despite the latest emphasis on gender dysphoria. Recently there have been fervent promoters of depathologizing trans, sex/gender expansive and intersex people.[5] The depathologization advocates argue that trans, sex/gender expansive and intersex sexed/gendered experiences around the world are still considered pathologies (Adams et al, 2017), despite healthcare policies and clinical literature stating otherwise (WPATH, 2012; APA, 2013; WHO, 2018). For instance, in the *ICD-11 beta draft* (WHO, 2015), the proposal of the Working Group on the 'Classification of sexual disorders and sexual health' section indicated that they should remove trans-related categories from the 'Mental and behavioural disorders' chapter and include it in another called 'Conditions related to sexual health'. They proposed to continue with the classification of gender diversity in childhood as gender incongruence. While some activists have suggested that these are indeed gains, others suggest that we are led to believe that these diagnoses are based on scientific discoveries rather than the ordering of (non)pathological characteristics. I suggest that these new diagnoses are in fact created from an assumption that normal people can be divided into two and only two sex/genders, that there is such a material thing as masculinity and femininity, and that the tacit sense-impressions of psychiatrists and sexologists about them are the only ones that count. The diagnostic policies reflect these clinical sense-impressions.

Sense-impressions of trans, sex/gender expansive and intersex people

According to Cohen et al (1997), sense-impressions in psychiatric consultations with trans people have been understood through two distinct schools of thought. The first consists of those who understand that the 'psychopathology' of trans people emerges from causal psychiatric disturbances, for example, cross-sex/gender identification is the result of underlying pathological processes. The second school suggests that trans people develop independently of psychopathology, but can become impaired due to the psychological stressors that manifest from occupying a place in society that is stigmatized and difficult to coordinate, and that gives rise to difficulties associated with a new physical, social and psychological identity, as Fleming and Feinbloom (1984: 747) argue. However, these two approaches can only account for dichotomous and essentialist models of sex/gender and sexuality, in which they assume that individuals seek to embrace one('s) true identity (male or female, heterosexual, gay, lesbian, bisexual). Psychiatric consultations, as we have seen, are in fact a matter of how clinicians tacitly understand their sense-impressions in ways derived from their school of thought, which affects the person in front of them, rather than the nature of patients' own self-image. I will turn now to qualifying my claim.

The Utrecht Gender Dysphoria Scales (UGDS) – Female and Male respectively (UGDS-F and UGDS-M) – are widely used in clinics in Europe. It is difficult to ascertain who constructed them, however, some members of the European Network for the Investigation of Gender Incongruence (ENIGI) seem to be using them as part of their diagnostic practice. The ENIGI consists of:

four major West European gender identity clinics [...] a collaboration [... t]o facilitate cross-country and cross-clinic comparisons, the participating gender identity clinics (Amsterdam, Ghent, Hamburg, and Oslo) now have *one diagnostic protocol and use the same assessment battery* [...] By using similar instruments and procedures, the collaborating clinics aim to gain better insight in the phenomenon of GI [gender incongruence] and its treatment effectiveness, and to explain some of the contradicting findings in the literature. (Kreukels et al, 2012: 446, emphasis added)

The UGDS test consists of 12 items, which seems to be aimed at children or adolescents, with the use of the words 'boys' and 'girls' within the scale. An online search takes you to a chapter about the validation of the test, which was apparently accepted for publication in the *Archives of Sexual Behavior* in 2013, but never seemed to appear there. In 2016, however, a validation study was conducted of both the Gender Identity/Gender Dysphoria Questionnaire for Adolescents and Adults (GIDYQ–AA) and UGDS which did appear in the journal (Schneider et al, 2016). Content validity (nature of response to items), internal validity (internal consistency or reliability), criterion validity (strength of relationship with a related variable) and construct validity (strength of relationship with an underlying variable) are important to understand in diagnostic and treatment protocols it seems (see Reis and Judd, 2014). Likert scale measures are used to quantify attitudes towards a particular series of statements about a topic in both questionnaires, arguably tapping into the cognitive and affective components of patients' attitudes. However, for a measurement method to be meaningful and useful it must be shown that it is reliable, accurate and consistent insofar as it measures similar levels in stable participants and valid insofar as it must measure what it intends to (Carmines and Zeller, 1979), for example, a health-related questionnaire's ability to actually assess in our case sex/gender identification, gender dysphoria and gender incongruence. These tests seem to be consistent with an emphasis on distress and with the latest gender dysphoria diagnosis in the *DSM-5* (APA, 2013). Arguably, distress is understood as the clinical problem rather than the sex/gender identification per se. Also the 'new' diagnostic indicators of 'a strong desire to be rid of one's primary and/or secondary sex characteristics because of a marked incongruence with one's experienced/expressed gender', 'a strong desire for the primary and/or secondary sex characteristics of the other gender', 'a strong desire to be of the other gender', and 'a strong conviction that one has the typical feelings and reactions of the other gender' in the latter test, and in addition experiencing a 'clinically significant impairment in social, occupational, or other important areas of functioning' (APA, 2013: 452–453) in the former all seem to be congruent with diagnostic posturing of how trans people 'feel'. It is important, however, to critique the claims of validity being espoused. Interpretive research philosophies arguably lead to incompatible formulations of validity posing numerous problems for positivistic validity measures (Berg, 1989). Free-text boxes, for example, are not available in the GIDYQ–AA and UGDS tests. This of course reduces the infinite ways of responding, while safeguarding numeric 'validity' testing. Although free-text boxes would allow space for a detailed explanation of individual trans, sex/gender expansive and intersex people's desire to explore phenomena in more detail, they are never included in the tests to uncover insights into patients' self-perception about their sex/gender identification, gender dysphoria or gender incongruence. These tools produce diagnoses through what Burt (1979: 144–173) would call 'conversations with silent patients'. Idiographic measures that incorporate patients' own descriptions of their condition and what it means to them can provide a much-needed patient voice in research outcome measures. The underlying impetus of the informed consent model, which I will turn to in a later section of this chapter, should urge physicians to talk to each patient in turn rather than using a statistical abstraction; as Burt (1979: 129) noted years ago, the questionnaire approach may seem scientific, but it only 'reiterates stereotypic depiction of choiceless/choice-making role allocations while reciting the litany of mutual consent'.

The tests continue to be about how the clinicians view the symptomatology of trans, sex/gender expansive and intersex people rather than the views of patients themselves or even taking account of mutual consent. Clinicians have already established, indeed territorialized, 'true' trans, sex/gender expansive and intersex phenomena within a pathological framework, rather than understanding it through numerous other possibilities. We can suggest that what Latham calls the axiomatization of a 'true' trans person is reasserted (Latham, 2019) through the latest diagnostic assemblage. However, there are both limitations and benefits to this axiomatization. While clinical axiomatization can work as foundational in the diagnostic field, and can, in many current healthcare systems, be productive for health intervention claims for resources, insurance payments and systematized logging of codes for costing and commissioning purposes, it will always lack the ability to incorporate new discoveries and any new self-perceptions of the patients whom psychiatrists are meant to serve. In fact, these psychiatric symptoms have not changed a great deal in the successive diagnostic manuals, except perhaps semantically, since the early days of institutionalized trans healthcare and from Benjamin's (1966, 1971) 'true transsexual' symptomatology. In the case of sex/gender expansive and intersex people this axiomatization is an even more peculiar basis upon which to claim any form of validity, as explored later in this chapter. The practitioners, patients, data, diagnostic tools, and the published validation of the tools used for analysis work and the medico-legal system constitute a diagnostic assemblage. If we look at the diagnostic tools that underpin psychiatric diagnosing of trans, sex/gender expansive and intersex people through an assemblage lens, we could describe it in the following way: the assemblage territorializes the cognitive content through retrospective consolidation of a (clinical) consensus (DeLanda, 2016). As such, we can claim that any diagnostic relationship may support intervention, but must be seen as territorializing trans, gender expansive and intersex conditions. It is important to note here that trans, gender expansive and intersex conditions are not now considered psychiatric diseases (WPATH, 2012), and should be seen only as producing sense-impressions for psychiatrists who have been awarded the power to support or hinder self-determination of sex/gender transitions.

Precocious or delayed puberty and medical sense-impressions

In this section, I would like to draw attention to the different ways that sense-impressions work within the healthcare assemblage for trans, sex/gender expansive, intersex and cis children. The *DSM-5* (2013) diagnostic criteria adopt a distress or marred social functioning model for trans, sex/gender expansive and intersex children, adolescents and adults in relation to their bodies. In children, they often have to prove their distress for long periods of time. We know this is not the case for cis sex/gender people in relation to their bodies. A general practitioner can refer a cis child whom they suspect is exhibiting precocious puberty to a specialist. Cis sex/gender adolescents sometimes undergo hormone suppressing therapy, commonly known as hormone blockers or hormone supplements, in situations when puberty does not follow the expected trajectory and timescales. This medical intervention has been available for several years now (Boot et al, 1998). According to Rogol, a pharmacologist, the goals of androgen therapy for cis sex/

gender adolescent boys are to promote corporeal growth and secondary sexual characteristics while allowing an increase of muscle mass and bone mineral content. Additionally, administration of androgens in Rogol's (2005: 1319) cases, is to treat delayed puberty in cis sex/gender boys who 'feel that they look too young, are not considered a "peer" in their age group and have difficulty competing in athletic endeavours'. Rogol's analysis can be understood to situate some cis sex/gender boys within a marred social functioning narrative.

If we accept at face value that the assertion of the diagnostic manuals (*ICD-11, DSM-5*) that identification with a sex/gender other than that assigned at birth is not pathological, and that the diagnosis should relate only to the potential distress or impairment, then this of course is similar to the cis sex/gender person's impaired functioning, such as not being considered a peer in 'their' sex/gender group or having difficulty in other areas of life. If physicians believe that being trans, sex/gender or intersex is not pathological, and that it is the distress that this may cause that is the diagnosable factor, then one would have to presume that they should make no categorical distinction between a cis sex/gender boy and a trans boy who both strongly desire to enter the usual male-type puberty, develop secondary sexual characteristics in line with their desires about their future sex/gender, and be able to function in line with their peers and their 'self-determined' desire. Two major aspects need to be considered, however: first one of these children has been assigned as a female/girl or intersex and, second, they *may* have different types of reproductive organs, which would warrant different medical observations to be made and potentially different approaches in understanding the meanings of the measurements of the blood tests done to try to make sure that no untoward harm is being done by administering these interventions.

If we look at the prescribing of hormone inhibitors or hormone blockers from another angle, one may assume them to be prescribed for similar reasons to do with dysphoria or incongruence. A recent *Panorama* programme (Burns and Parks, 2019) on the BBC in the UK 'debated' and 'assessed' whether it is correct for clinicians to administer hormone blockers and/or hormones to the rising numbers of trans and sex/gender expansive children who are being referred to the only specialized service in the UK. Puberty blockers offer youth significant benefit as they relieve some gender dysphoria by preventing unwanted physical changes (Janicka and Forcier, 2016). These hormone blockers postpone the type of puberty that children often say they are fearful of, because the development of particular bodily characteristics will ultimately defy who they feel they are in relation to their bodies, producing further distress due to the unwanted pubertal changes (Riley et al, 2011; Olson and Garofalo, 2014). Remember, the same types of hormone blockers have been administered to cis children diagnosed with precocious puberty for many years as noted earlier. Precocious puberty symptoms include any or all the following: breast development, pubic or underarm hair development, rapid height growth, onset of menstruation and acne before 7 or 8 years of age in girls. Before the age of 9, boys' symptoms can be an enlargement of the testicles or penis, pubic hair growth, underarm or facial hair development, rapid height growth, voice deepening and acne (Prété et al, 2008; Roy et al, 2009). In the television programme Dr Kirkland, the presenter, who is also a family general practitioner and journalist, recognized that doctors have been prescribing these drugs for cis children experiencing 'precocious puberty' at a young age, for many years. But Kirkland claimed that in some way trans children might be different, saying 'less is known about their safety in transgender medicine, in relation to brain development'. It seems odd that he seems to be suggesting that the cerebral, material and embodied development in trans children would potentially be markedly different to that of cis sexed/gendered children, and that they will not react biologically in similar ways to those with precocious puberty.[6] There may of course be adverse reactions to these treatments, as with all treatments, including those with cis sex/gender children, but if this happens this would be dealt with as with all drug reactions. Perhaps this was just a faux pas by Dr Kirkland, or perhaps his sense-impressions about trans, sex/gender expansive and intersex children are that they are in fact a distinct species with a vastly different biology.

This is not to deny that there will be molecular effects from the interventions for trans and sex/gender expansive and intersex children. Indeed, the reason for using such treatments is to generate molecular effects. Nonetheless, these interventions have been prescribed for trans and sex/gender expansive children at the University of Amsterdam's gender clinic for over twenty years now, and for a shorter time in other countries. The physicians at the Amsterdam gender identity clinic do not 'provide any physical medical interventions before puberty' (de Vries and Cohen-Kettenis, 2012: 309) and, following extensive eligibility criteria being met by the child and the family, such as the child reaching Tanner stage 2–3 of puberty[7] and the family members being supportive, they can be prescribed GnRHas, if so desired and consented to. When a child satisfies the eligibility criteria it usually means that physicians are satisfied that they are likely to continue their treatment with more permanent medical interventions regardless of whether GnRHas are prescribed or not. Prior to this time parents are recommended to adopt an attitude of watchful waiting until the child 'arrives' at puberty.

However, critics of the treatment have argued that 'persistence' and 'desistence' of cross-sex/gender desires are influential factors in whether puberty blocking treatment ought to be given to children. In the *Panorama* film it was correctly said that there is not a vast amount of longitudinal evidence systematically generated or assessed in relation to trans (and potentially sex/gender expansive) children. However, there are several difficulties with this line of argumentation. There is some evidence from discussion of whether puberty blockers are a clinically just treatment for children to suggest that this results in less gender dysphoria and reduces suicide ideation and suicide for trans and sex/gender expansive children.[8] While more research in this area is necessary to be secure in our knowledge of the material outcomes, endocrinologists have used puberty blockers (GnRHas) and accelerators with many cis sex/gender, intersex and trans adolescents over many years, and while there is little research on the outcomes of these interventions, such research is still available.

The endocrinological treatment debate, particularly for sex/gender expansive and trans children, has also centred on a rather curious argument relating to the legalization of cannabis and the potential for it to lead on to more dangerous and addictive drugs. The argument is that hormone blockers will lead onto more permanent trans medical interventions, such as hormone therapy and surgery, and thus is something to be avoided if possible (see Roy et al, 2009). The critics do not acknowledge that the interventions have been used extensively to delay (or advance puberty) for intersex children and cis sex/gender children going through precocious puberty. The claim regarding risk, and thus the focus of contention, is that children who are treated with puberty blockers are more likely to transition to a sex/gender not assigned to them at birth, which is regarded by some as a clinical and social failure. On methodological and scientific grounds this likelihood of more permanent transitions is just not known, nor can it ever be. Therefore, this claim of causality is a rather tenuous one to make, as Zucker and Seto (2015) argue that any randomized controlled study looking at treatment and no treatment for children would be difficult (and unethical). Pursuing this type of 'gold-standard' research in today's ethically stringent climate would probably be forbidden. Also, any such study would have to be a rather long longitudinal study, as it is widely accepted that because there are multiple forms of trans sexing/gendering, transitioning can occur at any point throughout the lifespan, whether that be within the binary sex/gender system or trying to move beyond it. Within the argument of persistence/ desistence, transitioning tends also to be understood as the worst possible scenario, as opposed to being gay, lesbian and, of course, the standard: cis sex/gender. The critics' ability to proffer a hypothesis and their inability to provide evidence either supporting or opposing it is unscientific and filters through to the wider debate about the ethics of self-determining one's sex/gender. While safety is important and can be monitored, my analysis was not about whether it is morally right or wrong, but about whether physicians' sense-impressions about patient-centred care and self-determination are the same for cis and trans, sex/gender expansive and intersex patients, which I conclude they are not.

Not competent enough to self-determine their treatment!

Hilário (2020: np) argues that psychiatrists are sometimes 'allowing room for trans people to define themselves in their own terms'. I argued a number of years ago, however, that patients often offered stereotypical answers to questions that the psychiatrist asked them in the clinic to try to ensure that they received the interventions that they desired (Davy, 2010). These kinds of responses were like the axiomatic narratives outlined by Latham (2019) mentioned earlier. While seemingly, within some medical communities a patient's self-definition of sex/ gender identification and what constitutes an authentic trans person, is being challenged with the advent of informed consent models, in the UK there have been and continue to be trans (affirmative) clinicians working within the confines of protocols, clinical standards and diagnostic restrictions, which of course is not that surprising. These policy effects nonetheless are perhaps best understood through some controversies that have occurred in the UK. The outcomes of the controversies provide insights into how the diagnostic assemblage is enlarged and shrinks through time with different patients and with different clinicians.

While some psychiatrists like Christine Richards are demonstrating a more nuanced perspective on depathologization within the medical community than those, previously described, of some of her colleagues, there continue to be territorializing biopolitical forces at play resulting from medical policy and practice. These forces affect the micro and macro planes of immanence and the co-production of self-determining healthcare interventions. Nettleton (2004) describes how the contemporary landscape in healthcare is developed in part by health consumers on the net. Pearce (2018) suggests that these chatroom health seekers are researching their health concerns distributed through IT systems at the same time as trying to break out from orthodox (sex/gender) medicine. The internet has inevitably generated new types of connections and relationships with healthcare providers. Nettleton (2004: 674) states:

> Medical knowledge is therefore no longer exclusive to the medical academy and the formal medical text. It has 'escaped' into the networks of contemporary info-scapes where it can be accessed, assessed and re-appropriated. Rather than being concealed within institutional domains of medicine, knowledges of the biophysical body (hitherto medicine's most sacred object) seep out into cyberspace …

And this allows subjects to emerge, demanding nuanced approaches and co-constituting innovations as part of their right to consume healthcare. This is particularly so with the emergence of web-connected trans, sex/gender expansive and intersex people and their ability to share knowledge and information about healthcare, sex/gender affirming care, sex/gender terms and identifying (with) others who may be desiring or undergoing similar treatments (see for example Evans et al, 2017). Patients now are demanding approaches beyond, or other than the standardized and often outdated modes of healthcare delivery. In other words, healthcare consumers are more affective in their consultations, shifting them from a medical-led to a medical–consumer co-productive relationship. When the co-productive relationship is not forthcoming, actions are taken that are supported by the human rights principle of self-determination in many cases. However, there is much contemporary evidence to suggest that these affects are less effective in sex/gender medicine. For instance, psychiatrists and psychotherapists are rarely called upon to become gatekeepers for medical interventions other than those offered in trans, sex/gender expansive or intersex healthcare (Budge, 2015). As such, there is one form of moral status applied to trans, sex/gender expansive and intersex patients and another to cis sex/gender patients. The two moral statuses distinguish between those who are deemed able to articulate their desire in relation to their 'condition' (cis sex/gender) and those who must submit themselves and prove their rationality and distress (trans, sex/gender expansive and intersex), resulting in healthcare rights being disproportionally distributed. As Florence Ashley (2019a: 481) asserts:

Gender dysphoria assessments misrepresent trans embodiment and devalue the experiences of those who wish to alter their bodies for reasons other than gender dysphoria. Those who want to take HRT because of gender euphoria or creative transfiguration must lie about their fundamental experience of gender or be refused the gendered body they want – something cisgender people almost invariably get to have [...] lying or not obtaining the desired care, are unpalatable and dehumanising. Because they don't see self-reported desire for medical transition as sufficient a justification to obtain a HRT prescription, mental health referral requirements fail to recognise the value of trans self-actualisation.

What Ashley is referring to here is an informed consent self-determination argument, similar to the Kantian argument that a rational person, because of their humanness, warrants dignity as an end in itself and merits the moral status of being able to choose for themselves what happens to them and their body (Düwell, 2013). Düwell (2013), however, offers us an interesting dilemma in relation to the Kantian formulation when healthcare is needed and offered, or not, as the case may be. Here, legal consent is meaningless for protecting a physician/surgeon, particularly in de jure states that require a psychiatric diagnosis prior to their patient getting the secondary gains of body modification if so desired. Now, in many healthcare assemblages, the theoretical possibility of a physician/surgeon intervening on the body of someone who may change their mind later on requires that the patient demonstrate that they are a 'true' and 'responsible' trans, sex/gender expansive and intersex person according to the diagnostic manuals. Liability is distributed in case of future legal cases against those who have provided interventions and this safeguards, for example, the surgeons and endocrinologists involved. Perhaps, then, co-production of sexed/gendered bodies with surgery and hormones requires new relational ethics that elevates the role of the surgeon and endocrinologist.[9] A different form of 'relational ethics' is required then in which a 'circle of beneficiaries' (Düwell, 2013: 115) negotiate equitably with each other without psychiatric involvement. I will shortly turn to the question of whether the activists' depathologization praxis, which calls for this new relational ethics assemblage to proceed in order to claim self-determination in an equitable and ethical way, but first I would like to consider intersex people in order to illustrate further the battle within sex/gender healthcare of who gets to decide who is pathological and who is not, which has long been pursued, for reasons unknown, by the psychiatric sector.

The pathologizing of intersex people, in all their variety – their singularities – in the *DSM-5* (APA, 2013: 451) is bolstered by using the term *disorders of sex development*. This denotes 'conditions of inborn somatic deviations of [the] reproductive tract from the norm and/or discrepancies among the biological indicators of male and female'. However, this is a strange inclusion in the psychiatric manual deemed to be concerned with psychiatric conditions. Of course, the inclusion of intersex people is based on them suffering from gender dysphoria, which seems to me inappropriate. My colleague and I (Davy and Toze, 2018) have previously suggested that intersex people seem to be clinically assessed comparably to trans people if their assigned sex/gender at birth causes them distress for at least six months. Moreover, they can be assessed based on experiencing two or more symptomatic indicators in the manual. These diagnostic indicators are: 'a strong desire to be rid of one's primary and/or secondary sex characteristics because of a marked incongruence with one's experienced/expressed gender', 'a strong desire for the primary and/or secondary sex characteristics of the other gender', 'a strong desire to be of the other gender', and 'a strong conviction that one has the typical feelings and reactions of the other gender'. It is unclear to us which indicators can encapsulate intersex people in relation to a marked incongruence with their experienced/expressed gender and identification with the other gender, or desire to be of the other gender, or strong conviction that one has the typical feelings and reactions of the other gender. What is the *DSM-5* referring to when it uses the term 'the other gender?' (Davy and Toze, 2018). As we saw earlier, intersex infants are often operated on at a very young age and assigned an 'optimal' sex/gender. Therefore, if the 'optimal' sex/gender is what intersex people are gender dysphoric about, then this would mean that the original assignment was not optimal, and that means the medical team, in effect, caused the person to become gender dysphoric. This puts intersex people in a rather curious position insofar as they would need to produce the same symptoms as trans and sex/gender expansive people in the clinic because of the inappropriateness of the sex/gender forced on them at birth. Moreover, it seems to me, following Deleuze and Guattari (2007), that there is no inherent singular 'other sex/gender' in relation to intersex people but *n sexes*. This pathologization of trans, sex/gender expansive and intersex people is, nonetheless, rightly being challenged.

Sex/gender self-determination as political healthcare praxis

Changes in human rights discourses in recent decades have seen significant social and cultural transformations surrounding bioethics, biolaw and human principles in relation to biomedical developments (Muller, 1994; Rendtorff and Kemp, 2000; Rendtorff, 2002; Halpern, 2005; Schramme, 2008; Gordon, 2012; Ivanović et al, 2013). As we saw previously, the literature on the 'ethics of the body' (Shildrick, 2005) offers significant analytical insights into the complexity of rights-based claims of the patient and, to a lesser degree, the practitioner, the activist and the lawyer. Bioethics and biolaw, however, tend to be fixed within normative templates that often assume people in varying bioethical and medico-legal relationships have relatively stable standards of neutral judgement. And that these standards of judgement are underpinned by a determinable calculus of harms and benefits made by the rational and impartial person (Shildrick, 2005). Laclau (2005: 70) argues that, to exist as a political subject in the first place, a social movement in its 'totality' (that is, as 'a people') must 'have access to the field of representation'. We have seen however that trans, sex/gender expansive and intersex people do not have extensive scope in relation to their own representations in relation to their transitioning desires in the clinic. Representations are being produced by them nonetheless elsewhere and particularly in health social movements. In this section I will describe the main interventions that the trans and intersex health social movement wants from health systems and show the implications of these representational demands for health policy in insurance and welfare-state systems.

First, though, I would like to start to look at the political representational work, originating particularly from some trans and sex/gender expansive people, about being 'born this way'. Trans and sex/gender expansive people have previously defined their sex/gender identifications with reference to Cartesian dualism, in which the body is distinct from the mind. This dualism was most commonly depicted through a 'wrong body' narrative that was differentiated from how the mind experiences and feels (Prosser, 1998); however, due to the availability of vernacularized neuroscience, the narratives in some trans people accounts have been refined and they have adopted a more sophisticated but, I will go on to argue, a no less problematic and unhelpful, biogenetic narrative. Since the rise in the social status of neuroscience, and of course the role that DNA plays in the way we look, what we are supposed to 'be' and what we supposedly can 'do', the 'dumbed down' scientific languages that surround them for public consumption and use have entered trans, sex/gender expansive and intersex vernacular without much critique. In some trans and sex/gender expansive people's claims to womanhood or manhood, and indeed beyond these representations, the structure of the brain takes centre stage as a biological fact, with inner feminine and masculine traits. Some of the trans advocates' claims now imply that they have a cerebral intersex condition (Transgender London, 2011; Brain, 2012). Drawing on a misreading of biological research from Kruijver et al (2000) and Zhouet al (1995) – research based on a very small sample, not replicated, and thus scientifically flawed – then truncating these research findings, these advocates have suggested that sex/gender identities are a product of innate biological dispositions caused by hormonal influences in the fetus which affect the brain. In spite of these early studies, and a large review incorporating biological 'evidence' (Besser et al, 2006) suggesting that there are various bodies of work showing the *possible* link to trans, sex/gender expansive and intersex identities, I would like to qualify my critique that this research is flawed insofar as it tries to, but does not successfully show that hormonal influences produce feminized or masculinized neurological brain structures which then direct a post-natal desire to transition. This, I argue, cannot take account of the material, behavioural and morphological developments that manifest through time and through life. Researchers (Shonkoff and Phillips, 2000; Giedd, 2004) have described synaptic growth in the brain and this evidence considered demonstrates that in early childhood, adolescence and into young adulthood the brain is much more materially affected by behaviour and environment, and is co-constitutive along with biology, which we can see in neurological structures through scans. Although the variable of sex/gender is used in these studies to understand empirical 'differences', they are rarely understood in sexed/gendered terms, but in morphological terms, which is explained by Giedd (2004: 79) as:

> male brains are approximately 12% larger on average than those of females. This difference remains statistically significant, even when controlling for height and weight. Of course, gross size of structures may not reflect sexually dimorphic differences in neuronal connectivity or receptor density [... and] should not be interpreted as imparting any sort of functional advantage or disadvantage [...] the brain undergo[es] dynamic changes.

Other researchers have argued that the brain can rewire or reshape itself in response to new stimuli, which has been called neurogenesis (Maguire et al, 2006; Woollett and Maguire, 2011). The leap from brain structures to femininity and masculinity 'in' brains misses out a fundamental stage of inquiry, which is paramount for these claims to be warranted, that of social forces impacting the judgement of what are coded as masculine and feminine behaviours and how masculinity or femininity are assembled in a single sex/gender.

As such, it is not clear why this activist strategy of seeking an essentialist explanation about being trans, sex/gender expansive or intersex through an appeal to the 'truth' of scientific language has currency in contesting professional expertise (see Pearce, 2018). The point is, it ought not to be the case that we use an insecure, 'competing universality' to justify our sense of becoming and to be able to self-determine ourselves. What I suggest we need to produce and represent is how (human and non-human) modes of becoming affect each body at each moment. Moreover, we must suggest that there are material aspects that will always exceed our knowledge. We can never know in advance the affective capacities of a body, the effects of which it is capable, 'in a given encounter, a given arrangement, a given combination' (Deleuze, 1988: 125). What we can know, however, is our desire, our will to produce ourselves.

Informed consent models

The WPATH's *SOC 7* (2012), produced by clinicians, researchers and occasionally trans health social movement activists, has attempted to establish a looser language, which shifts trans healthcare from a gatekeeper model to a collaborative model, due to widespread problems with access, provision and delivery of health services for trans and sex/gender expansive people. The *SOC 7* stresses that it is important for healthcare professionals to recognize that trans people's health interventions are foremost a patient's decision and the responsibility of the professional is to assist patients with making fully informed decisions.

Trans activists have been at the forefront of challenging healthcare professionals in the NHS to incorporate a self-determination approach, but with little success. Problematic research, such as that which promotes a pathologizing view of trans, sex/gender expansive and intersex people, is also challenged with little effect. The consequences of pathologization can include human rights violations, which negatively impact access to healthcare for trans, sex/gender expansive and intersex people, the right to bodily integrity, and limit the right to a self-determined personality. Nonetheless, trans, sex/gender expansive and intersex depathologization discourses, together with anti-psychiatric perspectives, have started to discuss how psychiatric diagnosis can be coercive, even in the face of a widespread shift in health policies towards patient-centred medicine (Davy et al, 2018). When such research is acknowledged within medicine, then perhaps we will see some developments in patient-centred medicine in parity with other healthcare practices given to cis sex/gender people. First, though, the health assemblage must desire that another healthcare economy is possible, beyond the binary model of 'biological' pathologies for trans, sex/gender expansive and intersex people.

The biologism debate mentioned earlier often stands opposed to the self-determination approach for claiming healthcare interventions and demanding policy and practice changes. To be essentially a woman or essentially a man or neither is what Nick Crossley (2001: 34) calls 'vulgar materialism', which fails to allow for the intersection of politics, science, philosophy and biology, and therefore the question of applying new materialist approaches is raised again. As such, biologism on its own is immaterial to whether trans, sex/gender expansive and intersex people can be at the forefront of producing their sex/gender and healthcare, if the healthcare sector truly desires patient-centred care for all.

Describing sex/gender diversity as pathological or otherwise abnormal is groundless, discriminatory and without demonstrable clinical utility (Castro-Peraza et al, 2019). By contrast, the informed consent model for gender affirming treatment seeks to acknowledge and better support the patient's right to, and capability for, autonomy, bodily integrity and self-determination in choosing care options without the mandatory involvement of a psychiatrist. New developments surrounding informed consent models of healthcare for trans, gender expansive and intersex people are, however, at an embryonic stage and are often limited to certain medical interventions, such as hormone therapy (see Deutsch, 2012). Nonetheless, this approach is forcing open the obvious gaps in the traditional pathologizing theories, and through these gaps, people can question the empirical basis upon which sex/gender healthcare services are constructed.

The informed consent model has been described by the WPATH (2012) as consistent with the guidelines presented in the *SOC 7*. WPATH argues that these are flexible clinical guidelines which support the personalized tailoring of interventions co-constituted by the individual and health professionals. However, in spite of

WPATH's 'flexibility', and before it can be applied, first it is the role of a(n) (experienced) mental health professional to 'directly assess gender dysphoria in children and adolescents' (WPATH, 2012: 174). Similarly, for adults, WPATH states that '[i]nitiation of hormone therapy may be undertaken after a psychosocial assessment has been conducted and informed consent has been obtained by a qualified health professional', and the person should have 'well-documented gender dysphoria' (WPATH, 2012: 187). While WPATH seems to be edging towards informed consent, the guidelines do not fully embrace the model outlined by advocates. Continued reliance on mental health professionals to determine eligibility and readiness for treatment sends a clear message that the patient is not really in the position to self-determine their bodily interventions if so sought. Informed consent does not enable hormone treatments or surgeries on demand but supports patients' and clinicians' collaborative determination of the best available treatment (see Cavanaugh et al, 2016). This, as we have seen with Helen Webberley, who was providing private care to some trans and sex/gender expansive children in the UK, and the (failed) attempt to bring charges of malpractice against Richard Curtis, undermines rather than complements the informed consent model for legally competent people to make decisions about their healthcare.

One more point I would like to demonstrate is the assertion that assessment of gender dysphoria is required. While the *DSM-5* (APA, 2013) was produced a year after the *SOC 7*, and although *DSM-5* accepts that the 'phenomenology' of trans and sex/gender expansive people is much more diverse than was previously acknowledged in the clinical literature, the reliance on evaluating gender dysphoria is problematic. For instance, the *DSM-5* (APA, 2013: 453) states curiously that not all individuals will experience distress as a result of incongruence, despite a strong desire for medical interventions. It is far from transparent, then, how a mental health professional can look for and provide a well documented evaluation of someone's gender dysphoria when for some it may not be there in the first place (Davy and Toze, 2018).

International medico-legal assemblages and self-determination

I wish now to focus on three developments that challenge the omnipotence of the medical field over trans, sex/gender expansive and intersex bodies. A number of medico-legal models are being applied internationally. For example, the Argentinian Gender Identity

Law, enacted in 2012, provides the right to state-funded trans healthcare within an informed consent model. The act introduced an unprecedented law for trans people based on human rights principles. No medical diagnosis or treatment is required for a change of legal gender, and the act allows children to consent to change their legal gender when supported by their legal representatives. This law now sets a reference point for the development of other national legal frameworks and health policies, and is cited by many trans activists as incorporating their rights for human dignity, bodily integrity and self-determination (Davy et al, 2018).

According to Davy et al (2018), the Maltese Gender Identity, Gender Expression, and Sex Characteristics Act, adopted in 2015, fulfils many of the demands of the depathologization movement. The act pledges the right of all Maltese citizens to the acknowledgement of their sex/gender identity, and the recorded sex/gender can be amended without a diagnosis or medical treatment being required. Any change of a recorded sex/gender is self-declarative. Additionally, the act protects the bodily integrity and physical autonomy of children against treatment and/or surgical intervention. An amendment to the Maltese act, in 2016, outlawed the pathologization of sex/gender identity or sex/gender expression as classified in *ICD* or other internationally recognized classification manuals, such as the *DSM-5*. Unlike the Argentinian law, however, trans-specific state-funded healthcare is not guaranteed in Malta.

And the final example: Ireland passed the Gender Recognition Act 2015, which allows legal sex/gender changes without an assessment by the state or its norm entrepreneurs. Sex/gender amendments are possible through self-determination for any person over the age of 18 who is listed in Irish birth or adoption registers. Anyone between the ages of 16 and 18 must secure a court order to exempt them from the normal requirement to be at least 18 years of age. Ireland is one of only four legal jurisdictions in the world where people may legally change sex/gender through self-determination. All these examples show a trend towards autonomy, bodily integrity and self-determination; however *n sexes* are caught up in multiple medico-legal assemblages across the world that are always in the process of becoming. This challenges the understanding of the utility of sex/gender assignment at birth on numerous planes of immanence.

Concluding remarks

Trans, sex/gender expansive and intersex people's healthcare is caught up in complex healthcare assemblages consisting of government funding, governing institutions, educational standards, revalidation processes, de jure state psychiatric agencies and the more recent development of – but much less heard – patients' voices. Sex/gender transitions have always been co-produced but constrained by psychiatric practices because of both tacit healthcare practices and economic reasoning within an assemblage distributing affects and being affected by other cultural and political assemblages. This has led some trans, sex/gender expansive and intersex people to tailor their narratives in line with psychiatrically established representations to claim their healthcare desires. Nonetheless, health assemblages develop in nomadic ways. The nascent informed consent model is gradually forcing healthcare practitioners and governing institutions to think that another healthcare economy is possible, beyond a binary model of 'biological' pathologies for trans, sex/gender expansive and intersex people. I will now turn to school cultures in the UK, to look at how sex/gender assignment is being awarded less force in producing sex/gender. This will show how these cultures connect to the biopolitical assemblage that regulates the citizen body and highlight that the sex/gender assemblage in school cultures produces citizenship status differently to the sex/gender assemblage in UK medicine.

5

Self-determination
in school cultures

Introduction

In this chapter I will look at different assemblages that affect and are affected by trans and sex/gender expansive children and their parents.[1] In the school-education assemblage there are forces that intensify, affecting trans and sex/gender expansive children and their parents. This is the same for cis people too. The relevant qualities that everybody has are not inherent, but are gripped in specific assemblages. The qualities are not archetypal or phylogenetic, but are grasped/desired in assemblages, becoming-human and/or becoming-social (Deleuze and Guattari, 2004). There is a growing evidence base that promoting self-determination has positive effects on students (Wehmeyer, 2014). Generally, students with various physiological and psychological differences have been the focus in building self-determination theory in schools (Eisenman and Chamberlin, 2001; Wehmeyer et al, 2003; Wehmeyer, 2014). Educationalists have developed what they refer to as self-determination interventions in order to support and motivate students by developing strategies that may help them succeed through school. These interventions are meant to be worked out with the students and through considering the goals that are meaningful to the student. This enhances students' engagement with the curricula and strengthens their chances of completing school (Abery et al, 1995; Eisenman, 2007). Whether these strategies, motivations and self-determination opportunities can be implemented rests on the chances that educators and the curriculum allow (Eisenman and Chamberlin, 2001) alongside other systemic forces, such as policy incentivizations and wider public pressures.

Self-determination models in education have been developed from the social model of disability activists and academics who were highlighting how difference was used to fuel discrimination against those considered to be educationally, physically and/or mentally impaired. The social model of disability has influenced many self-determination models, including those related to trans, sex/gender expansive and intersex people. There are some contemporary international school policy initiatives for trans, sex/gender expansive and intersex children at school. This development comes at a time when the legal recognition of trans, sex/gender expansive and intersex people has been awarded varying degrees of legal (as opposed to cultural) and citizenship rights within sex/gender systems in many different nation states. These developments have contributed to the re-emergence of an older legal and policy debate: should a person's sex/gender be legally relevant when considering equal rights legislation?

Those who view boys, girls, men, women, intersex, sex/gender expansive and trans as inherently the same except in reproductive function and bodily aesthetics, and regard any other observable differences as the results of social conditioning, would perhaps not see that sex assignment has much meaning. However, those who suggest that we live with historical inequality between the sexes, suggest that we require binary sex differentiation in order to equalize and amend the wrongs of the past. K.R. Browne's (1984) social evolutionary theory of binary sex differences, however, could never deal with the differences within each social sex/gender. He stated that:

> states must be prepared to show that sex classifications are in fact better than other classifications that could be made. The author parts company with others on this issue and would allow considerations of efficiency and administrative convenience to be included in the decision making calculus. Where strong enough, these considerations should be determinative.

While K.R. Browne (1984: 619) was only looking at binary sex differentiation for legal purposes, he suggests that:

> A recognition of [binary] sex differences does not compel an acceptance of all forms of sex discrimination. Much discrimination has nothing to do with genuine sex differences […] A recognition of differences does mean, however, that not all discrimination is invidious, and thus an inquiry must be made into the particulars of each case.

If each case of discrimination should be looked at through the recognition of sex/gender differences, then at what point on the dividing line do we say that one person is male and another person is female? This question emerges from the fact that biology has shown us that humans do not necessarily fall into such discrete sides of the binary, a point that is acknowledged by K.R. Browne but summarily dismissed. A second issue that presents itself to me and prompts me to question the premise of Browne's argument are the intensities that produce human and non-human bodies within medico-legal assemblages are not purely biologically driven. In light of this, Browne is looking for an easy-to-administer definition of sex/gender but can derive little from the biological research he cites because sex/gender is not strictly biological, and works through particular assemblages with varying intensities that may or may not support social norms. Desires produce particular goals as well as underpin sociopolitical hierarchies that maintain certain opportunities, rights and privileges because of the morphology of the body (Karkazis, 2019). Nonetheless, he suggests that to execute 'a sex-blind legal order on a two-sexed species may not be successful without considerable coercion by the state' (Browne, 1984: 620); a rational policy, he argues, whose objective is to regard the sexes/genders fairly, must take into account the differences between the sexes. He then goes on to contradict his assertion about the two-sex model by suggesting that: 'Of course, any kind of determinist view is usually an oversimplification' (Browne, 1984: 650). If the two-sex model is an oversimplification then why do we not have, in the words of Deleuze and Guattari (2007), '*n sexes*', indicating that sexes/genders can be reconfigured and (can) matter in multiple ways? To relinquish difference in favour of a universal corporeality and approach the meeting of human and non-human bodies within the medico-legal assemblage will inevitably undermine health and self-determination.

We can look to Deleuze and Guattari's (2004) concept of a 'series' of things, where psychological and behavioural similarities occur in particular populations and where they are interpreted or represented in particular ways. However, Deleuze and Guattari also warn that this epistemological approach is not innocent but nebulous, because it does not acknowledge heterogeneity. While Browne's assertions are now quite dated, a similar set of claims has reared its head again at the beginning of the 21st century in the guise of gender critical ideology, which has attempted to take to task parents and groups that are supportive of trans and sex/gender expansive children. Gender critical feminists suggest that trans people are unable to change sex/gender because of their biology, that is, chromosomes, gametes and procreative potential. This form of epistemic posturing by gender critical feminists, to paraphrase Audrey Lourde (2018), demonstrates an arrogance in assuming that any discussion of feminist theory ought not to examine our many differences. Lourde (2018: 48) rhetorically asks: 'What does it mean when the tools of racist patriarchy [essentialism] are used to examine the fruits of that same patriarchy? It means that only the most narrow perimeters of change are possible and allowable.' Nonetheless, those who have heightened visibility through platforms such as the mainstream media continue to suggest that children do not fully understand their desires to live differently or beyond the sex/gender assignment they were given, and it is others, and particularly parents, who are influencing their children's desires, by forcing a 'transgender ideology' on them. As we saw earlier, gender critical feminists further suggest that these children should be coerced 'back' to their original assignment. However, as Kennedy and Hellen (2010: 40) have argued:

> if a school system tried to coerce any other group of individuals to become people they are not, to regard an inner core of their identities as illegitimate, and prevent them from freely expressing their identities freely [...] it would be regarded as barbaric.

The gist of Kennedy and Hellen's argument is, I believe, correct, insofar as nobody should be coerced into a life that they do not want to have; I also agree that it would be regarded barbaric if other groups had to put up with life policing in the same insidious way as young trans and sex/gender expansive children do. However, I take issue with the inherent essentialism in their argument. While the desire to transition to something different from the sex/gender assigned at birth is unmistakable for these children, there are only processes of becoming.

Victor Madrigal-Borloz, in his capacity as United Nations' independent expert on the protection against violence and discrimination based on sexual orientation and gender identification, made an unparalleled argument before the General Assembly in 2018 (see United Nations Office of the High Commission, 2019). He argues that any legal, social or cultural obligations to abide by dichotomous sex/gender norms violate human rights law. Madrigal-Borloz drew upon decades of scholars' and activists' critiques of the idea that biological sex inherently determines gender identity through a fixed process or universal formula. A key claim was that sex/gender norms obstruct everybody's right to self-determination (United Nations Office of the High Commissioner for Human Rights, 2019). Before this declaration by Madrigal-Borloz, however, the Maltese government arguably had introduced one of the most inclusive nationwide policies about sex/gender and schooling, stating that:

The Trans, Gender Variant and Intersex Students in Schools Policy is developed within the context of the Framework for the Education Strategy for Malta 2014–2024 [...] and the values promoted through the Respect for All Framework [...] Every student, in the present and in the future will be provided with the necessary knowledge, skills, competences and attributes for citizenship and employability within an inclusive, safe, secure and motivating school environment that inspires and facilitates learning. (Agius et al, 2015: 5)

The aims of this policy are to:

1. Foster a school environment that is inclusive, safe and free from harassment and discrimination for all members of the school community, students and adults, regardless of sex, sexual orientation, gender identity, gender expression and/or sex characteristics. 2. Promote the learning of human diversity that is inclusive of trans, gender variant and intersex students, thus promoting social awareness, acceptance and respect [and] 3. Ensure a school climate that is physically, emotionally and intellectually safe for all students to further their successful learning development and well-being, including that of trans, gender variant and intersex persons. (Agius et al, 2015: 5–6)

This policy acknowledges that trans, sex/gender expansive and intersex students and their parents are often embroiled in situations at school in which they are critiqued, either face to face or through other more subtle means, such as restrictive policies and unspoken social norms. The Maltese policy puts the rights of *everyone* at the heart of schooling and awards protections rarely seen before.

At micro levels within schools in the UK, these wider sex/gender norms are being debated and sometimes implemented based on 'self-determination' policy from the EU. Some affirmative parents and teachers are supporting trans and sex/gender expansive children, producing the ground upon which students are able to make some choices about sex/gender expression that mingle and collide with other human and non-human bodies in assemblages with distinct forces. These forces are productive but with uncertain outcomes.

Deleuze's notions of affect and intensity have been central to key ideas in educational settings more recently. Pedagogical scholars and related disciplines have drawn on Deleuze's work to develop 'affective pedagogies' (Probyn, 2004; Hickey-Moody, 2009a, 2009b). This scholarship considers education and learning spaces as facilitating intensive processes of affective and material production of (posthuman) bodies. Forces, sensations and intensities are transmitted between human and non-human bodies in ways that transform trans and sex/gender expansive children's distinctive capacities. In this chapter, I will draw on my own research in the UK and a growing body of international empirical work (Ehrensaft, 2012, 2016; Hidalgo et al, 2013; Pyne, 2014a, 2014b, 2016; Temple Newhook et al, 2018; Winters et al, 2018) that looks at school cultures and the advocacy-school assemblage being produced by parents, teachers and other human and non-human bodies who are supportive of trans and sex/gender expansive children. Through the concept of nomadic subjects which, as we saw earlier, is styles of living through transitions and passages without predetermined destinations, we can explore the potential that emerges in relation to 'self-determining' sexes/genders in school cultures. Braidotti (2006b: np) suggests that 'nomadism refers to the kind of critical consciousness that resists settling into socially coded modes of thought and behaviour. It is the subversion of set conventions that defines the nomadic state, not the literal act of travelling' (Braidotti, 2006b: np).

As noted earlier, this chapter will draw on my own empirical work with parents (in the UK) who are supportive of their trans and sex/gender expansive children and explore the challenges they face in advocating alongside them in schools. I intend to illustrate how sex/gender 'self-determination' is situated as a possibility within school cultures. Particularly, I will be looking at the intended and unintended outcomes of parents' advocacy, in which some become proponents in the virtual field of nomadic ethics and sex/gender 'self-determination' by proxy. As such, the premise of many supportive parenting strategies is that the children are the experts regarding their sex/gender experiences, and that they should be able to express themselves without restriction, criticism or ostracism, and that the adults are their translators at certain junctures (Ehrensaft, 2016: 16).

Moreover, I will show how parents need to become *expert witnesses* on any of their nomadic journeys with their children while countering many negative critiques. In this role, parents attempt to find gaps in the policy and public discourses where 'sex' is used as an arbitrary segregationally limiting approach in dividing people. They also find gaps in new relationships with in-group and out-group norms, the points of weakness and false genesis of sex/gender determination.

Drawing on Deleuze's (1992) account of bodies, affects and assemblages I will reject the notion that people have innate capacities, which are then realized in particular situations; I will instead show that through these gaps, through co-productive forces and through coincidental paths, resistance and change occurs with regard to parents' trans and sex/gender expansive children at school, not by asking what trans and sex/gender expansive children are but by asking what their bodies can do.

Contextualizing schooling in the UK and internationally

School has been the place to both educate and socialize children, and generally mirrors the social, cultural and economic modes of reproduction (Kamens et al, 1996; Miller, 2018). This is reflected in early documents produced by the Council of Europe, which suggest that fundamental transformations in education and other connected institutional domains should be carried out in each of the member states, according to its national context and traditions. The first key policy I want to consider here states that there:

> was no sphere [that] should be exempt from engaging in intercultural dialogue – be it the neighbourhood, the workplace, the education system and associated institutions, civil society and particularly the youth sector, the media, the arts world or the political arena. Every actor – whether NGOs, religious communities, the social partners or political parties – is implicated, as indeed are individuals. And every level of governance – from local to regional to national to international – is drawn into the democratic management of cultural diversity. (Council of Europe Ministers of Foreign Affairs, 2008: 10)

These aspects of cultural diversity socialization for citizens, while being trained to become economically and socially productive, and relational to other culturally diverse citizens, are subsumed within the social contract with the de jure state, and are referred to in many national educational policies. Citizens and de jure state functionaries, in the form of expert witnesses, ought to all come together in producing society and develop economic and social progressiveness through promoting better intercultural practices. These foci are incorporated into mechanisms implemented to measure how schools are doing in, for example, their attainment goals and actual exam and assignment results, and this is especially prominent in children's later years of schooling, when they are being prepared for their potential career paths, employment, training or university places. In many modern societies, especially in such places as the UK, concepts of cultural diversity and values in education are often contested.

Cultural diversity is problematized because of many contending cultural learning traditions that are not accepted in majority culture or even understood fully by all teachers. In the UK, this has resulted in a series of faith schools, state schools, academies and private schools having different degrees of autonomy in relation to the curriculum and the subjects taught. Different forms of schooling have been researched in relation to implementing cultural diversity and the evidence suggests that difficulties in incorporating it into teaching are exacerbated because there is no clear definition of multicultural education (Gay, 1979; Appleton, 1983; Grant and Sleeter, 1986). Some teachers also think that cultural diversity does not fit into disciplines, such as maths or science, or that it would put too much strain on the time available for key curricula (Ogbu, 1992). Suzuki (1984: 295), adds that:

> even many well-intentioned educators promote multiculturalism in rather superficial ways – for example, by highlighting ethnic foods, holidays, or costumes [...], such approaches can contribute little to solving the problems faced by schools in a multicultural society and to improving these schools in the ways envisioned by some of the more serious, thoughtful advocates of multicultural education.

The studies often focus on the cultural traditions in relation to faith, spirituality and ethnicity rather than, for example, sex/gender diversity. While of course this focus is important, the faith-based traditions that are introduced to learners are often celebrated as fundamental to, and unwavering from, an original set of customs. However, as we saw earlier, citizenship and values surrounding the nation, faiths and customs are continually being contested and thus evolve.

In a postcolonial world, the merging of customs – both faith-based customs and wider cultural practices – is deftly debased. For example, anthropologists have long argued that pre-colonial cultures were often 'more accommodating to sex/gender differences than present-day homophobes allow'. In the case of some African countries' traditional customs, these largely reflect 'imported Christian missionary ideology and colonial law' (Epprecht and Egya, 2011: 369).[2] Similarly, sex/gender systems are produced differently across the world but are rarely the focus of multicultural teaching.

Freire's (2000) contributions to the emancipation of consciousness along sex/gender lines was not developed in his early work, which tended to promote cultural and class-based struggles, and particularly indigenous struggles, against colonial oppression. Sexuality and gender as culturally based issues were pushed aside, as in much of the Marxian approach to pedagogy. The principles of engagement with Freire's teaching and learning techniques nonetheless have been taken up by feminists like bell hooks (1993, 1994). She tells us without sentimentalism that we need to love, without making our differences invisible,[3] to truly promote a democratic and a racism-free life. This message is not backward-looking insofar as we, as humans, are inherently loving, but a projection of what could be produced if we let ourselves love others different to ourselves.

The debasing of original customs has not been lost on the Council of Europe (2016) who have developed a relatively new report entitled: *Competences for democratic culture: Living together as equals in culturally diverse democratic societies*, which tries to cultivate the cultural competences of the education sector across Europe on account of the multicultural societies that we live in. Rather than looking back to cultural practices and customs, educators are encouraged to look forward towards a state of accommodation by working through the inevitable conflicts that will emerge with numerous people with multiple customs and traditions living together within a nation state.

The Council of Europe (2016: 15) announced that competences 'need to be acquired by learners if they are to participate effectively in a culture of democracy and live peacefully together with others in culturally diverse democratic societies'. The list of competences that schools are encouraged to develop are divided into values, attitudes and skills, and comprises valuing human dignity and human rights, cultural diversity, democracy, justice, fairness, equality and the rule of law; being open to cultural otherness and to other beliefs, worldviews and practices; being respectful; being civic-minded; taking responsibility; partaking in self-efficacy; being tolerant of ambiguity while pursuing autonomous learning, critical analytical and thinking skills alongside listening and observation skills. In light of this, students must demonstrate empathy, flexibility and adaptability, linguistic and communicative abilities, being cooperative, while learning conflict-resolution competences and developing a critical understanding of the world and the self. This extensive list is indeed perhaps generally something that liberal pluralist societies should strive for.

Chantal Mouffe (1996: 10) suggests, however, that the types of liberal ideals outlined in the EU policy assume that the 'moral' requirements of a just society are being led by the 'free exercise of public reason' and are supposed to develop through rational and reasonable discussions toward a consensus with which we are all happy. This of course, she is arguing, diminishes the real and sometimes violent nature of conflicts and power struggles within society, all of which seem to disappear into thin air in this abstract list of goals. Instead we must work through the conflict, aided by dialogue, with the understanding that some rights just might trump some others (Smith, 1998). This is especially the case for those conflicts where it may never be possible able to find common ground with everyone involved within a particular space and time, or solutions that will ever be supported by the governing parties, the self-regulating professional bodies, or the people in them who are meant to facilitate the ideals.

Notwithstanding my critique of EU competences listed earlier, I am in agreement with Anne Marie Smith's (1998) interpretation of Laclau and Mouffe, who she understands as demonstrating that the regulatory frameworks of government and the people tasked to implement changes on macro and micro planes of immanence seem to retain some imaginary authority; that is, people look to these authorities to deal with cultural differences, not because the authorities are unrelenting static entities and have a simple form of power over the powerless, but because hegemonic articulations have been seen to shift (back and forth) through their power,[4] which can be adapted to organic crises in many cultural domains. The extensive list of competences described earlier of course has implications for the way that the hegemonic cultural articulations within policy may transpire for different people, that is, the articulations that are developed and incorporated and those that are ignored. For example, the implications of the (non-)implementation of competences will potentially be different for children and parents than for teachers and other school staff, who are all key for children's acquisition of those competences and in facilitating them while the children are at school. There is an assumption that teachers and other staff at the school both believe in and will practise the competences that the liberal pluralist viewpoint recommends in national and international policy, an argument I will pick up on later. Another assumption is that those competences do not affect the facilitators' own belief systems negatively. Nonetheless, even if two viewpoints diverge, it seems from the EU policy goals (Council of Europe, 2016) that, like the physicians in the previous chapter, it is expected that those who provide social services will potentially forgo their own 'self-determination' for the assumed wider good of democratic liberal pluralism. This is most passionately described by the Council of Europe (2016: 10):

All cultures are internally heterogeneous, contested, dynamic and constantly evolving. And all people inhabit multiple cultures that interact in complex ways. The concept of 'intercultural' is also examined in this section. It is proposed that intercultural situations arise when an individual perceives another person or group as being culturally different from themselves. Intercultural dialogue is therefore defined as dialogue that takes place between individuals or groups who perceive themselves as having different cultural affiliations from each other. It is noted that [...] intercultural dialogue is extremely important for fostering tolerance and enhancing social cohesion in culturally diverse societies.

One interesting contestation of cultural equality in the school system in the UK is people's outpourings against trans and sex/gender expansive children. These 'debates' often do not take place on school grounds; actions to influence how trans and sex/gender expansive differences are understood are pushed more intensely through mail-outs and visual materials arguing for a gender-critical stance while teaching children about sex, sexuality and relationships. Many more critics of trans and sex/gender expansive children, however, are debating the issue in the liminal space of feminist and neo-conservative Twitter feeds and in closed meetings, often speaking to their echo chamber about their sex/gender politics. Nonetheless, some arguments that challenge the authenticity of trans and sex/gender expansive children have appeared in the national newspapers. Self-determining sex/gender, either within or beyond the binary sex/gender system, and the recognition of trans and sex/gender expansive children and their parents' rights, are clear examples of an intra-cultural diversity. This diversity has given rise into vitriolic (social) media coverage which, I argue, stirs up contempt and ridicule for sex/gender minorities as well as much support. It is unclear how a meaningful dialogue can take place due to the violent rhetoric being peddled about, for example, parents supporting their younger children in social transitions and their older adolescent children, if they so desire, with medical support and interventions.

Social transitions for pre-pubertal trans and sex/gender expansive children is a way of removing the sexed/gendered obstacles that inhibit them from living freely (Winters et al, 2018). Medical support and interventions for these children can include psychotherapy and/ or puberty blockers. Medical intervention, such as psychotherapy and GnRHas for those adolescents who have reached Tanner Stage

2–3 of puberty may be offered, if deemed suitable by the attending physicians, parents and the children themselves. Other forms of intervention such as surgery can be provided, but only at the age of other surgeries in any given country's policy directives regarding age restrictions, unless, as we have seen, the intervention is regarded as a medical emergency. Generally, surgery must be recommended by at least one psychologist or psychiatrist. Violent rhetoric is peddling fear around these interventions, suggesting that children are incompetent to consent and, when they are of legal age, still too young and duped by an evil trans ideology; there is a belief that, if coerced out of this thinking, they would eventually live as cis sex/gender people.

Sex/gender coercion

Coercive approaches have been a site of contention for many years. They were most notably exercised early on by Richard Green (1987), targeting boys who were sexed/gendered as effeminate, and most controversially by Zucker whose policy was for children to learn to accept their assigned sex/gender and behave accordingly. Zucker reported to news outlets, following accusations of him performing reparative therapy, that he was actually 'lowering the odds that as such a kid gets older, he or she will move into adolescence feeling so uncomfortable about their gender identity that they think that it would be better to live as the other gender and require treatment with hormones and sex-reassignment surgery' (Smith Cross, 2015: np). For example, when children demonstrated sex/gender 'non-conforming' behaviours, parents often took them to a psychologist to intervene to change their child's interests to those more in line with stereotypical play, pastimes and clothing. These 'psychotherapeutic' interventions were asked for more so for those sexed/gendered males rather than for those sexed/gendered female at birth. Those sexed/gendered females could display a degree of so-called masculinity and were often known in both lay and psychiatric terminology as tomboys. One US psychiatrist (among a number of them) had the opinion that sex/gender non-conforming behaviour, alongside boys rejecting 'their male role', constitute 'symptoms of child gender disturbance' and that was enough for clinical intervention (Rekers et al, 1977: 3; see also Rekers et al, 1976). These assumptions about the pathological nature of cross-sex/gender behaviours and expressions were taken up in psychiatric circles. For one psychiatrist, Zucker (2008), the solution to halting what he believes are cross-gender activities lies in supporting children to live with the sexed/gendered assignment they were given. He argues:

it is my clinical impression that many of these youngsters, and their families, respond quite effectively to psychotherapeutic interventions. Although I have no doubt that the changes that one can observe in these youngsters can, in part, be attributed to 'spontaneous remission', if I dare use such a term, I believe that the situation is more complex than this. In other words, I think that therapeutics can work with young children with GID [gender identity disorder] [... and it is] legitimate to want to make youngsters comfortable with their gender identity (*to make it* correspond to the physical reality of their biological sex). (Zucker, 2008: 358)

He further suggests that there are three components to his therapeutic approach: treatment of gender identity disorder in the 'naturalistic environment'; treatment of the parents; and treatment of the child. Zucker explains that, for the child, this may include the promotion of same-sex peer relations; encouraging gender-typical and neutral activities; and what he calls 'limit-setting' of cross-gender behaviours, and dialogues about gender between parent and child (Zucker, 2008: 360). What these cross-gender behaviours are, or what the dialogues would be about, seems vague. As a practising psychosexual therapist, working in the UK's NHS, May (2002) suggests that heterobinarisms – dominant cultural standards of heterosexuality, hegemonic masculinity and femininity – do not often cohere with her own understanding of sexed/gendered expressions.

Moreover, one interesting and connected interpretation of Zucker's (2008) approach is that it is also the parents' nameless 'pathology' that needs therapeutic intervention. One key aspect of his 'therapy', he states, is the use of 'dialogues *on gender* between parent and child' (Zucker, 2008: 360, emphasis added). It seems that due to their children's experiences, the parents' psyches relating to sex/gender need to be overhauled and their parenting practices need amending. If we accept that, in general, psychiatric knowledge and practice is primarily organized through a biogenetic lens that views psychopathology as being molecular and biochemical in nature, and that mental ill health is founded on a logic of loss and deficit, then it should seem strange to infer, through a diagnosis of gender dysphoria, that a child's or indeed an adult's sex/gender desires are created through inadequate socialization. This must assume two things. First, 'dialogues on gender' suggests that there are agreed upon and ontologically secure sex/gender characteristics that can be universally classed as masculine or feminine and can be related to a 'physical reality'. For decades, however, in the discipline of gender studies and in other areas of inquiry, masculinity and femininity have been shown to be socially constructed, ephemeral, ontologically insecure and not necessarily associated with bodily materiality (Butler, 1990, 1993; Lorber, 2000; Berkowitz et al, 2010). Second, Zucker (2008: 360) states: 'In my view, early parental tolerance or reinforcement of cross-gender behavior has been the rule, not the exception' with the children he sees with gender identity disorder.'[5] Drawing on Green's (1987) early assumptions, which also blamed the parents, Zucker (2008) suggests that there is some form of (sexual) trauma that triggers what are ostensibly subconscious elements, contributing to the tolerance of 'cross-gender behavior'. He argues, these traumas – although he never provides empirical evidence for them – once therapeutically addressed within the family, the child's expressions, feelings and desires would be 'reverted'. The behavioural recourse Zucker claims would be in line with 'his' or 'her' 'biological reality' and sexed/gendered assignment. A number of papers published by Zucker and his colleagues (see for example Zucker and Bradley, 1995; Zucker and Seto, 2015), however, also claim that there is evidence pointing to the possibility that genetics and/or prenatal hormones are influential in the development of trans and sex/gender expansive and intersex people. Following on from this, it is unclear why – if one believes that there is gendered behaviour that is masculine/male and feminine/female in so-called non-pathological people, which can be affected by different genetics and levels of hormones that are inevitably assembled in numerous configurations – one would retain a binary model to pathologize others. Moreover, why would anyone insist on trying to align non-harmful behaviours with a binary system which is really outside the potential of any calculation, and thus obviously not fit for purpose, while at the same time blaming the (mother) parent for their apparent psychopathology? This of course is not what is happening. What is happening is a clinical reprimand of the children's and parents' desires, and an attempt to take recourse in these norm entrepreneurs' utterances about masculine or feminine traits, resulting in the dismissing of the children's self-determination.

Following a number of critiques about the unethical practice of reparative/conversion therapies, in particular for gay and lesbian people, the practice has since been widely condemned by various psychological associations in operation.[6] For example, Hidalgo and colleagues (2013: 285) suggest that:

The major premises informing our modes of practice include: (a) gender variations are not disorders; (b) gender presentations are diverse and varied across cultures, therefore requiring our cultural sensitivity; (c) to the best of our knowledge at present, gender involves an interweaving of biology, development and socialization, and culture and context, with all three bearing on any individual's gender self; (d) gender may be fluid, and is not binary, both at a particular time and if and when it changes within an individual across time; (e) if there is pathology, it more often stems from cultural reactions (e.g., transphobia, homophobia, sexism) rather than from within the child.

Considering this new psychotherapeutic approach, and the increasing number of de jure states passing laws prohibiting conversion therapy for young people, makes it seem that the days of this unethical practice are a thing of the past.

Sex/gender policing

While the style of psychotherapy practised by Zucker on children and their parents has been widely rejected as a clinical intervention by Hidalgo, Ehrensaft and other psychotherapists, the pressure to conform to culturally specific sex/gender norms nonetheless does still go on, sometimes in more obvious as well as in more subtle ways. Cultural, religious, familial sex/gender, school norms, alongside more mundane fields such as toy shops, clothing stores, television programmes and other cultural products, for example, are similarly directive and (unwittingly) 'recruited' in a panoptic apparatus that functions to underwrite 'properly' sexed/gendered subjects.

Another pernicious sex/gender form of policing has recently surfaced within critical gender feminist, right-wing parties and evangelical Christian social media,[7] and has occasionally made it into mainstream media. Accusations of child abuse against parents who are supporting their trans and sex/gender expansive children, on occasion, have been investigated by child protection services. These accusations infer that not only is the child wrong (or pathological) in pursuing their desires of self-determining their sex/gender, but also that the parents have pathological tendencies for facilitating or supporting their child in this way. We have seen this in the earlier aetiological approaches to trans and sex/gender expansive children in Green's (1987) and Zucker et al's

(1994) work, which suggest that parental attitudes and behaviours regarding psychosexual socialization are key to whether a child will consolidate a 'cross-sex/gender' identification. Zucker (2008: 358) is often cited or alluded to in these accusations, which often take something like this form:

> *The reasons for such tolerance or encouragement seem to vary.* In some instances, it appears related to an intense desire on the parent's part, particularly the mother's to have a child of the opposite sex [...] This wish, which is not 'fulfilled,' appears to then influence subsequent maternal socialization that affects the child's emerging gender identity. (Zucker et al, 1994: 58).

Like much of psychological theory, such authors leave the door open to lines of flight in which the reasons vary, however they lean towards the pathological story they want to advocate for. In this case blaming the mother for, in effect, her Munchausen syndrome by proxy, where the caregiver of a child, most often a mother, either makes up fake symptoms or causes real symptoms to make it look like the child is sick. Social studies considering supportive mothers indicate that such mothers feel that others judge them as being too permissive or 'crazy' in allowing their children to develop and explore their sex/gender (Johnson and Benson, 2014).

There are, however, some nuanced differences between the earlier blaming of parents in the aetiology of trans and sex/gender expansive children's behaviours by psychiatrists and the critical gender feminists', right-wing parties' and evangelical Christians' more recent take on it. The latter arguments are centred on how the 'transgender lobby', through their 'propaganda', has infiltrated the consciousness of parents who then openly pursue trans and sex/gender expansive services for their children – resulting from a form of duped consciousness – rather than believing that the child had any input into the desired trajectory of their lives. This warrants further critique.

The logic manifested in these attacks reinforces the well-established hierarchy of sexed/gendered ways of being. Note, however, that according to the critics' logic, sex/gender normativity is changeable through ideological forces that change a person's consciousness. In this formulation, sex/gender norms are more unstable than trans, gender expansive or intersex planes of immanence. A person may stop being sex/gender normative by simply being exposed to 'propaganda'. However, one cannot 'stay' sex/gender normative by simply by watching sex/gender normativity on for example television or seeing it in magazines, in toy shops or schools, within the home, or indeed anywhere. Instead the critics defend the dated and sometimes illegal forms of 'conversion practices' to create a form of sex/gender normativity. The issue is that the critics do not recognize that sex/gender is fluid, unstable and elusive (for a similar argument in relation to Russian sexualities, see Kondakov, 2020). Another fact that the critics miss is that very little is known about parents who support their trans or sex/gender expansive children, and that the theories were based on psychiatrists' normative assumptions, and perhaps derived from their own ideas being developed through the sex/gender propaganda from television programmes and family structures and cultural practices.

Much of the contemporary debate about self-determining sex/gender, it is worth noting, has been interconnected with arguments about sex-segregated spaces being eroded for 'women born women' and girls, particularly on the part of some academic Tweeters. These attacks have seeped through to wider discourse, as one Tweeter states: 'transgender ideology [is] a direct attack on the hard-won rights of women and children – which, again, is WHY the lobby seemingly has to work in the dark, without public debate'.[8] Given this visible divide between trans and sex/gender expansive people and gender critical feminists and other parties, it is unclear how the idealism of (intra) cultural diversity dialogue (Smith, 1998) can be ever resolved or even debated at a societal level just yet.

Nonetheless, feminist social scientists, anthropologists and philosophers have been debating the binary sex/gender-differentiated body in relation to cross-cultural and intra-cultural societies for many years now. Linda Nicholson (1994: 83) states that we:

> cannot look to the body to ground cross-cultural claims about the male/female distinction [...] In this alternative view the body does not disappear from feminist theory. Rather it becomes a variable rather than a constant, no longer able to ground claims about the male/female distinction across large sweeps of human history, but still there is always a potentially important element in how male/female distinction gets played out in any specific society.

We must understand that here the biological body is assumed to be the basis upon which cultural meanings are constructed. This, Nicholson (1994: 81) suggests, is the 'biological foundational' approach, which asserts that while cultural diversity is possible, the fundamental commonality observed and represented across the species is two sexes, male and female. This representational commonality, she asserts, forecloses several inquiries. For example, she suggests that we are unable to comprehend an expansion of the two sex/gender model by looking at sex/gender diversity both intra-culturally and cross-culturally. This is because, through time and in space, the materiality of the outer body increasingly took on the role of providing testimony to the nature of the self it contained, because of the dominance of metaphysical thought (Braidotti, 1994). Many feminists (see, for example, Fox-Keller and Longino, 1983; Longino and Doell, 1983; Lorber, 1994) have raised concerns over the connection between body morphology at birth, behavioural sex differences aligned to that morphology, and the resultant understanding of human nature, and argue that retaining this simple formula may generate sufficient justifications for maintaining rather than disrupting social and legal inequalities that biological determinists have successfully augmented. For instance, Lorber (1994: 53) suggests that 'men's social bodies are the measure of what is human' and that any created differences between women's social bodies will always be measured against men's humanness (see also MacKinnon, 1987). What we do not get a sense of is the way that humanness unfolds in these debates. Despite us all always being in processes of becoming, the development of boys and girls, women and men, was seen to embody certain inherently fixed traits along a particular developmental path that corresponded to their 'biological sex'.[9] This is still starkly entertained by philosophers, social scientists, scientists and wider publics who have accepted the 'objective' descriptive claim of a binary biological sex/ gender difference, in spite of the incredible work by many second wave feminists who highlight the dangers of biological essentialism.

I can confidently claim, following Butler who, following Foucault, suggested that a given body is not an innocent descriptive claim about biological sex. The feminist biologist Anne Fausto-Sterling similarly argues that: '[T]hose looking to biology for an easy-to-administer definition of sex and gender can derive little comfort from the most important of these [research] findings' (cited in Karkazis, 2019: 1898). This is because 'sex' is not a static, discrete characteristic that exists prior to the relations and practices that produce it. Indeed, evolution would not make sense if this was the case. 'Sex' is not even strictly biological and works through multiple intensities that can support social norms and particular goals as well as underpin sociopolitical hierarchies that maintain certain opportunities, rights and privileges because of the morphology of the body (Karkazis, 2019). Butler argues that this supposedly neutral act of interpolating binary biological sex/

gender categorization is central to sexism, and hetero- and sex/gender normativity (Butler, 1992). To take this to its logical conclusion, this would mean that those feminists who work with the 'womyn born womyn' discourse to suggest a clear division between a biological male and female may unwittingly contribute to the sexist contexts and intensities in societies.

Numerous feminist historians have also demonstrated the sexist nature of schooling that drew on 'biological evidence', particularly for those people sexed female, who were 'thought' to have the biological constitution for only certain academic subjects.[10] Even now, educational outcome studies tend to pursue analyses that situate binary sexes/genders as somehow fundamentally different, and sex/gender still has much weight as a variable in understanding differences in educational attainment, for example. However, Spielhofer et al (2004) argue that there is quite a lot of evidence that girls now tend to pursue subject choices that were stereotypically chosen by boys. This is obviously not because of any fundamental changes in the biological potential or constitution of those sexed female at birth, their chromosomes or procreative potential. Many of the changes in behaviour result from practice in using the body and performing tasks (Young, 1990). As Fine et al (2013: 550) argue, as humans we have 'evolved an adaptively plastic brain that is responsive to environmental conditions and experiences, and the modulation of endocrine function by those experiential factors contributes to that plasticity'. The brain is constantly under construction through the years; however, the relation between volumes of structures of the brain and behaviours and desires have never been established (Giedd, 2004). Brain plasticity is also witnessed in related research which provides all-round evidence that girls' grades are slightly higher in some countries (Daly, 1996); however, this finding becomes much more complex when variables such as socioeconomic status, ethnicity and motivation are included in the analysis. The point is that analysts of this kind should seek to account for their own processes of reification and seek to look at the forces that produce, at certain moments, the reality of that moment, rather than reinforcing and reifying essentialist or indeed constructionist 'identity' categories, which can also uncritically determine 'girls' and 'boys', 'ethnicity' and 'race', and so on as significant categories of analysis (Brubaker and Cooper, 2000). As Brubaker and Cooper (2000) have noted, in these types of analyses we often find an amalgam of both constructivist and essentialist language in the analytical categories. This is because the former language is semantically attached to the stability of an 'identity' and the latter language to its essential nature.

Despite a seemingly reversed understanding about boys' and girls' schooling and attainment outcomes in some countries, the variables of sex/gender continue to be used to reiterate differences in much science and pseudoscientific evaluations that have little to do with biology – their use is epistemological. This has led feminist critics to conclude that it is not only that the outputs of such (pseudo)science contribute to scientifically unjustified cultural understandings of female–male relations as fixed, inevitable and ordained by nature, but also that such (pseudo)science that pursues sex/gender binaries, rather than complexity, is itself flawed and unenlightening (Fine, 2010; Fine et al, 2013). While, of course, we still live in a sex/gender-segregated time and space to a large degree, the vestiges of 'sexual difference' based on an arbitrary binary sex/gender differentiation at birth tells us little about biology and material bodies or our productive potential, and perhaps tells us more about the social divisions in society.

All this points towards other micro intensities within assemblages affecting school outcomes, which seems obvious, but is important to highlight. Within all these analyses the sexed/gendered girls and sexed/gendered boys are shown to be socialized into sex/gender roles and ways of being that – time and again – have been demonstrated to have material intensities and are key elements in the operations pursued by human and non-human bodies through de jure state apparatuses (Smith, 1998), rather than biological determinism per se. Suffice to say, sexing/gendering at birth materially affects young people's schooling because of the intensities beyond and within the body assemblage. As such, can we talk about self-determination at all when such practice is there from the moment one is born? This is especially witnessed when a child decides that they want to live a different sex/gender or beyond the established sex/gender system. The journey we have been on in this section was important to show some of the debates and arguments that the parents I interviewed were contending with in their daily lives. One of the key challenges that parents faced was at home.

Social transitions in supportive homes

There are many ways that children and adolescents 'come out' as trans or sex/gender expansive (Ehrensaft, 2012, 2016; Platero, 2014; Davy and Cordoba, 2020). The emergence can be a slowly dawning affair, and/or facilitated by set of conversations about clothing, toys, pastimes and sex/gender desires and/or fears, or bullying, but no matter which way these desires emerge they are ongoing and are produced through time. 'Coming out' is not a once-and-for-all episode, and can go on for many years, when it is understood to be relevant (Nealy, 2017). Parents suggested that their children approached them, their friends, and sometimes their teachers. Sometimes, however, parents suggested that it emerged in semi-solitary situation, where their child developed ideas about themselves both with and without the use of the internet. Generally, there has been an increase in affirmative parenting of trans and sex/gender expansive children, evidenced in the newly formed self-help and charity groups being set up and staffed by parents.

There is, it seems, an increase too in support from people beyond the immediate family, which has recently started to be evidenced in the social sciences and which suggests that positive outcomes for trans and sex/gender expansive children are dependent on social and/or parent/peer support (Hill and Menvielle, 2009; Hill et al, 2010; Kuvalanka et al, 2018; Davy and Cordoba, 2020).[11]

'Coming out' as a trans or sex/gender expansive child at home is not simply about deciding to follow a line of flight, ending up as trans or sex/gender expansive. Coming out is negotiated through time and to different degrees with different family members, friends, school staff and parents of other children at the school and, depending on the maturity of the child, the vitriolic and pathologizing arguments that circulate around their bodies. Nonetheless, the multidimensionality surrounding experiences of 'coming-out' does not privilege a single mode of development and thus has multiple narratives of sex/gender realness. As Vaccaro (2013: 100) asserts, the child is 'doing not being' and that should be enough to engender any recognition to make room for things to happen if desired, or not if not desired. Parents facilitating their child's self-determination challenges the way that trans and sex/gender expansive identities are commonly defined, measured and made to 'measure up'. The multiplicity of forces in play while 'coming out' at home impacts both the material non-human bodies and the materiality of the young person's body.

The child's coming out results in a complex set of experiences for parents too (Nealy, 2017; Davy and Cordoba, 2020) – some of whom find it challenging, despite offering their support, while others suggest that it is a 'that makes sense' moment. Parents that I spoke to often felt that they too need to come out, on many occasions, alongside their children (Davy, 2020). Saeger's (2006) case study is useful to illustrate some of the affective intensities that parents and their children encounter during these periods. Parents go through 'stages' of acceptance, including discovery, turmoil and decision-making, and attempting to find balance. These experiences, regardless of the age of the child, are generally co-coordinated by the child and parent(s) through productive processes. These produce an initial set of social selves formed through economic, political, historical and environmental conventions – an assemblage – that affects their next move. This provides some evidence for the reciprocal influence theories of childhood socialization developed in the 1980s by Glass et al (1986), which suggests that the affectivities of socialization are developed through time, with multi-directional forces, resulting in the family unit sometimes acting as an agent of, rather than an impediment to, change. It is widely acknowledged that there are often distinctive intensities and issues facing all children now, and these are different from the forces that perhaps confronted their parents in the past. It is, however, the parental generation that is often responsible for interpreting their children's desires and then mediating on behalf of their children, if they feel it is appropriate. This can often lead to intergenerational and intra-social transmission of different attitudes towards sex/gender.

As such, sex/gender is not static, and is produced by the intensities of human and non-human bodies that people encounter (Brooks and Bolzendahl, 2004). The changing matter of sex/gender is a co-productive emergence of ideas and desires. While external influences inevitably impact ideas about sex/gender socialization, there is much evidence to suggest that children's desires within the family generally have more force than has been previously thought (Ehrensaft, 2016; Davy and Cordoba, 2020). Glass et al (1986) demonstrated reciprocal influence in the 1980s by considering radical social changes that were taking place, which they argued had much influence. But who and/or what produced these 'radical social changes' if not the populations and non-human bodies emerging?

As there are now more imaginable and desirable sexed/gendered possibilities for many, the practicalities of engaging with human and non-human bodies often need confronting by parents of trans, sex/gender expansive and cis sex/gender children. Most parents of trans and sex/gender expansive children in my study started to obtain as much information as possible to try to better understand their child and what they may need to do to prepare the school and for the school to prepare for their child(ren). Maintaining regular discussions with their child about names, pronouns, clothing, hair styles and the desires they have about school proved to be an effective strategy that parents said helped them and other immediate family members adjust and make plans. As Aveline,[12] a parent of a young trans girl, states:

'So the name change came about two years ago and the pronoun a year ago. [Name] is referred to by her name by the family, in the community, at school and anywhere that we go [...] So it is a journey that we are all on.'

Many parents in the study drew on the metaphor of a staggered journey without a final endpoint. There were various pathways that they co-produced, similar to Deleuze and Guattari's 'lines of flight'. The following exchange between me and two parents demonstrates multiple possible lines of flight.

Paul: He will be in year 6 next year.

Mary: On weekends we would see him as ['female name 1'] or ['female name 2'].

Paul: Sometimes when he got home from school he would be ['female name 2'].

Mary: ['Female name 2'] is very sassy, and very exhausting [laughs].

Zowie: Is that because femininity is hard work?

Paul: He also would say that he is agender, but not as often.

Mary: We try not to ask everyday who are you, what are you? But if he is specifically asking to be called.

Paul: Yes he is able to be free and come to us and say that today please call me whatever he wants to be called.

Zowie: What were your initial thoughts in relation to this very fluid existence?

Paul: It was a relief to see this, him being able to explore this and you could see a weight come off him when he was able to explore, like how happy he seems when he is just figuring things out or how happy he is when he can just explore how he is feeling. It is nice to see.

Mary: I think before he did feel that he needed to be in that boy box. To tick that box. Again, I think that it was reassuring for him as well that he doesn't have to.

This type of productive engagement, many parents said, also provided the grounds upon which their children were being acknowledged, and that this allowed them the freedom to explore their sex/gender (see also Pyne, 2016).

Parents did not have a definitive knowledge of their children's sex/gender, but co-engendered a process of ongoing, nomadic ethics often in the face of not knowing (Pyne, 2016: 22). Prior to the realizations of their children's exploration of their sex/gender, parents' understanding about 'it' was often at a territorialized state of naïve consciousness

(Freire, 2000). Freire suggests that people without experience live passively, thinking that their fate is out of their hands, and in many respects it is. Perhaps 'fate' is the wrong way to describe something as it connotes that something is predetermined as if it is in the lap of the gods. Perhaps it is better to understand this passivity as having different ideas and desires. Through the concept of nomadic subjects which, as we saw earlier, is a style of living through transitions and passages, I suggest that most of the parents' passivity was a form of habit or repetition (Deleuze, 2004). But with the child's desire, parents' ideas emerge in relation to 'self-determining' sexes/genders. Because many parents had rarely had to think about sex/gender in such profound ways, many of them had to develop productive strategies in light of their children's desires and because of the new knowledge originating from their research surrounding sex/gender systems, segregation, medicine, fear, grief and social support. The research that parents undertook led to numerous imaginaries, and some new worrying limit-situations arising from new interactions. Parents imagined that they would encounter many negative forces from humans and non-humans alike, because, like them, they have not grappled with the phenomena of trans and sex/gender expansive children. Freire understands people can nonetheless move through naïve consciousness to a critical consciousness – naïve transitivity – in which people learn about possibilities available to them and how to contribute to producing new horizons (Freire, 2000).

A few of the parents were more cognizant of (trans) sex/gender matters, potentially due to them identifying as trans or sex/gender expansive themselves. However, despite these parents' trans and sex/gender expansive experiences, they still sought practical information about contemporary school environments, such as human rights, school policies and legal frameworks, as they knew they were in a different social context now to when they were at school. The possibilities around trans and sex/gender expansive children at school seemed to have opened up, although they were by no means understood to be safe and welcoming places. The fears about their child going to school were overwhelmingly affected by the potential dangers and possible ostracisms, and their inability to fully shield their child from any negativity that they may face from teachers, peers and parents of other children (Brill and Pepper, 2008; Pepper, 2012; Pyne, 2016). Therefore, seeking practical information for trans and sex/gender expansive parents was similar to that of the cis sex/gender parents who contributed to the study and who were supporting their trans or sex/gender expansive child going to school.

The parents of trans and sex/gender expansive children all started to research how best to develop the support they thought they would need to make their children's schooling as safe and productive as possible (Davy and Cordoba, 2020). Prior to, and during the time I met with the parents, there had been several press articles, radio shows and documentaries aired in the UK debating medical, social and ethical approaches to trans and sex/gender expansive children (*Women's Hour*, 2014; Nagesh, 2017; Reed, 2017; Roberts, 2017).[13] Many of the parents referred to these media portrayals, some positively and some negatively. On the positive side, they knew they were not alone. On the negative side, each parent began to assume there was an oppressive (school) culture that their trans or sex/gender expansive child might have to face. This was despite some of the shows and radio programmes highlighting some favourable outcomes in the lives of young trans and sex/gender expansive people. This, alongside acknowledging the practicalities of day-to-day living, led them to reflect on how best to help facilitate their child's freedom to explore their sex/gender within their particular school culture.

A number of parents sought out support groups and organizations, gaining knowledge about trans and sex/gender diversity, which also helped them build up their confidence to start meeting with key people in the school to discuss and address some of the processes that their children required immediately. and to talk through some things that they might potentially require in the future. For instance, name and pronoun changes that staff and children had been habituated to at the school, sometimes for several years, needed changing. There were also many external forces to be considered, such as antagonistic school staff and parents of other children; worries about sexed/gendered segregated spaces and sports, and an intense fear of bullying and violence.

Co-producing sex/gender at school

For several years now pedagogical research has emphasized the potential of and need for self-determination in the classroom. Fostering productive relationships is thought to be key in developing self-determination in children (Field and Hoffman, 2012). It seems that this is no different for the parents who were beginning to advocate with and on behalf of their trans and sex/gender expansive children. Throughout the school coming-out period, decisions were made with their children about the actions needed in the school. These decisions were supplemented with information from their own research. Parents began to approach relevant people within the school, such as the head teacher or head of year, for them to begin acknowledging their trans or gender diverse child. The initial meetings with school staff created the grounds upon which to start discussing actual and imaginary limit-situations (Freire, 2000) and enact any changes needed in the school. Antonia Darder (2017) argues that identifying those who are given the opportunity to be problem-posers and engage in a culture of questioning in the classroom foregrounds the crucial issue of who has control over the conditions of learning and how specific modes of knowledge, identities and authority can influence classroom relations. When parents presented the conundrums about sex/gender transitions and gender expansivity, and these were recognized by school staff and used in pedagogical situations as circumstances relating to trans and sex/gender diverse children's daily lives, the perceived oppression sensed by the parents decreased. This also alleviated somewhat the intensity of stigma that was experienced. These parents, then, were at the forefront of negotiating the sexed/gendered forces at the school by developing suitable practices for their children's coming out with some support from education professionals. Many of the parents sensed a movement from the previously perceived limit-situations as they developed working relationships with staff at the schools.

Nearly all the parents suggested that coming out to others in the school was a stepped process. These stepped processes were also dependent on the age of the child. Hilary and Collin's quotation is representative of most parents in the study:

Collin: I think they [the school] have dealt with [this] well in the beginning in as much as, I don't think that they encouraged them [the child] to take too many steps at once. Because our approach in the beginning was: OK I hear what you are saying and we'll take it on board, and I think that we parked it for a little bit, you are still young, let's see how it goes, it will take the path that it takes sort of thing. Rather than say that's great what are we going to do now sort of thing, or you can forget that sort of thing? I think that they followed the same path.

Hillary: Yes and allowed it to develop at a pace it, well we said earlier everybody's different and it shouldn't be forced, but equally it has to be supported.

Parents regarded the school system as a set of junctures, where teachers may be reproducing and reinforcing sexed/gendered processes, yet these were seen as changeable, through prompting a critical consciousness (Freire, 2000) and bringing about changes to systems, such as name and pronoun changes on registers. Although it was relatively easy to change names and pronouns on the registers, thus establishing the student under a self-declared name and sex/ gender marker, changes to examination documentation were not possible unless a legal change of name had been recorded. If this legal process had not been completed, the examination documents would retain the student's original name and birth assigned sex/gender. Parents reported that this was a source of distress, particularly for older children who were in the process of sitting their examinations. Nonetheless, the measures taken within the classroom validated their child's sex/gender identification and expression. Here we can witness how the assemblage functions with differing intensities in relation to a rather arbitrary public change of name producing sex/gender in its singularities.

Sometimes limit-situations were candidly acknowledged by school staff themselves. Following an equality and diversity policy being discussed at a school governors meeting, Katherine said:

> 'I went to see the head afterwards and I said: 'You do know that you have forgotten the trans bit?' She said: 'Oh yes I can see that, of course we will put it in.' She said, 'This is personal, isn't it?' And I said yes. [...] She was brilliant, and she said that there are all sorts of things that we have to think about residentials, where will she sleep? Which toilets will she use?' (Katherine, parent of AFAB [assigned female at birth] prepubescent girl)

The school in this case was responsive, trying to ensure that equitable practices and processes were in place. One parent said that their child 'went under the radar', because at that point they did not need any institutional changes, for example, using spaces that were outside those that they felt comfortable using or changing their registered name. As such, parents of gender expansive children suggested that their child was officially unrecognized, even though their sexed/ gendered aesthetic was highly visible and often accommodated at school. Other parents with sex/gender expansive children suggested that they were misunderstood, which led to toxic environments. Following the school's positive reception of their child coming out as a girl, Sally and Peter speculated that, if in the future their child came out as non-binary, while it would not be an issue for them, it might cause an event within the school that would have to be thought through again:

> 'Because [name] is 100 per cent girl [now], I am not sure as she gets older there is a potential to consider something that is not now in her terms of reference, like non-binary, gender fluid or anything like that. I think that would be challenging. So while she is 100 percent gender binary, it's kind of easy. But if she stepped into an in-between space, it will be difficult [at school].' (Sally, parent AMAB [assigned male at birth] prepubescent girl)

What this analysis suggests is that changes in school practices that reconfigure sex/gender identities to include those that go from one sex/gender to the 'other' may not, at this moment in time, bring about change for those who do not identify within the binary system of sex/gender. The process for sex/gender expansive people seems to be different than for those children who identified within a binary sex/gender system, and similarly complex in relation to sexed/ gendered freedoms.

Generally, though, the democratization of binary sex/gender transitions has permeated into school cultural assemblages at least for many in this cohort of parents. The language of human rights, equality and diversity for all children was reported to be widespread in school cultures in this research. This is not to say that all schools facilitated these transition processes easily. Parents worked hard at demonstrating that the rights of their trans and sex/gender diverse children are of the utmost importance. Most of the parents, however, suggested that although there were many complex situations to be negotiated while coming out, the schools generally supported their children on the basis of how the child wished to be referred to, demonstrating that, at certain junctures, trans and sex/gender expansive children's bodies were reterritorialized beyond the instrumental logic of binary sex/ gender biopolitical forces. The schools' reception of the children's coming out, however, varied from total support and being facilitative towards the child's needs to not making a big deal out if it – and only very rarely with antagonism.

Social transitions

The development of trans or sex/gender expansive children and adolescents has been described as a set of stages contributing to 'transgender emergence' (Lev, 2004). Lev describes the stages as, first, the child understanding that they are trans, followed by information seeking and potentially searching for others who may be like them and whom they may like to be in contact with. The next stage, according to Lev, is the disclosure to significant others, followed by a consolidation around their identities and how to label themselves. The next key stage is a resolution of what Lev describes as gender dysphoria and further acceptance of their gender identification. An exploration of any issues surrounding clinical interventions, such as puberty suppression alongside choices surrounding sex/gender presentation, such as pronoun use, clothing and names, then leads on to engaging with and integration in social spaces and peer groups resulting in pride. While Lev (2004) suggests that the stages should not be regarded as linear, and that children and adolescents may or may not do some or all of these things from stage to stage, or even go through each of the stages, this research describes a potentiality of some of the key factors that the children and adolescents have identified about their desire to live beyond the sexed/gendered assignment at birth. This is often regarded as a social transition. Social transitioning is frequently about being reconfigured in numerous ways at each and every colliding point from when a child was sexed/gendered at birth as one sex/gender, and either wants to be referred to as the other, or something more expansive. We often lose sight of the ways that human and non-human bodies impact the configuration of (trans and sex/gender expansive) children, which, of course, can only offer us a representation about some lives.

Parents supporting social transitions may not necessarily be about the younger trans and sex/gender expansive children moving towards a particular medical path, but rather about acceptance and having faith in their child's sex/gender self-determination, and affirming how and what they want their roles, expressions, identities and desires to become (Davy and Cordoba, 2020). Ashley (2019b: 88) suggests that:

> [i]n keeping faith, parents are encouraged to see how their established moral identi[fication] should lead them to accept their children's gender [identification]. In trying on, parents are encouraged to creatively explore the various possible futures that are open to them, inviting them to imagine how their relationship with their child could evolve, in the hopes that they realize that acceptance is the best way forward, however painful and difficult it can be.

The family members, then, are nomadic in the sense that multiple factors are pursued on open pathways which are non-generalizable. The children, parents, teachers, and other human and non-human bodies connect, circulate, move on and are the matter of emotions, bonding, coalitions and interconnections (Braidotti, 1994: 35). The transitions are singularities through which multiple forces intersect. The forces create complexity with which the children, parents, teachers and so on move, which of course will have some similarities with others' movements, but also many differences. As Kathleen Stewart (2007: 12) shows us, we can see 'what happens to people, how force hits bodies, how sensibilities circulate and [can] become [...] collective' in relation to other movements. In other words, desire is a productive force within an assemblage and not an endpoint. Massumi (2002: 250) describes affective desire as a 'vital movement' that can be 'collectively spread'. One such similarity is the desire for the use of respectful and congruent language (for example, names, pronouns and that documentation reflects their ontological self). This set of linguistic forces is a major part of the assemblage of trans and sex/gender expansive children's lives, and is often regarded by them as a matter of basic human dignity towards acknowledging their self-determination (Winters et al, 2018). Rosalind described how this was attempted in collaboration with her daughter's teacher:

> 'So, when she transitioned, [name] would have just gone into the school the next day as a girl, but we were wanting to support [name] in a more gradual way at school. At that point, she had socially transitioned at home, but at school she had still been wearing male-ish clothes. So, we would buy her girls' trousers and she would feel ok because they were girls' trousers, which was great, but she wanted to wear the full dress and skirt. So, with the school we decided that we would first of all change [name's] name, and the teacher did that in a very straightforward subtle way, bearing in mind they were only [age]. The teacher just said her name, the way that she wanted it to be on the register one day, and just to let you know this name is now going to be that name and she did the register and that was that. Nobody asked any questions. The following week, the teacher changed the pronouns with my child and she again, being [age], there was only so much that that she wanted to do, so they just accepted that as well. She said we are all going from he to say she and that is how we are going to talk about your

friend [...] At that point it was all fine. [name] was able to wear whatever she wanted to school. We did it in stages to help the other children as well, so it was almost not such a big deal for them.'

The coalitions at school deterritorialize socially recognized 'truths' and the scientifically 'valid' 'corpo-r(e)ality of the subject' (Braidotti, 1994: 41) and produce new forms of mattering.

Although some parents are unsupportive of their children with their social and/or medical transitions due to the very real trauma to and disruption of their imagined future lives, many families that initially reject their child eventually settle on varying levels of support (Ashley, 2019b). Nonetheless, social and/or medical transitions for trans and sex/gender expansive children are co-constituted by parents and their children alongside other human and non-human forces on multiple planes of immanence, while all contending with the elimination of both imagined and real limitations imposed on them. The metaphysical vision of the trans and sex/gender expansive child has often been theorized within the structure/agency, subjected/self-determined nexus, which often misses the proliferation of forces producing the planes of immanence upon which the child, parent, teacher, policy, sex/gender assignment and so on function in the explorations of sex/gender possibilities. The question of trans and sex/gender expansive embodiment is 'self-determined' insofar as it emerges (continuously) among a proliferation of human, political and social science discourses about 'life', bodily matter and human and non-human desires.

Backlash

There has been a concerted backlash against parents and their children. Intermittent media flurries about trans and sex/gender expansive kids have drawn attention to the fact that they are increasingly visible within the school system in the UK. Children who are expressing themselves beyond their sexed assignment, while being supported by their parent(s), have been bombarded with criticisms over the last few years.[14] The criticisms range from anti-trans feminists, who suggest that parents are forcing trendy trans activists' ideology on innocent children (Glass, 2018), or from parents who were stated to 'lobby the government and the NHS against what they claim is "coerced medicalization" – propelling vulnerable young people convinced they are the wrong gender towards treatments that risk leaving them infertile' (Walsh and Griffiths, 2019: np), to the age-old fear of contagion, which was widely reported when some Christian parents removed their own children from a school (Nagesh, 2017) and accusations of child abuse from religious far-right commentators (Jacob, 2019). Mermaids – a support group set up in England for trans and sex/gender expansive children and their families – reported on their website that Professor Paul Baker of Lancaster University, using Corpus Linguistics methodology, analysed a range of recent news articles in the British press. The author of the report found that:

> An analysis of 100 random cases in 2018–19 found 56 cases where transgender children were described as existing and/or requiring support. Thirty-seven cases were more disapproving, either suggesting that children who identify as trans should not be supported in transitioning or that efforts to support them are unnecessary. A further seven cases appear more neutral.

While it seems that most articles were supportive or at least acknowledged that trans and sex/gender expansive children exist, over a third were disparaging about supporting these children. There have also been similar negative views published from a few academics, psychologists and parents in recent edited collections (see Brunskell-Evans and Moore, 2018; Moore and Brunskell-Evans, 2019. These collections generally suggest that supporting children 'who identify' as trans or sex/gender expansive is physically and psychologically experimental, and dangerous for the children; and that it is adult (trans) people, utilizing and enforcing 'transgender ideology' within school literature, at the gender clinics and in consultations in policy domains, who have invented and augmented the phenomena of trans and sex/gender expansive children (Moore and Brunskell-Evans, 2019).[15]

Critics emphasize the contingency of losing girls' and women's rights, particularly on the grounds of people assigned male at birth, who identify as female, invading sex-segregated spaces developed for females.[16] Another tactic is the claim that if there was no such thing as 'gender ideology' then the people sexed female at birth who identify as male would just emerge as lesbians. In a sense this strand of feminist argumentation has been rehashed from the 1980s and 1990s, from Janice Raymond (1980, 1994) and the similar work of Sheila Jeffreys (1997, 2006, 2012, 2014) later, whose trust in the metanarrative of binary biological sex differences and sex/gender assignment on the basis of a glance by physicians at the genital area of infants is unwavering, leading to the argument that trans, sex/gender expansive and intersex people ought not to have rights to self-determine their sex/gender because this removes women's and girls' rights. They further suggest that they are helping these children by stopping them from making a mistake if they pursue their desire, because it is a false desire. These criticisms are all wrapped up in the assumption that it is better not to be trans or sex/gender expansive. Perhaps it is better not to be trans and sex/gender expansive, but only when there is complicity between schools, prejudice in wider society and critics' cultural values and norms in denying their existence and their self-determination. There is a certain irony in the critics' claims about the trans and sex/gender expansive children being invented insofar as they do not seem to be aware of the perpetuation of (symbolic) violence and ostracism that they are manifesting against the children that they assume they are helping. By suggesting that they are helping the children to not make life-diminishing decisions about their sex/gender, they are also arguing that their evaluation of the child's life should occupy a privileged position, and that their vision of life is the only valuable existential interpretation of life. However, trans and sex/gender expansive children do exist, and their supportive parents are generating, I will demonstrate in the next section, more expansive school cultural norms through a number of processes that shift the personal limits (Freire, 2000) placed on their children. Additionally, parents reframe, then attempt to co-realize, their children's equitable membership in (school) cultures.

While we should not deny trans and sex/gender expansive child's experiences, or suggest that their desires can ever be fully understood, I would like to suggest that the unity of trans and sex/gender expansive experiences is mistaken by many. Often the body appears then disappears on several planes of immanence, producing flows within numerous assemblages. Parents, friends, policy, schools, judgements, law and so on converge at different junctures and reconfigure the trans and sex/gender expansive bodies, on multiple planes. As I have suggested elsewhere: 'Each body is constantly in processes of becoming through its proximity and movement with and through other bodies, artefacts, institutions and so on' (Davy, 2019: 90). As such, trans and sex/gender expansive children despite or even because of their material bodies are always in processes of becoming. They constantly produce the '*production of productions*, of actions and of passions; *productions of recording processes*, of distributions and of co-ordinates that serve as points of reference' (Deleuze, 1984: 4, emphasis in original).

School receptivity, policy and procedures

An affirmative approach with trans and sex/gender expansive children is contingent on expressing a positive response to their sex/gender productions. This is what Ehrensaft (2016) calls the 'listen and act' model. Promoting the possibility for nomadic explorations does not presume that a child will inevitably transition to a sexed position not assigned to them at birth, but instead acknowledges the plane of immanence in such a way as to see the production of affects that can affirm their contemporaneous desires. The parents, however, suggest that these affirmative approaches at school do challenge the 'business as usual' way that schools operate. At various schools the limits to sex/gender self-determination were being tested out through the development of school policies and procedures, which often surpass the medico-legal frameworks that try to halt or rigidly control the direction of productive flows and movements, by creating biopolitical parameters within which the children are encouraged to operate.

Several schools that were already trans and sex/gender expansively aware, as Cressida suggested, had done their research beforehand. The head teacher, during a meeting Cressida had with him, said that:

> 'He was talking about the practical solutions, like the changing rooms, the PE lessons, toileting, any other potential problems with children. He was prepared and helpful because he had done that.'

This teacher and a few others had already accommodated trans or sex/gender expansive children at their school before, without any issues. The strategies were of a practical nature. Changing names and pronouns were similarly tackled without much fanfare. Freya said that she:

> 'discovered that they had had trans people before in the 6th form. When I filled in the data at the beginning, [name] said that they have got me down as female, you have got to ask to change my gender, they had changed the name, because by that time we had done the Deed Poll, so I just ticked male.'

Whereas Hilary and Collin said:

> 'the school have been supportive. They approached us about [name] being able to be called [name] at school. They

would change the register before we had got any deed poll, or anything along those lines, which I thought was really encouraging. That they were educated enough and had the processes to manage that.'

These overwhelmingly positive interactions between the staff at school, the child and parent(s) commonly instilled a sense of unexpected acceptance of their children's contemporaneous sex/ gender explorations. As Davy and Cordoba (2020: 11) suggest, these reactions engender a co-productive process that affects their children's right to grow as:

> human beings in an education system free from disapproval and violence[, which] was often upheld on democratic grounds. The equality principle and the international right of self-determination allowed a gradual emergence of the critical consciousness necessary to analyze what potential limits may manifest for their child's struggle for identification, self-respect and self-determination.

Concluding remarks

The promotion of self-determination in schools seems to engender forces that positively affect trans and sex/gender expansive children and their parents. While these forces can be objectively good or bad, they are not contingent upon a moralizing consciousness we often see in the arguments against children co-producing their sex/gender in these complex assemblages. They are good and bad because human and non-human bodies act upon another and produce good or bad affects that either increase or decrease the power to act, or as Deleuze and Guattari (2004) would suggest, it is good when the affects open a line of flight that was previously blocked. This then leads us to the question of relational ethics within the assemblages that are produced in ongoing ways. If people's action increases the capacity to act out desires then this is objectively good and supports a deterritorializing line of flight, but if that action decreases our power to act this is bad and blocks us; as Deleuze and Guattari (2004: 284) say:

> we know nothing of a body until we know what it can do, in other words, what its affects are, how they can or cannot enter into composition with other affects, with the affects of another body, either to destroy that body or be destroyed

by it, either to exchange actions and passions with it or to join with it in composing a more powerful body.

As such, trans and sex/gender expansive children self-determining their nomadic lives beyond the sex assignment at birth may engender what Deleuze and Guattari frame as a resistance to micro-fascisms in everyday lives. What they also challenge is the notion of 'self-determination' itself, and therefore we must consider the co-productive forces around us in order to avoid the common hierarchized forms of sex/gender found in much of the literature.

Concluding remarks

The book has posed several questions about how self-determination is conceived, achieved, contested and materially lived through in (some) historical realities of sex/gender. My intention was not to answer all the questions posed, because we cannot securely retrieve them due to the productively fleeing, eluding, flowing, leaking and disappearing nature of sex/gender self-determination in complex assemblages developed *vis-à-vis* legal statutes, healthcare protocols and pedagogical cultures. I have instead tried to pose dilemmas, paradoxes and look at power games that assert forces within debates about sex/gender self-determination. Nonetheless, I have tried to draw out the singularities of trans, sex/gender expansive and intersex people and show how, in our examples, they connect to bioethics (in the form of research relations), biopolitics (in the forms of sex/gender assignments and the connected citizenship and policy frameworks), and the wider population (in their singularities). The one clear force that I wanted to highlight, even though this force is affected and affective differently in all these nomadic connections, is the birth designation made by physicians and recorded by parents. This led me to the questions: Is sex/gender assignment at birth fit for purpose? Do sex/gender assignments have a medical purpose? and What challenges can be levelled at the practice in light of human rights declarations surrounding the rights of people to their bodily integrity, autonomy and 'self-determination'? I demonstrated that sex/gender assignment at birth is only ever a clumsy representation that cannot cope with those bodies that do not, will not, or indeed cannot be constrained within the parameters of those vague designations in use across the world. This form of sex/gender 'recognition', as we have seen, is on shaky ground in the areas of biology, law and personal desires. I suggest that, to paraphrase Braidotti (1994), we may want to displace established expectations about sex/gender essentialism and sex assignment at birth and blur them gracefully but firmly, and acknowledge the constantly nomadic interactions that we all have with our desires to self-determine our lives.

Notes

Chapter 1

1. The ideological project of reproducing a 'moral' discourse in relation to representations of a (western) binary sex/gender system, to paraphrase Rosi Braidotti (1994: 100), treats (sex) difference as a subset of characteristics constituting a sexed identity. She states that: 'The subject is defined in terms of sameness, as equation to a normative idea of a Being that remains the same in all its varied qualifications and attributes. The univocity of metaphysical discourse about the subject [...] rests on a [sic] inherently normative image of thought' (Braidotti, 1994: 100). This, she asserts, needs problematizing. There needs to be an affirmation of a multiplicity of differences that will enable us to understand the potential scope of what humans and non-humans can become. In our case, it is an understanding of the diversity of trans, sex/gender expansive and intersex people alongside cis sex/gender people. This can emerge only if we refuse any dualisms to judge, for example, 'subversive' and 'duped' sex/gender practices, and instead incorporate nomadic assemblages as both an ethical and methodological necessity (Davy, 2019).

2. The International Covenant on Civil and Political Rights, Article 24 (United Nations, 1966) states in Article 24 that:

   > 1. Every child shall have, without any discrimination as to race, colour, sex, language, religion, national or social origin, property or birth, the right to such measures of protection as are required by his status as a minor, on the part of his family, society and the State. 2. Every child shall be registered immediately after birth and shall have a name. 3. Every child has the right to acquire a nationality.

3. Jeffreys (2005) suggests that trans women fetishize having sex as women or are sexually aroused by the thought, or image, of themselves as women, drawing on Blanchard's (1991) typology in which he calls this 'Autogynephilia'. Blanchard also suggests that trans women who oppose his typology are in denial. He states: 'I've published two studies that suggest at least some transsexuals who deny autogynephilic arousal are consciously or unconsciously distorting their histories' (cited in Blanchard, 2008: 437). For a critique of the views of Blanchard and his followers see Serano (2007, 2010, 2016).

4. Alex Sharp (2015) has described a recent legal phenomenon of successful sexual offence prosecutions for 'gender fraud' in the UK. Three of the defendants in the different cases identified as trans men at the time of the alleged offences.

5. This argument has long been a feminist understanding and was most famously stated, I would argue, by Simone de Beauvoir, who suggests that women are not born but become women. She states: 'Woman? Very simple, say the fanciers of simple formulas: she is a womb, an ovary; she is female – this word is sufficient to define her. In the mouth of a man [or woman, or others] the epithet *female* has the sound of an insult' (de Beauvoir, 1997: 35). The insult is steeped in the fact that the body determines, or rather has effects, in society, resulting in many false notions of what a woman is or what she can become. The issue is not that all

women do not have wombs, ovaries and so on, but rather that sex/gender-based socialization impedes our abilities to express ourselves in multiple ways, or, indeed, self-determine our different pathways in emergent ways. This should be enough to encourage us to ask the question: is sex assignment in relation to medicine useful? It seems to me that diagnosis, prognosis and healthcare requires knowledge of bodily parts and their functioning together, rather than the simple distinction 'female' or 'male', which may tell us nothing about those parts and their actual biological functioning. In this sense, assignment at birth can only ever make you into a representation that cannot cope with those bodies that do not, cannot or will not be constrained within the parameters of that designation. In light of this, it is not surprising there has been an increase in demands, like the declaration written by Dan Christian Ghattas (2015) for Organisation Intersex International Europe and International Lesbian, Gay, Bisexual, Trans and Intersex Association (ILGA) Europe, calling for an end 'to mutilating and "normalizing" practices such as genital surgeries, psychological and other medical treatments [for intersex people]. Instead, intersex people must be empowered to make their own decisions about issues that affect their bodily integrity, physical autonomy and self-determination', as well as from regional groups, such as the Australian and Aotearoa/New Zealand community statement that called for an end to legal classification of sex, stating that all are based on structural violence and fail to respect diversity and a 'right to self-determination' (Black et al, 2017).

6   In her article 'Will gender self-declaration undermine women's rights and lead to an increase in harms?', Alex Sharpe (2020) skilfully demonstrates that the premise of gender critical feminists' argument about trans women being inherently the same as cis sex/gender men in relation to violence (in sex-segregated spaces) does not hold with the available evidence. The article responds to a key claim that gender critical feminists publicize widely, about their fears regarding proposed amendments to the Gender Recognition Act (GRA, 2004) in the UK, arguing that if a legal self-declaration process of sex/gender birth certificate amendments is implemented, this will ultimately lead to the rights of women and girls being eroded. In other countries where self-declaration has been implemented, there has not been an increase in sexual assaults against women or girls in sex-segregated spaces.

7   What I mean by non-surgical trans people is those whose identification is with either a man/boy or woman/girl but who do not want to pursue genital surgery, or cannot due to them not being able to obtain a psychiatric referral, or because they have impairments which would make pursuing surgery too risky, or they cannot for financial reasons.

8   See, for example, Hughes (2008), who suggests that intersex embodiment recognized at birth is often described as an endocrine and/or a surgical 'emergency'. On many occasions, so-called ambiguous genitalia that 'indicate' an intersex embodiment to physicians, do not meet the medical criteria for a life-threatening emergency. He suggests, however, that it is difficult and distressing for the parents and the extended family to have a child who cannot be immediately placed within the binary sex/gender system.

9   I have developed this argument elsewhere (Davy, 2019) in relation to trans and non-binary people and will explore the policy implications in more depth later.

10 I have argued (Davy, 2011b) that bodily aesthetics are generative and function in the habitus, which emerges temporally within multiple fields (subcultures, social arenas, healthcare clinics, sexual spaces and so on). The forces generated by bodily aesthetics shift depending on place, time, people involved and so on, showing

us the lack of inherency in the bodily aesthetic. Bodily aesthetics are, however, affective. I have suggested that the individual tries to maximize their social worth, which can help explain the emergence of body projects within sex/gender orders; but the affective outcomes are not foreseeable. Bodily aesthetics are generative, and affect and transform social relations. It is my contention, then, that it would be more helpful to think about the aesthetics of sex/gender as central to people's social fields and as rhizomatic affectivities. This, however, tells us little about health processes, nor can it tell us anything about material experiences of the molecular.

11 See Sarah Richardson's book *Sex itself: The search for male and female in the human genome*, which explores the cultural interactions with chromosomes and theories of genetic sexual difference. She argues that both science and popular literature are rich with the sexing of the X and Y chromosomes but use culturally dominant inferences in their representations. She states that there is 'nothing essential about the X and the Y in relation to femaleness and maleness' (2013: 6).

12 Surgical interventions were/are often performed before 2 years of age, and thus the likelihood that the child would have many memories about the consultations and surgery is minimal.

13 In Scotland a consultation ran from 9 November 2017 to 1 March 2018, and in England from 3 July 2018 to 22 October 2018. The High Court in England, on 10 March 2020, ruled that they would not sanction the use of an 'x' on official documents for those who are non-male or non-female.

14 In the Suicide Act 1961 in the UK, the law whereby it was a crime for a person to commit suicide was abrogated. Now it is an offence if: (a) a person does an act capable of encouraging or assisting the suicide or attempted suicide of another person, and (b) a person's act was intended to encourage or assist suicide or an attempt at suicide.

15 These analogues act on the pituitary gland, inhibiting hormone secretion and temporarily suppressing the endogenous production of oestrogen and testosterone respectively.

16 See for example:

https://www.theguardian.com/uk-news/2020/jan/22/high-court-stop-nhs-giving-puberty-blockers-children

https://www.telegraph.co.uk/news/2019/03/07/nhs-transgender-clinic-accused-covering-negative-impacts-puberty/

https://womansplaceuk.org/2019/10/14/no-child-is-born-in-the-wrong-body-with-michele-moore-heather-brunskell-evans/

https://twitter.com/CamScholars/status/1181166829638766592

Chapter 2

1 Numerous regulatory bodies are regularly invoked wittingly or unwittingly by people in the UK. For example, the Office for Standards in Education, Children's Services and Skills, the Environment Agency, the Financial Conduct Authority, the Charity Commission for England and Wales, the Care Quality Commission, the Health and Safety Executive, the Bar Standards Board, the Office of the Gas and Electricity Markets, the Advertising Standards Authority and so on. These regulatory bodies contribute to setting up a whole system of reterritorializations on the signified, and on the signifier itself, and block or hinder lines of flight. Nonetheless, they are also what Deleuze and Guattari (2004) call a collective assemblage of enunciation, from which statements are made and can take on

importance since such statements transform social character intercorporeally. These enunciations affect the non-human bodies alongside the bodies of people and other factors and can be defined as a set of intercorporeal transformations in each society.

2   I perhaps ought to have emphasized *his* freedom at this point, because in these early revolutionary times it was those who were sexed male who were the beneficiaries of these developments more than people sexed female. Trans, sex/gender expansive and intersex were never considered at this time in Europe in relation to freedoms. Through time, however, political rights have become more equitable in some countries; but differences in the form of 'freedoms' for different (human and non-human) bodies remain. For example, abortion, consent, rape, homosexuality, and trans and intersex healthcare in many cultures generate diverse medico-legal considerations about bodily integrity and 'self-determination' rights at a molar level that affects the molecular level.

3   People themselves provide the security, as Ronen (1979) argues: it is not the de jure state that fights, but the people who make up the armed forces and the wider populace who provide support for the fighters.

4   People can of course leave the nation, as many do by choice or necessity, attempting to find a better life offered by a different host territory.

5   See: https://twitter.com/juliaftacek/status/1170368790011494402?lang=en

6   At the time of publication Canada, Belgium, the Netherlands, Luxembourg, Colombia, Switzerland, parts of the United States and the state of Victoria in Australia have frameworks to assist death.

7   First, I am using suicide in a literal sense of taking one's life. Many social theorists have developed understandings about suicide in relation to the 'secularization' of society (Durkheim, 1951), the strength of community ties facilitated by religion (Pescosolido and Georgianna, 1989) or the lack of relatedness with social network ties (Tilly, 1984). While these theoretical contributions seem to account for 'why' people may want to die by suicide, Foucault (1986) suggests that the act of suicide is productive and constitutes the ultimate challenge to the biopolitical administration of life by the de jure state. There is ample evidence regarding the fear of suicide on the part of successive governments across Europe and what has been called 'depopulation anxiety' (Miller, 2016: 17). While dying by suicide was illegal or against God's will, abortion and contraception were also depicted as population suicide and crimes against the integrity of the race/nation. I am also using 'suicide' here as a metaphor for killing off one's whole identification, consisting of a national essence, and replacing it with identified forms of subordination, in order to struggle against them (Mouffe, 1992). We can also use the term metaphorically, if one decides to migrate elsewhere without papers. This kills off the identity by severing the political ties and the social contract with the nation state of origin. This severing also demonstrates these ex-pats' lack of consent to the governing elites. Nonetheless, this also means a 'rebirth', which requires a new territorial base in which a new 'consensual' contract needs to be established. This may indeed generate a line of flight to something different in relation to a new life, but will reterritorialize their capabilities, utility and value within another (capitalist) economic system.

8   Co-production here should not be read as having a value. Co-production is a concept that means simply something being co-produced. The value of the production is subsequently added by people.

9   This form of rhetoric is seen more and more in education too, particularly in higher education, where the student voice is encouraged to help determine

the education they receive. A different assemblage is being produced in school education, where parents are encouraged to discuss what is taught to their children, despite a national curriculum (except for academies and private schools in the UK). There are conceptual similarities between health and education insofar as liberal individualist approaches are premised on the rhetoric of 'service users' having more say in how services are delivered, and what is delivered, while making the providers more accountable. It is not my position here to say whether this does or does not generate better or worse standards, or make the service providers more accountable, but to illustrate the rhetorical and paradoxical representations that have been and continue to be used *vis-à-vis* autonomy, bodily integrity and self-determination.

[10] Patients with cancer can feel as if the body is being invaded by both the disease and the physicians, resulting in them losing control of their sense of self (Waskul and van der Riet, 2002). Frank (2002) describes cancer tumours as being possessed by a 'savage God', while Sontag (1979) represents cancer as a 'demonic pregnancy'. These all have a common theme of something extraneous invading the autonomous body.

[11] Squier (1996) provides a history of the ways that the fetus is represented as a separate entity from the 'carrier' figuratively, technologically and scientifically, which emerged in the 19th century. These representations resonate with sonographers and many pregnant people as signs of both humanness and selfhood. In Australia 'Zoe's Law', a bill which recognized the fetus as a person in certain contexts, was introduced into the New South Wales Parliament, however, it was not enacted because the Upper House delayed voting on it.

[12] The refusal to treat trans people is documented in the media. For example, many de jure state laws in the US and elsewhere protect the autonomy of physicians over that of trans, sex/gender expansive and intersex patients. See https://www.vice.com/en_uk/article/j5vwgg/doctors-refuse-to-treat-trans-patients-more-often-than-you-think

[13] See, for example, Catholics for a Free Choice (CFFC) https://www.catholicsforchoice.org/. Also, in predominantly Catholic countries, such as Eire, Portugal, Argentina, Malta and Spain, governments have introduced some of the most unconventional laws in the world that support trans, sex/gender expansive and intersex people. For example, the Argentine Senate enacted Law 26.743 in 2012, the first of its kind, to assure access to legal gender recognition for trans people without judicial, psychiatric or medical intervention. Also, access to free and voluntary healthcare for transition allows children to consent to change their legal sex/gender when supported by their legal representatives (Davy et al, 2018).

[14] On the latter point, trans and sex/gender expansive surgical interventions have often been objected to on the grounds that this is experimental and not evidence-based care, but procedures that intersex people have, which are similar, are rarely mentioned in these contexts.

[15] While often condemning the cultural practice of genital cutting of girls, doctors have turned a blind eye to other problematic types of genital cutting, such as intersex surgeries, which Fausto-Sterling (2000) sees as 'cosmetic surgery performed to achieve a social result', and circumcision in boys.

[16] I will take up this point in Chapter 3 in relation to self-regulation. I will demonstrate that the shift from early to contemporary physicians' regulatory frameworks, which are produced by 'elite' practitioners in positions of power, attempts to secure their powerful position in healthcare provision while also trying to grapple with the question of markets versus beneficence and non-maleficence.

[17] See: www.image.guardian.co.uk/sys-files/Guardian/documents/2007/05/25/reid. PDF

[18] GnRHas inhibit the secretion of sex hormones and the onset of pubertal changes in the body, and thus stop the development of unwanted morphological characteristics, such as facial hair and the deepening of the voice, or the development of breasts and menstruation for trans and sex/gender expansive children.

[19] See https://www.gendergp.com/how-did-i-get-here-an-open-letter-from-dr-helen-webberley/

[20] Sex/gender affirmation surgery is regulated through national rules for surgery in Belgium, Bulgaria, Cyprus, Estonia, France, Germany, Greece, Hungary, Luxembourg, Romania, Slovakia, Slovenia and the United Kingdom. There are two countries in Europe – Malta and Ireland – where requests can be made for surgery at 16 years old, and in Austria, Croatia, Czech Republic, Denmark, Finland, Italy, Latvia, Lithuania, the Netherlands, Poland, Portugal, Spain and Sweden it is restricted to those aged 18. As such, headlines which make it into the tabloid press, such as 'Sex-change treatment for kids on the rise' (see https://www.cbsnews.com/news/sex-change-treatment-for-kids-on-the-rise/), if interpreted as referring to surgical intervention, are technically incorrect. If it interpreted as including psychotherapy and GnRHas for a minority of adolescents then they are technically correct. However, the age at which 'sex-change' surgery is provided, for instance, is mostly found near the end of these news articles. The articles generally follow the format: ' "Gender-reassignment surgery, which may include removing or creating penises, is only done by a handful of U.S. doctors, on patients at least 18 years old," Spack said. His clinic has worked with local surgeons who've done breast removal surgery on girls at age 16' (Anonymous, 2012: np).

[21] See for example: https://www.bmj.com/content/366/bmj.l5647, https://www.bmj.com/content/366/bmj.l5647/rapid-responses, https://www.thetimes.co.uk/article/experts-investigate-use-of-puberty-blockers-on-transgender-children-6l695lflf, https://www.transgendertrend.com/puberty-blockers/

Chapter 3

[1] In England and Wales, the Births and Deaths Registration Act 1953 and in Northern Ireland the Births and Deaths Registration (Northern Ireland) Order 1976 require that the birth of every child born be registered within a period of 42 days. Regulations set out the particulars to be registered but they must include a sex. In Scotland, it is a requirement to register the child's birth and the sex within a period of 21 days (Government Equalities Office, 2019).

[2] There are now many legal acts across the world that allow trans people to amend their birth certificates, however, each nation has its own route that the person must take to do so. Very few nations allow for self-declaration of sex/gender, but (at the time of writing) Argentina (2012), Malta (2015), Ireland (2015), Norway (2016), Belgium (2017), Denmark (2018), Portugal (2018), Luxembourg (2018) and, Uruguay (2018) do. Thirty-three countries in Europe require a mental health diagnosis of Gender Dysphoria or Gender Identity Disorder before identity documents can be adapted.

[3] In the case of intersex people in the UK and elsewhere, physicians have been criticized (see Bauer et al, 2016) for carrying out unnecessary surgical interventions that contravene the Convention on the Rights of the Child (CRC). Moreover, the CRC declaration does not state that a male or female sex needs to be

registered: 'The child shall be registered immediately after birth and shall have the right from birth to a name, the right to acquire a nationality' (United Nations Office of the High Commissioner, 1989: np), which warrants that, in light of the fact that we all ought to be treated equally in the eyes of the law, there is no need for sex designation.

[4] I am using 'physician(s)' here as a catch-all term for those who administer medical care (including psychiatrists).

[5] In *The history of medical education*, O'Malley (1970) has demonstrated a rise in the academic learning of medicine in Italy, France, Germany and England from the 12th century onwards.

[6] See: https://www.gmc-uk.org/education/standards-guidance-and-curricula/guidance/shape-of-training-review

[7] There are different schools of thought on what constitutes 'psychopathologies' and their 'cures', and different views on suitable treatment strategies and outcomes resulting from professionals' education and in practice.

Chapter 4

[1] The post-transition specifier was modelled on the concept of 'remission'; however, this does not make sense for those people who are non-dysphoric or non-impaired, but still desire transitioning interventions. The *DSM-5* states that 'not all individuals will experience distress as a result of [...] incongruence' (APA, 2013: 451). If a patient is non-dysphoric/non-impaired then, logically, no remission of dysphoria can take place. Diagnosing non-dysphoric/non-impaired people would result in a false positive diagnosis (Davy and Toze, 2018). The diagnosis used in this way is to persuade health insurance companies to pay out for treatments rather than functioning as a medical diagnosis.

[2] See: https://gic.nhs.uk/about-us/the-team/dr-james-barrett/

[3] See: https://gic.nhs.uk/about-us/the-team/dr-james-barrett/

[4] I have used (pseudo) hermaphroditism here to indicate the term was used historically. People who are intersex have repudiated this term for many years. Many also contest the term 'disorders of sex development' (DSD), now mostly found in clinical literature (see Reis, 2007; Diamond, 2008).

[5] See Cabral and Viturro (2006), Winter et al (2009), Cabral (2010), Reisner et al (2015, 2016) Kara and Cabral Grinspan (2017), Winter (2017), Suess Schwend et al (2018), Suess Schwend (2020); Winters (2008, 2013).

[6] Dr Kirkland did not offer any evidence about the cerebral impact on cis children either.

[7] Tanner stage 2–3 tends to be a few years later than the age when they are prescribed to cis children due to clinical desire for children to have some cognitive emotional maturation (de Vries and Cohen-Kettenis, 2012).

[8] Go to http://transhealth.ucsf.edu/pdf/ Transgender-PGACG-6-17-16.pdf

[9] Gonsalves (2020) argues that the more visible aspects of the sexed/gendered body helps elevate the role of the surgeon; however, this disregards the power that psychiatry retains within the medico-legal assemblage.

Chapter 5

[1] I am unable to consider intersex children in this chapter because of the lack of empirical work in this area, which requires much more visibility, if intersex children

are willing to share their stories. This must be led by intersex people themselves, however. As the activist Mauro Cabral Grinspan argues:

> for all those people who enjoy being visible and have the privilege of accessing spaces thanks to their personal and political contacts: thank you, but we do not need you to do us the favor of making us visible; what we need is that you and your contacts run from the middle, this will allow us to be visible. (https://www.facebook.com/search/top/?q=mauro%20cabral%20grinspan&epa=SEARCH_BOX)

2   See also El-Rouayheb (2005) for an analysis from the Middle East, Durban-Albrecht (2017) for the Caribbean, Evans-Pritchard (1970) for an example from Africa, and Blackwood and Wieringa's (1999) edited collection about same-sex and trans gender practices across the world.

3   See: http://www.newschool.edu/lang

4   I am particularly thinking of one key shift 'back' and 'forth' in the UK: the decriminalization of homosexuality in the 1950s followed by the policy introduced in Thatcherite Britain, when any promotion in schools of homosexuality was criminalized through what is known as Section 28. The Local Government Act 1988 added Section 2A, which included Section 28, to the Local Government Act 1986, which affected England, Wales and Scotland, and was enacted on 24 May 1988. Section 28 stated that a local authority 'shall not intentionally promote homosexuality or publish material with the intention of promoting homosexuality', or 'promote the teaching in any maintained school of the acceptability of homosexuality as a pretended family relationship' (Local Government Act 1988: np). Section 28 [note 8] was repealed by Members of the Scottish Parliament as part of the Ethical Standards in Public Life Act on 21 June 2000. The Labour government introduced the Local Government Act 2003 on 18 September if that year and Section 28 was finally repealed.

5   This was the name of the diagnosis at the time that Zucker's paper was published.

6   Conversion therapy has been denounced for being harmful by dozens of medical and human rights organizations around the world including the WHO, the Canadian Psychological Association, the American Medical Association, Human Rights Campaign, Amnesty International. See for example https://www.psychiatry.org/newsroom/news-releases/apa-reiterates-strong-opposition-to-conversion-therapy, https://www.apa.org/news/press/releases/2015/04/therapies-sexual-orientation and https://cpa.ca/docs/File/Position/SOGII%20Policy%20Statement%20-%20LGB%20Conversion%20Therapy%20FINALAPPROVED2015.pdf in relation to LGB people and https://www.noconversioncanada.com/what-is-conversion-therapy in relation to trans and sex/gender expansive people.

7   See, for example, https://twitter.com/UKIP/status/1115746893064228864

8   See https://twitter.com/OsborneInk/status/1201620625783164928

9   Human development approaches were often understood in stages (see, for example, Havighurst, 1948; Erikson, 1950, 1982; Freud, 1965). If children did not develop through these normative stages, and were known to social services for example, interventions were often enforced in families to try to 'elevate' them to pre-perceived normative standards of development. In contemporary childhood and youth studies these stage standards have been modified and made more complex, but still make numerous assumptions about optimal emotional and social development for the child to succeed in school, work and society.

[10] This literature is vast, and I do not have the space to review it here. Suffice to say that girls' schooling historically, if indeed they did go to school, was to provide a moral, literary and domestic education for their futures as women, good wives and mothers (see, for example, Dyhouse, 1977; Jordan, 1991).

[11] See Grossman et al (2005) for the negative consequences for those trans and sex/gender expansive children who do not have the support of their parents.

[12] All parents' names have been anonymized.

[13] Some documentaries were also shown while we were analysing the interviews for this book, see for example: *Trans kids: Why medicine matters* (Burns and Parks, 2019).

[14] See for example: https://www.theguardian.com/society/2019/jul/27/trans-lobby-pressure-pushing-young-people-to-transition, https://www.thetimes.co.uk/article/parents-battle-state-sponsored-sterilisation-of-trans-children-mb55fxt60, https://news.sky.com/story/nhs-over-diagnosing-children-having-transgender-treatment-former-staff-warn-11875624.

[15] See: https://www.lifesitenews.com/news/cold-calculated-institutionalized-child-abuse-experts-comment-on-child-gender-transitions. For some more affirmative action that counters the 'child abuse' discourse, see: https://www.mermaidsuk.org.uk/exclusive-new-research-reveals-the-truth-about-newspaper-coverage-of-trans-issues!.html and https://www.genderspectrum.org/explore-topics/parenting-and-family/.

[16] See for example multiple Twitter entries from these authors and their political allies https://twitter.com/PJaxParker/status/1213532387801477121, https://twitter.com/OurDutyGrp/status/1211329037186084868, https://twitter.com/brunskellevans/status/1207681803454205960.

References

Abery, B., Rudrud, L., Arndt, K., Schauben, L. and Eggebeen, A. (1995) Evaluating a multicomponent program for enhancing the self-determination of youth with disabilities. *Intervention in School and Clinic*, 30(3): 170–179.

Abraham, J. and Lewis, G. (2000) *Regulating medicines in Europe: Competition, expertise and public health*. London: Routledge.

Abulof, U. (2016) We the peoples? The strange demise of self-determination. *European Journal of International Relations*, 22(3): 536–565.

Adams, N., Pearce, R., Veale, J., Radix, A., Castro, D., Sarkar, A. et al (2017) Guidance and ethical considerations for undertaking transgender health research and institutional review boards adjudicating this research. *Transgender Health*, 2(1): 165–175.

Agamben, G. (1998) *Homo sacer: Sovereign power and bare life* (D. Heller-Roazen trans.). Stanford, CA: Stanford University Press.

Agius, S., Calleja, G., Cristiano, C., Caruana, B. and Baldacchino, R. (2015) *Trans, gender variant and intersex students in schools' policy*. Malta: Ministry of Education and Employment. Available from: https://education.gov.mt/en/resources/Documents/Policy%20 Documents/Trans,%20Gender%20Variant%20and%20Intersex%20 Students%20in%20Schools%20Policy.pdf

Ahmed, S. (2006) *Queer phenomenology: Orientations, objects, others*. Durham, NC: Duke University Press.

Ahmed, S. (2008) Open forum imaginary: Preliminary remarks on the founding gestures of the 'new materialism'. *European Journal of Women's Studies*, 15(1): 23–39.

Aizura, A.Z. (2006) Of borders and homes: The imaginary community of (trans)sexual citizenship. *Inter-Asia Cultural Studies*, 7(2): 289–309.

Allsop, J. and Mulcahy, L. (1996) *Regulating medical work: Formal and informal controls*. Buckingham: Open University Press.

Andersson, J., Salander, P. and Hamberg, K. (2013) Using patients' narratives to reveal gender stereotypes among medical students. *Academic Medicine*, 88(7). Available from: https://journals.lww. com/academicmedicine/fulltext/2013/07000/Using_Patients__ Narratives_to_Reveal_Gender.35.aspx

Annandale, E. and Hunt, K. (eds) (2000) *Gender inequalities in health*. Buckingham: Open University Press.

Annandale, E. and Hunt, K. (1990) Masculinity, femininity and sex: An exploration of their relative contribution to explaining gender differences in health. *Sociology of Health & Illness*, 12(1): 24–46.

Anonymous (2020) Sex-change treatment for kids on the rise. *CBS News*, 20 Feb. Available from: www.cbsnews.com/news/sex-change-treatment-for-kids-on-the-rise/

Ansara, Y.G. (2015) Challenging cisgenderism in the ageing and aged care sector: Meeting the needs of older people of trans and/or non-binary experience. *Australasian Journal on Ageing*, 34(S2): 14–18.

Ansara, Y.G. and Hegarty, P. (2012) Cisgenderism in psychology: Pathologising and misgendering children from 1999 to 2008. *Psychology and Sexuality*, 3(2): 137–160.

APA (1994) *Diagnostic and statistical manual of mental disorders: DSM-IV*. Washington, DC: American Psychiatric Association.

APA (1995) *Diagnostic and statistical manual of mental disorders: DSM-IV: international version with ICD-10 codes*. Washington, DC: American Psychiatric Association.

APA (2000) *Diagnostic and statistical manual of mental disorders: DSM-IV-TR*. Washington, DC: American Psychiatric Association.

APA (2008) Transgender, gender identity, and gender expression non-discrimination. Available from: www.apa.org/about/policy/transgender.pdf

APA (2013) *Diagnostic and statistical manual of mental disorders: DSM-5*. Washington, DC: American Psychiatric Association.

Appleton, N. (1983) *Pluralism in education: Theoretical foundations*. New York: Longmans.

Ashley, F. (2019a) Gatekeeping hormone replacement therapy for transgender patients is dehumanising. *Journal of Medical Ethics*, 45(7): 480–482.

Ashley, F. (2019b) Puberty blockers are necessary, but they don't prevent homelessness: Caring for transgender youth by supporting unsupportive parents. *American Journal of Bioethics*, 19(2): 87–89.

Association of American Medical Colleges (2007) *Joint AAMC-GSA and AAMC-OSR recommendations regarding institutional programs and educational activities to address the needs of gay, lesbian, bisexual and transgender (GLBT) students and patients*. Washington, DC: Association of American Medical Colleges.

Axtell, J.L. (1970) Education and status in Stuart England: The London physician. *History of Education Quarterly*, 10(2): 141–159. Available from: www.jstor.org/stable/367022

Balint, E. (1969) The possibilities of patient-centred medicine. *Journal of the Royal College of General Practitioners*, 17(82): 269–276.

Barker, M. J. and Richards, C. (2015) Further genders. In C. Richards and B.M. John (eds), *Handbook of the psychology of sexuality and gender* (pp 166–182). Basingstoke: Palgrave Macmillan.

Barrett, J. (ed.) (2007) *Transsexual and other disorders of gender identity.* Oxford: Radcliffe.

Bassett, V., Conron, K.J., Landers, S. and Auerbach, J. (2002) Public health infrastructure: Building LGBT competency into health care, institutions, and policies. *Clinical Research and Regulatory Affairs,* 19(2–3): 191–222.

Bauer, M., Truffer, D., Greenberry, H., Vago, D., Jaye, L. and Hayes-Light, J. (2016) *Intersex genital mutilations: Human rights violations of children with variations of sex anatomy.* NGO report to the 5th periodic report of the United Kingdom on the Convention on the Rights of the Child (CRC). Zurich: StopIGM.org/ Zwischengeschlecht.org.

Beauchamp, T.L. and Childress, J.F. (2001) *Principles of biomedical ethics* (5th edn). Oxford: Oxford University Press.

Becker, H.S., Geer, B., Hughes, E.C. and Strauss, A.L. (1960) *Boys in white: Student culture in medical school.* Chicago, IL: University of Chicago Press.

Benjamin, H. (1966) *The transsexual phenomenon.* New York: Julian Press.

Benjamin, H. (1971) Should surgery be performed on transsexuals? *American Journal of Psychotherapy,* 25(1): 74–82.

Benner, P. (2000) The roles of embodiment, emotion and lifeworld for rationality and agency in nursing practice. *Nursing Philosophy,* 1(1): 5–19.

Berg, B.L. (1989) *Qualitative research methods for the social sciences.* New York: Allyn & Bacon.

Berkowitz, D., Manohar, N.N. and Tinkler, J.E. (2010) Walk like a man, talk like a woman: Teaching the social construction of gender. *Teach Sociology,* 38(2): 132–143.

Berlant, J.L. (1992) *Profession and monopoly: A study of medicine in the United States and Britain.* Los Angeles, CA: University of California Press.

Besser, M., Carr, S., Cohen-Kettenis, P.T., Connolly, P., De Sutter, P., Diamond, M. et al (2006) Atypical gender development – a review. *International Journal of Transgenderism,* 9(1): 29–44.

Billings, D.B. and Urban, T. (1996) The socio-medical construction of transsexualism. In R. Ekins and D. King (eds) *Blending genders: Social aspects of cross-dressing and sex-changing* (pp 99–117). London: Routledge.

Binkley, S. (2011) Psychological life as enterprise: Social practice and the government of neo-liberal interiority. *History of the Human Sciences*, 24(3): 83–102.

Birke, L. and Best, S. (1980) The tyrannical womb: Menstruation and menopause. In L. Birke, W. Faulkner, S. Best et al. (eds), *Alice through the microscope: The power of science over women's lives* (pp 89–107). London: Virago.

Black, E., Bond, K., Briffa, T., Carpenter, M., Cody, C., David, A. et al (2017) *Darlington statement: Joint consensus statement from the intersex community retreat in Darlington, March 2017*. Sydney. Available from: https://eprints.qut.edu.au/104412/1/Darlington-Statement.pdf

Blackless, M., Charuvastra, A., Derryck, A., Fausto-Sterling, A., Lauzanne, K. and Lee, E. (2000) How sexually dimorphic are we? Review and synthesis. *American Journal of Human Biology*, 12(2): 151–166.

Blackwood, E. and Wieringa, S.E. (eds) (1999) *Female desires: Same-sex relations and transgender practices across cultures*. New York: Columbia University Press.

Blanchard, R. (1991) Clinical observations and systematic studies of autogynephilia. *Journal of Sex & Marital Therapy*, 17(4): 235–251.

Blanchard, R. (2008) Deconstructing the feminine essence narrative. *Archives of Sexual Behavior*, 37: 434–438.

Blashfield, R.K., Keeley, J.W., Flanagan, E.H. and Miles, S.R. (2014) The cycle of classification: DSM-I through DSM-5. *Annual Review of Clinical Psychology*, 10(1): 25–51.

Bonifacio, H.J. and Rosenthal, S.M. (2015) Gender variance and dysphoria in children and adolescents. *Pediatric Clinics of North America*, 62(4): 1001–1016.

Boot, A. M., de Muinck Keizer-Schrama, S., Pols, H.A., Krenning, E.P. and Drop, S.L. (1998) Bone mineral density and body composition before and during treatment with gonadotropin-releasing hormone agonist in children with central precocious and early puberty. *Journal of Clinical Endocrinology & Metabolism*, 83(2): 370–373.

Bosk, C.L. (2003) *Forgive and remember: Manging medical failure*. Chicago, IL: University of Chicago Press.

Bowie, P., Bradley, N.A. and Rushmer, R. (2012) Clinical audit and quality improvement – time for a rethink? *Journal of Evaluation in Clinical Practice*, 18(1): 42–48.

Braidotti, R. (1994) *Nomadic subjects: Embodiment and sexual difference in contemporary feminist theory*. New York: Columbia University Press.

Braidotti, R. (2002) *Metamorphoses: Towards a materialist theory of becoming*. Cambridge: Polity Press.

Braidotti, R. (2006a) The becoming minoritarian of Europe. In I. Buchanan and A. Parr (eds), *Deleuze and the contemporary world* (pp 79–94). Edinburgh: Edinburgh University Press.

Braidotti, R. (2006b) Difference, diversity and nomadic subjectivity. Available from: www.translatum.gr/forum/index.php?PHPSE SSID=6cd2392338786b806c251b6e6e2bb5cf&topic=14317. msg107006#msg107006

Brain, A. E. (2012) Another part of the puzzle. Available from: http://aebrain.blogspot.co.uk/

Brill, S. and Pepper, R. (2008) *The transgender child*. San Francisco, CA: Cleis Press.

Brilmayer, L. (1991) Secession and self-determination: Territorial interpretation. *Yale Journal of International Law*, 16(1): 177–202.

Briscoe, A.M. (1978) Hormones and gender. In E. Tobach and B. Rosoff (eds), *Genes and gender 1* (pp 31–50). New York: Gordon Press.

Brody, D.S. (1980) The patient's role in clinical decision-making. *Annals of Internal Medicine*, 93(5): 718–722.

Brooks, C. and Bolzendahl, C. (2004) The transformation of US gender role attitudes: Cohort replacement, social-structural change, and ideological learning. *Social Science Research*, 33(1): 106–133.

Browne, K. (2009) Womyn's separatist spaces: Rethinking spaces of difference and exclusion. *Transactions of the Institute of British Geographers*, 34(4): 541–556.

Browne, K. (2011) Beyond rural idylls: Imperfect lesbian utopias at Michigan womyn's music festival. *Journal of Rural Studies*, 27(1): 13–23.

Browne, K.R. (1984) Biology, equality, and the law: The legal significance of biological sex differences. *Southwestern Law Journal*, 38(2): 617–702.

Brubaker, R. and Cooper, F. (2000) Beyond 'identity'. *Theory and Society*, 29(1): 1–47.

Brunskell-Evans, H. and Moore, M. (eds) (2018) *Transgender children and young people: Born in your own body*. Newcastle: Cambridge Scholars Publishing.

Budge, S.L. (2015) Psychotherapists as gatekeepers: An evidence-based case study highlighting the role and process of letter writing for transgender clients. *Psychotherapy*, 52(3): 287–297.

Burchell, G. (1996) Liberal government and techniques of the self. In A. Barry, T. Osborne and N. Rose (eds), *Foucault and political reason* (pp 19–36). London: University College London Press.

Burkitt, I. (1999) *Bodies of thought: Embodiment, identity, and modernity*. London: Sage.

Burns, L. (Producer) and Parks, J. (Director) (2019) *Trans kids: Why medicine matters* [Video/DVD]. London: British Broadcasting Corporation. Available from: www.bbc.co.uk/programmes/m0002tw1

Burt, R.A. (1979) *Taking care of strangers: The rule of law in doctor–patient relations*. New York: The Free Press.

Butler, J. (1990) *Gender trouble: Feminism and the subversion of identity*. London: Routledge.

Butler, J. (1992) Sexual inversions. In D.C. Stanton (ed.), *Discourses of sexuality: From Aristotle to AIDS* (pp 344–361). Ann Arbor, MI: University of Michigan Press.

Butler, J. (1993) *Bodies that matter: On the discursive limits of 'sex'*. London: Routledge.

Butler, J. (2004a) *Precarious life: The powers of mourning and violence*. London: Verso.

Butler, J. (2004b) *Undoing gender*. New York: Routledge.

Butler, J. (2015) *Notes toward a performative theory of assembly*. Cambridge, MA: Harvard University Press.

Butler, J., Laclau, E. and Žižek, S. (2000) *Contingency, hegemony, universality: Contemporary dialogues on the left*. London: Verso.

Cabral, M. (2010) 'Autodeterminación y libertad'. 22 October. Available from: www.pagina12.com.ar/diario/suplementos/soy/1-1675-2010-10-22.html

Cabral, M. and Viturro, P. (2006) (Trans)sexual citizenship in contemporary Argentina. In P. Currah, R.M. Juang and P.S. Minter (eds) *Transgender rights* (pp 262–273). Minneapolis, MN: University of Minneapolis Press.

Caldon, L.J.M., Collins, K.A., Reed, M.W., Sivell, S., Austoker, J., Clements, A.M. et al (2010) Clinicians' concerns about decision support interventions for patients facing breast cancer surgery options: Understanding the challenge of implementing shared decision-making. *Health Expectations*, 14(2): 133–146.

Callis, A.S. (2014) Bisexual, pansexual, queer: Non-binary identities and the sexual borderlands. *Sexualities*, 17(1–2): 63–80.

Cannon, S. and Best, T. (2015) *Schools transgender guidance*. Available from: www.cornwall.gov.uk/media/13620644/schools-transgender_guidance_booklet-2015.pdf

Caplan, J. (1989) Postmodernism, poststructuralism, and deconstruction: Notes for historians. *Central European History*, 22(3–4): 260–278.

Careaga-Pérez, G. (2016) Moral panic and gender ideology in Latin America. *Religion and Gender*, 6(2): 251–255. Available from: https://doi.org/10.18352/rg.10174

Carmines, E.G. and Zeller, R.A. (1979) *Reliability and validity assessment*. Thousand Oaks, CA: Sage.

Carrera, M.V., DePalma, R. and Lameiras, M. (2012) Sex/gender identity: Moving beyond fixed and 'natural' categories. *Sexualities*, 15(8): 995–1016.

Castro-Peraza, M.E., García-Acosta, J.M., Delgado, N., Perdomo-Hernández, A.M., Sosa-Alvarez, M.I., Llabrés-Solé, R. et al (2019) Gender identity: The human right of depathologization. *International Journal of Environmental Research and Public Health*, 16(6): 978. Available from: www.mdpi.com/1660-4601/16/6/978

Catlin, A., Volat, D., Hadley, M.A., Bassir, R., Armigo, C., Valle, E. et al (2008) Conscientious objection: A potential neonatal nursing response to care orders that cause suffering at the end of life? Study of a concept. *Neonatal Network*, 27(2): 101–108.

Cauldwell, D.O. (1949) Psychopathia transexualis. *Sexology Magazine*, 16: 275–280.

Cauldwell, D.O. (2001) Sex transmutation-can one's sex be changed? There's but a thin genetic line between the sexes. *International Journal of Transgenderism*, 5(2). Available from: www.symposion.com/ijt/cauldwell/cauldwell_05.htm

Cavanaugh, T., Hopwood, R. and Lambert, C. (2016) Informed consent in the medical care of transgender and gender-nonconforming patients. *AMA Journal of Ethics*, 18(11): 1147–1155.

Chamberlain, J.M. (2009) *Doctoring medical governance: Medical self-regulation in transition*. New York: Nova Science Publishers.

Chandler, D. (2013) The world of attachment? The post-humanist challenge to freedom and necessity. *Millennium* 41(3): 516–534.

Chau, P. and Herring, J. (2002) Defining, assigning and designing sex. *International Journal of Law, Policy and the Family*, 16(3): 327–367.

Chiland, C. (2000) The psychoanalyst and the transsexual patient. *International Journal of Psychoanalysis*, 81(1): 21–35.

Chiland, C. (2005) *Exploring transsexualism*. London: Karnac Books.

Clough, P.T. (2008) The affective turn. *Theory, Culture & Society*, 25(1): 1–22.

Cohen, L., de Ruiter, C., Ringelberg, H. and Cohen-Kettenis, P.T. (1997) Psychological functioning of adolescent transsexuals: Personality and psychopathology. *Journal of Clinical Psychology*, 53(2): 187–196.

Colebrook, C. (2015) What is it like to be a human? *Transgender Studies Quarterly*, 2(2): 227–243.

Connell, R.W. and Messerschmidt, J.W. (2005) Hegemonic masculinity: Rethinking the concept. *Gender & Society*, 19(6): 829–859.

Connor, W. (1967) Self-determination: The new phase. *World Politics*, 20(1): 30–53.

Cordoba, S. (2020) Non-binary sexualities: The language of desire, practice, and embodiment. In Z. Davy, A.C. Santos, C. Bertone, R. Thoresen and S.E. Wieringa (eds), *Sage handbook of global sexualities* (pp 877–896). London: Sage.

Council of Europe (2016) *Competences for democratic culture: Living together as equals in culturally diverse democratic societies*. Strasbourg: Council of Europe.

Council of Europe Ministers of Foreign Affairs (2008) White paper on intercultural dialogue. 'living together as equals in dignity'. Strasbourg: Council of Europe.

Crenshaw, K.W. (1989) Demarginalizing the intersection of race and sex: Black feminist critique of antidiscrimination doctrine, feminist theory and antiracist politics. *University of Chicago Legal Forum*, 1989: 139–168.

Crenshaw, K.W. (1991) Mapping the margins: Intersectionality, identity politics, and violence against women of color. *Stanford Law Review*, 43(6): 1241–1299.

Croall, H. and Elder, A. (Producers) and Altman, K. (Director) (1999) *Paradise bent: Boys will be girls in Samoa*. [Video/DVD] Australia: Angle Pictures.

Crossley, N. (2001) *The social body: Habit, identity and desire*. London: Sage.

Curlin, F.A., Lawrence, R.E., Chin, M.H. and Lantos, J.D. (2007a) Religion, conscience, and controversial clinical practices. *New England Journal of Medicine*, 356(6): 593–600.

Curlin, F.A., Lawrence, R.E. and Lantos, J.D. (2007b) The authors reply. *New England Journal of Medicine*, 356(18) Available from: www.nejm.org/doi/full/10.1056/NEJMsa065316?query=recirc_curatedRelated_article#article_letters

Daly, P. (1996) The effects of single-sex and coeducational secondary schooling on girls' achievement. *Research Papers in Education*, 11(3): 289–306.

Darder, A. (2017) *Reinventing Paulo Freire: A pedagogy of love* (2nd edn). London: Routledge.

Davis, G., Dewey, J.M. and Murphy, E.L. (2016) Giving sex: Deconstructing intersex and trans medicalization practices. *Gender & Society*, 30(3): 490–514.

Davy, Z. (2010) Transsexual agents: Negotiating authenticity and embodiment within the UK's medicolegal system. In S. Hines and T. Sanger (eds), *Transgender identities: Towards a social analysis of gender diversity* (pp 106–126). New York: Routledge.

Davy, Z. (2011a) The promise of intersectionality theory in primary care. *Quality in Primary Care*, 19(5): 279. Available from: www.ncbi.nlm.nih.gov/pubmed/22186169

Davy, Z. (2011b) *Recognizing transsexuals: Personal, political and medicolegal embodiment*. Farnham: Ashgate.

Davy, Z. (2015) The DSM-5 and the politics of diagnosing transpeople. *Archives of Sexual Behavior*, 44(5): 1165–1176.

Davy, Z. (2019) Genderqueer(ing): 'On this side of the world against which it protests'. *Sexualities*, 22(1–2): 80–96.

Davy, Z. (2020) Freedom affects in trans erotica. In Z. Davy, A.C. Santos, C. Bertone, R. Thoresen and S.E. Wieringa (eds), *Sage handbook of global sexualities* (pp 969–991). Thousand Oaks, CA: Sage Publications.

Davy, Z. and Cordoba, S. (2020) School cultures and trans and gender-diverse children: Parents' perspectives. *Journal of GLBT Family Studies*, 16(4): 349–367.

Davy, Z. and Toze, M. (2018) What is gender dysphoria? A critical systematic narrative review. *Transgender Health*, 3(1): 159–169.

Davy, Z., Amsler, S. and Duncombe, K. (2015) Facilitating LGBT medical, health and social care content in higher education teaching. *Qualitative Research in Education*, 4(2): 134–163.

Davy, Z., Sørlie, A. and Schwend, A. S. (2018) Democratising diagnoses? The role of the depathologisation perspective in constructing corporeal trans citizenship. *Critical Social Policy*, 38(1): 13–34.

de Beauvoir, S. (1997) *The second sex* (H.M. Parshley trans.). London: Vintage.

de Bruijn, H. (2007) *Managing Performance in the Public Sector* (2nd edn). Abingdon: Routledge,

De Montfort University (2017) *Policy on support and procedures for trans, gender fluid and non-binary staff and students*. Leicester: De Montfort University.

de Vries, A.L.C. and Cohen-Kettenis, P.T. (2012) Clinical management of gender dysphoria in children and adolescents: The Dutch approach. *Journal of Homosexuality*, 59(3): 301–320.

de Vries, E., Kathard, H. and Müller, A. (2020) Debate: Why should gender-affirming health care be included in health science curricula? *BMC Medical Education*, 20(1): 51. Available from: https://doi.org/10.1186/s12909-020-1963-6

Deci, E.L. (1971) Effects of externally mediated rewards on intrinsic motivation. *Journal of Personality and Social Psychology*, 18(1): 105–115.

Deci, E.L. (1975) *Intrinsic motivation*. New York: Plenum.

DeLanda, M. (2006) *A new philosophy of society: Assemblage theory and social complexity*. London: Continuum.

DeLanda, M. (2016) *Assemblage theory*. Edinburgh: Edinburgh University Press.

Deleuze, G. (1983) *Nietzsche and philosophy*. New York: Columbia University Press.

Deleuze, G. (1988) *Spinoza: Practical philosophy* (R. Hurley trans.). San Francisco: City Lights.

Deleuze, G. (1992) *Expressionism in philosophy: Spinoza* (M. Joughin trans.). New York: Zone Books.

Deleuze, G. (1997) Immanence: A life. *Theory, Culture & Society*, 14(2): 3–7.

Deleuze, G. (2004) *Difference and repetition* (P. Patton trans.). London: Continuum.

Deleuze, G. (2006) *Two regimes of madness: Texts and interviews 1975–1995* (A. Hodges, M. Taormina trans.) New York: Semiotext(e).

Deleuze, G. and Guattari, F. (1984) *Anti-Oedipus: Capitalism and schizophrenia* (R. Hurley, M. Seem and H. R. Lane trans.). London: Athlone Press.

Deleuze, G. and Guattari, F. (2004) *A thousand plateaus: Capitalism and schizophrenia* (B. Massumi trans.). London: Continuum.

Deleuze, G. and Guattari, F. (2007) We always make love with worlds. In M. Lock and J. Farquhar (eds), *Beyond the body proper: Reading the anthropology of material life* (pp 428–432). Durham, NC: Duke University Press.

Department of Health (1989) *Working for patients*. London: The Stationary Office.

Department of Health (1997) *The new NHS: modern, dependable* (Cm 3807). London: The Stationery Office.

Deutsch, M.B. (2012) Use of the informed consent model in the provision of cross-sex hormone therapy: A survey of the practices of selected clinics. *International Journal of Transgenderism*, 13(3): 140–146.

Dewey, J.M. (2015) Challenges of implementing collaborative models of decision making with trans-identified patients. *Health Expectations*, 18(5): 1508–1518.

Diamond, M. (2000) Sex and gender: Same or different? *Feminism & Psychology*, 10(1): 46–54.

Diamond, M. (2002) Sex and gender are different: Sexual identity and gender identity are different. *Clinical Child Psychology and Psychiatry*, 7(3): 320–334.

Diamond, M. (2008) Human intersexuality: Difference or disorder. *Archives of Sexual Behavior*, 38(2): 172.

Dillon, M. and Lobo-Guerrero, L. (2009) The biopolitical imaginary of species-being. *Theory, Culture & Society*, 26(1): 1–23.

Doctors Opposing Circumcision (2016) Conscientious objection to non-therapeutic circumcision. Available from: www.doctorsopposingcircumcision.org/for-professionals/conscientious-objection/

Doyal, L. (2006) Sex, gender and medicine: The case of the NHS. In D. Kelleher, J. Gabe and G. Williams (eds), *Challenging medicine* (2nd edn, pp 146–161). London: Routledge.

Drescher, J. (2010) Queer diagnoses: Parallels and contrasts in the history of homosexuality, gender variance, and the diagnostic and statistical manual. *Archives of Sexual Behavior*, 39(2): 427–460.

Drescher, J., Cohen-Kettenis, P.T. and Winter, S. (2012) Minding the body: Situating gender identity diagnoses in the ICD-11. *International Review of Psychiatry*, 24(6): 568–577.

Duff, C. (2014) *Assemblages of health: Deleuze's empiricism and the ethology of life*. Dordrecht: Springer.

du Guy, P. (1996) *Consumption and identity at work*. London: Sage Publications.

Durban-Albrecht, E. (2017) Performing postcolonial homophobia: A decolonial analysis of the 2013 public demonstrations against same-sex marriage in Haiti. *Women & Performance: A Journal of Feminist Theory*, 27(2): 160–175.

Durkheim, E. (1951) *Suicide*. London: Routledge.

Durnová, A. (2018) Understanding emotions in policy studies through Foucault and Deleuze. *Politics and Governance*, 6(4): 95–102. Available from: www.cogitatiopress.com/politicsandgovernance/article/view/1528/1528

Düwell, M. (2013) *Bioethics: Methods, theories, domains*. Abingdon: Routledge.

Dworkin, R.B. (1992) Medical law and ethics in the post-autonomy age. *Indiana Law Journal*, 3: 727–742.

Dyhouse, C. (1977) Good wives and little mothers: Social anxieties and the schoolgirl's curriculum, 1890–1920. *Oxford Review of Education*, 3(1): 21–35.

Eckert, L. (2010) *Intervening in intersexualization: The clinic and the colony*. PhD thesis, Universiteit Utrecht, The Netherlands.

Eckert, L. (2017) *Intersexualization: The clinic and the colony*. New York: Routledge.

Ehrensaft, D. (2012) From gender identity disorder to gender identity creativity: True gender self child therapy. *Journal of Homosexuality*, 59(3): 337–356.

Ehrensaft, D. (2016) *The gender creative child: Pathways for nurturing and supporting children who live outside the gender boxes*. New York: The Experiment.

Eisenman, L.T. (2007) Self-determination interventions: Building a foundation for school completion. *Remedial and Special Education*, 28(1): 2–8.

Eisenman, L.T. and Chamberlin, M. (2001) Implementing self-determination activities: Lessons from schools. *Remedial and Special Education*, 22(3): 138–147.

El-Rouayheb, K. (2005) The love of boys in Arabic poetry of the early Ottoman period, 1500–1800. *Middle Eastern Literatures*, 8(1): 3–22.

Elston, M.A. (1991) The politics of professional power: Medicine in a changing medical service. In J. Gabe, M. Calman and M. Bury (eds), *The sociology of the health service* (pp 58–88). London: Routledge.

Endocrine Society (2019) Endocrine society urges policy makers to follow science on transgender health. *Endocrine News*, Oct. Available from: https://endocrinenews.endocrine.org/endocrine-society-urges-policymakers-to-follow-science-on-transgender-health/

Epprecht, M. and Egya, S.E. (2011) Teaching about homosexualities to Nigerian university students: A report from the field. *Gender and Education*, 23(4): 367–383.

Equal Rights Trust (2008) *Declaration of principles on equality*. Available from: www.equalrightstrust.org/ertdocumentbank/Pages%20from%20Declaration%20perfect%20principle.pdf

Erikson, E.H. (1950) *Childhood and society* (2nd edn). New York: Norton.

Erikson, E.H. (1982) *The life cycle completed: A review*. New York: Norton.

Esping-Andersen, G. (2000) The sustainability of welfare states into the twenty-first century. *International Journal of Health Services*, 30(1): 1–12.

Evans, Y.N., Gridley, S.J., Crouch, J., Wang, A., Moreno, M.A., Ahrens, K. et al (2017) Understanding online resource use by transgender youth and caregivers: A qualitative study. *Transgender Health*, 2(1): 129–139.

Evans-Pritchard, E. (1970) Sexual inversion among the Azande. *American Anthropologist*, 72(6): 1428–1434.

Fabre, C. (2008) *Whose body is it anyway? Justice and the integrity of the person*. Oxford: Oxford University Press.

Farmer, J.E., Jr (2017) Charting the middle course: An argument for robust but well-tailored health care discrimination protection for the transgender community notes. *Georgia Law Review*, 1: 225–266.

Farrell, C. (2004) *Patient and public involvement in health: The evidence for policy implementation*. London: The Stationary Office.

Fausto-Sterling, A. (1993) The five sexes: Why male and female are not enough. *The Sciences*, March/April: 20–24.

Fausto-Sterling, A. (2000) *Sexing the body: Gender politics and the construction of sexuality*. New York: Basic Books.

Field, S.L. and Hoffman, A.S. (2012) Fostering self-determination through building productive relationships in the classroom. *Intervention in School and Clinic*, 48(1): 6–14.

Fine, C. (2010) *Delusions of gender: The real science behind sex differences*. London: Icon Books.

Fine, C., Jordan-Young, R., Kaiser, A. and Rippon, G. (2013) Plasticity, plasticity, plasticity … and the rigid problem of sex. *Trends in Cognitive Sciences*, 17(11): 550–551.

Finn, G. (1998) Girl christened as boy wins right to new birth certificate. *Independent*, 2 Dec., p 3.

Fisher, B. and Tronto, J.C. (1990) Toward a feminist theory of caring. In E. Abel and M. Nelson (eds), *Circles of care: Work and identity in women's lives* (pp 36–54). Albany, NY: SUNY Press.

Fleming, M. and Feinbloom, D. (1984) Similarities in becoming: Transsexuals and adolescents. *Adolescence*, 19(75): 729–748.

Foucault, M. (1980a) *Herculine Barbin: Being the recently discovered memoirs of a nineteenth-century French hermaphrodite* (R. McDougall trans.). Brighton: The Harvester Press.

Foucault, M. (1980b) *Power/knowledge: Selected interviews and other writings, 1972–1977*. New York: Pantheon.

Foucault, M. (1986) Right of death and power over life. In P. Rabinow (ed.), *The Foucault reader* (pp 258–272). Toronto: Peregrine Books.

Foucault, M. (1990) *The care of the self: The history of sexuality* (R. Hurley trans.). London: Penguin.

Foucault, M. (1994a) Governmentality. In J.D. Faubion (ed.), *Power: Essential works of Foucault 1954–1984* (R. Hurley trans.) (pp 210–222). London: Penguin.

Foucault, M. (1994b) Society must be defended. In P. Rabinow (ed.), *Ethics: Essential works of Foucault 1954–1984* (pp 59–65). London: Penguin.

Foucault, M. (1995) *Madness and civilization: A history of insanity in the age of reason* (R. Howard trans.). London: Routledge.

Foucault, M. (1996) *The order of things: An archaeology of the human sciences* (A.M. Sheridan trans.). London: Routledge.

Foucault, M. (2003) *The birth of the clinic: An archaeology of medical perception* (A.M. Sheridan trans.). London: Routledge.

Foucault, M. (2006) 12th December 1973. In E. Lagrange (ed.), *Psychiatric power: Lectures at the Collège de France 1973–1974* (G. Burchell trans.). New York: Palgrave Macmillan.

Fox-Keller, E. and Longino, H. (eds) (1983) *Feminism and science.* Oxford: Oxford University Press.

Frank, A.W. (2002) *At the will of the body: Reflections on illness.* St Charles, IL: Houghton Mifflin Harcourt.

Frank, A.W. (2016) From sick role to narrative subject: An analytic memoir. *Health*, 20(1): 9–21.

Fraser, N. and Honneth, A. (2003) *Redistribution or recognition? A political-philosophical exchange.* London: Verso.

Freeman, L. and Ayala López, S. (2018) Sex categorization in medical contexts: A cautionary tale. *Kennedy Institute of Ethics Journal*, 28(3): 243–280.

Freidson, E. (1970) *The profession of medicine.* New York: Dodds Mead.

Freire, P. (2000) *Pedagogy of the oppressed* (M. Bregman Ramos trans.; 30th anniversary edn). New York: Continuum.

Freud, A. (1965) *Normality and pathology in childhood: Assessments of development.* New York: International Universities Press.

Freund, K. and Blanchard, R. (1993) Erotic target location errors in male gender dysphorics, paedophiles, and fetishists. *British Journal of Psychiatry*, 162(4): 558–563.

Frosch, D.L., May, S.G., Rendle, K., Tietbohl, C. and Elwyn, G. (2012) Authoritarian physicians and patients' fear of being labeled 'difficult' among key obstacles to shared decision making. *Health Affairs*, 31(5): 1030–1038. Available from: https://doi.org/10.1377/hlthaff.2011.0576

Fujimura, J.H. (2006) Sex genes: A critical sociomaterial approach to the politics and molecular genetics of sex determination. *Signs: Journal of Women in Culture and Society*, 32(1): 49–82.

Gabe, J., Kelleher, D. and Williams, G. (2006) Understanding medical dominance in the modern world. In J. Gabe, D. Kelleher and G. Williams (eds), *Challenging medicine* (pp xv–xxxiii). Abingdon: Routledge.

Garland, J. and S. Slokenberga (2018) Protecting the rights of children with intersex conditions from nonconsensual gender-conforming medical interventions: The view from Europe. *Medical Law Review*, 27(3): 482–508.

Gay, G. (1979) Changing conceptions of multicultural education. In H.P. Baptiste and M.L. Baptiste (eds), *Developing multicultural process in classroom instructions: Competencies for teachers* (pp 18–27). Washington, DC: University Press of America.

General Medical Council (1993) *Tomorrow's doctors*. London: General Medical Council.

General Medical Council (2003) *Tomorrow's doctors*. London: General Medical Council.

General Medical Council. (2009) *Tomorrow's doctors*. London: General Medical Council.

General Medical Council (2020) The duties of a doctor registered with the General Medical Council. Available from: www.gmc-uk.org/ethical-guidance/ethical-guidance-for-doctors/good-medical-practice/duties-of-a-doctor

Ghattas, D.C. (2015) *Standing up for the human rights of intersex people: How can you help?* ILGA Europe. Available from: www.ilga-europe.org/sites/default/files/how_to_be_a_great_intersex_ally_a_toolkit_for_ngos_and_decision_makers_december_2015_updated.pdf

Giaimo, S. and Manow, P. (1999) Adapting the welfare state: The case of health care reform in Britain, Germany, and the United States. *Comparative Political Studies*, 32(8): 967–1000.

Giddens, A. (1982) Class division, class conflict and citizenship rights. In A. Giddens (ed.), *Profiles and critiques in social theory* (pp 164–180). London: Palgrave.

Giedd, J.N. (2004) Structural magnetic resonance imaging of the adolescent brain. *Annals of the New York Academy of Sciences*, 1021(1): 77–85.

Gilbert, P. (1998) *The philosophy of nationalism*. Boulder, CO: Westview Press.

Gilman, S. L. (1999) *Making the body beautiful: A cultural history of aesthetic surgery*. Princeton, NJ: Princeton University Press.

Giordano, S. (2008) Lives in a chiaroscuro: Should we suspend the puberty of children with gender identity disorder? *Journal of Medical Ethics*, 34(8): 580–584.

Gladstone, D. (ed.) (2000) *Regulating doctors*. London: Institute for the Study of Civil Society.

Glass, J. (2018) Anti-trans activists hit out at 'parasitic' trans people at event in parliament. *Pink News*, 15 March. Available from: www.pinknews.co.uk/2018/03/15/anti-trans-activists-hit-out-at-parasitic-trans-people-at-event-in-parliament/

Glass, J., Bengtson, V.L. and Dunham, C.C. (1986) Attitude similarity in three-generation families: Socialization, status inheritance, or reciprocal influence? *American Sociological Review*, 51(5): 685–698.

Gonsalves, T. (2020) Gender identity, the sexed body, and the medical making of transgender. *Gender & Society*, online first. Available from: https://doi.org/10.1177/0891243220965913

Gordon, J. (2012) Human rights in bioethics – theoretical and applied. *Ethical Theory and Moral Practice*, 15(3): 283–294.

Government Equalities Office (2019) Variations in sex characteristics: Technical paper. Available from: www.gov.uk/government/consultations/variations-in-sex-characteristics-call-for-evidence/variations-in-sex-characteristics-technical-paper#chapter-6-sex-assignment-birth-registration-and-correcting-birth-certificates

GRA (2004) Gender Recognition Act 2004. Available from: www.opsi.gov.uk/acts/acts2004/ukpga_20040007_en_1

Grant, C.A. and Sleeter, C.E. (1986) Educational equity: Education that is multicultural and social reconstructionist. *Journal of Educational Equity and Leadership*, 6(2): 106–118.

Grant, J.M., Mottet, L.A. and Tanis, J. (2011) *Injustice at every turn: A report of the national transgender discrimination survey*. Washington, DC: National Center for Transgender Equality and National Gay and Lesbian Task Force.

Grant, J.M., Mottet, L.A., Tanis, J., Herman, J.L., Harrison, J. and Keisling, M. (2010) *National transgender discrimination survey report on health and health care*. Washington, DC: National Center for Transgender Equality and the National Gay and Lesbian Task Force.

Greco, M. (2004) The politics of indeterminacy and the right to health. *Theory, Culture & Society*, 21(6): 1–22.

Green, R. (1987) *The 'sissy boy syndrome' and the development of homosexuality*. New Haven, CT: Yale University Press.

Grimwood, T. (2010) "Gillick" and the consent of minors: Contraceptive advice and treatment in New Zealand. *Victoria University of Wellington Law Review*, 40(4): 743–769.

Grossman, A. H., D'Augelli, A.R., Howell, T.J. and Hubbard, S. (2005) Parents' reactions to transgender youths' gender nonconforming expression and identity. *Journal of Gay & Lesbian Social Services*, 18(1): 3–16.

Grosz, E. (1994) *Volatile bodies: Toward a corporeal feminism*. Bloomington, IN: Indiana University Press.

Grosz, E. (2005) Bergson, Deleuze and the becoming of unbecoming. *Parallax*, 11(2): 4–13.

Grosz, E. (2011) *Becoming undone: Darwinian reflections on life, politics and art.* Durham, NC: Duke University Press.

Grove, J. (2009) How competent are trainee and newly qualified counsellors to work with lesbian, gay, and bisexual clients and what do they perceive as their most effective learning experiences? *Counselling and Psychotherapy Research,* 9(2): 78–85.

Halpern, S.D. (2005) Towards evidence based bioethics. *British Medical Journal,* 331(7521): 901–903.

Hannum, H. (1996) *Autonomy, sovereignty, and self-determination: The accommodation of conflicting rights.* Philadelphia, PA: University of Pennsylvania Press.

Haraway, D.J. (1976) *Crystals, fabrics, and fields: Metaphors that shape embryos.* Berkeley, CA: North Atlantic Books.

Haraway, D. (1991) *Simians, cyborgs and women: The reinvention of nature.* London: Free Association.

Harding, S. (1991) *Whose science? Whose knowledge? Thinking from women's lives.* Ithaca, NY: Cornell University Press.

Hardt, M. and Negri, A. (2000) *Empire.* Cambridge, MA: Harvard University Press.

Hardwig, J. (1985) Epistemic dependence. *Journal of Philosophy,* 82(7): 335–349.

Hasenbush, A., Flores, A.R. and Herman, J.L. (2019) Gender identity nondiscrimination laws in public accommodations: A review of evidence regarding safety and privacy in public restrooms, locker rooms, and changing rooms. *Sexuality Research and Social Policy,* 16(1): 70–83.

Hausman, B.L. (1992) Demanding subjectivity: Transsexualism, medicine, and the technologies of gender. *Journal of the History of Sexuality,* 3(2): 270–302. Available from: www.jstor.org/stable/3704058

Hausman, B.L. (1995) *Changing sex: Transsexualism, technology and the idea of gender.* Durham, NC: Duke University Press.

Havighurst, R.J. (1948) *Developmental tasks and education.* Chicago, IL: University of Chicago Press.

HBIGDA (1990) Harry Benjamin International Gender Dysphoria Association standards of care. Available from: www.wpath.org/publications/soc

HBIGDA (2001) *The Harry Benjamin International Gender Dysphoria Association standards of care for gender identity disorders (SOC 6),* 6th version. Available from: www.hbigda.org/socv6.cfm

Heath, R.A. (2006) *The Praeger handbook of transsexuality: Changing gender to match mindset.* Westport, CT: Praeger.

Herdt, G. (ed.) (1993) *Third sex, third gender: Beyond sexual dimorphism in culture and history*. New York: Zone Books.

Hickey-Moody, A. (2009a) Little war machines: Posthuman pedagogy and its media. *Journal of Literary & Cultural Disability Studies*, 1(3): 273–280. Available from: www.muse.jhu.edu/article/365198

Hickey-Moody, A. (2009b) *Unimaginable bodies: Intellectual disability, performance and becomings*. Rotterdam: Brill Sense.

Hidalgo, M.A., Ehrensaft, D., Tishelman, A.C., Clark, L.F., Garofalo, R., Rosenthal, S.M. et al (2013) The gender affirmative model: What we know and what we aim to learn. *Human Development*, 56(5): 285–290.

Higgs, J. and Jones, M. (2000) Will evidence-based practice take the reasoning out of practice? In J. Higgs and M. Jones (eds), *Clinical reasoning in the health professionals* (2nd edn, pp 307–315). Oxford: Butterworth Heinemann.

Hilário, A.P. (2020) Rethinking trans identities within the medical and psychological community: A path towards the depathologization and self-definition of gender identification in Portugal? *Journal of Gender Studies*, 29(3): 245–256.

Hill, D.B. and Menvielle, E. (2009) 'You have to give them a place where they feel protected and safe and loved': The views of parents who have gender-variant children and adolescents. *Journal of LGBT Youth*, 6(2–3): 243–271.

Hill, D.B., Menvielle, E., Sica, K.M. and Johnson, A. (2010) An affirmative intervention for families with gender variant children: Parental ratings of child mental health and gender. *Journal of Sex & Marital Therapy*, 36(1): 6–23.

Hines, S. (2009) A pathway to diversity? Human rights, citizenship and the politics of transgender. *Contemporary Politics*, 15(1): 87–102.

Hines, S. (2010) Sexing gender; gendering sex: Towards an intersectional analysis of transgender. In Y. Taylor, S. Hines & M. Casey (eds), *Theorizing intersectionality and sexuality* (pp. 140–162). London: Palgrave Macmillan.

Hird, M.J. (2004) Feminist matters: New materialist considerations of sexual difference. *Feminist Theory*, 5(2): 223–232.

Holliday, R. and Sanchez Taylor, J. (2006) Aesthetic surgery as false beauty. *Feminist Theory*, 7(2): 179–195.

Honneth, A. (1992) Integrity and disrespect: Principles of a conception of morality based on the theory of recognition. *Political Theory*, 20(2): 187–201.

Honneth, A. (1995) *The struggle for recognition: The moral grammar of social conflicts* (J. Anderson trans.). Cambridge: Polity Press.

Honneth, A. and Margalit, A. (2001) Recognition. *Proceedings of the Aristotelian Society, Supplementary Volumes*, 75: 111–139. Available from: www.jstor.org/stable/4107035

hooks, b. (1993) bell hooks speaking about Paulo Freire – the man, his work. In P. McLaren and P. Leonard (eds), *Paulo Freire: A critical encounter* (pp 145–152). London: Routledge.

hooks, b. (1994) *Teaching to transgress: Education as the practice of freedom*. New York: Routledge.

hooks, b. (2013) *Writing beyond race: Living theory and practice*. New York: Routledge.

Horowitz, M. and Glassberg, K.I. (1992) Ambiguous genitalia: Diagnosis, evaluation, and treatment. *Urologic Radiology*, 14(1): 306–318.

Hossain, A. (2017) The paradox of recognition: Hijra, third gender and sexual rights in Bangladesh. *Culture, Health & Sexuality*, 19(12): 1418–1431.

Hossain, A. (2018) De-Indianizing hijra: Intraregional effacements and inequalities in south Asian queer space. *TSQ: Transgender Studies Quarterly*, 5(3): 321–331.

Houk, C. and Lee, P.A. (2011) The diagnosis and care of transsexual children and adolescents: A pediatric endocrinologists' perspective. *Journal of Pediatric Endocrinology and Metabolism*, 19(2): 103–110.

Howells, J. (1996) Tacit knowledge. *Technology Analysis & Strategic Management*, 8(2): 91–106.

Hughes, I.A. (2008) Disorders of sex development: A new definition and classification. *Best Practice & Research Clinical Endocrinology & Metabolism*, 22(1): 119–134.

Hughes, J. (2006) Beyond the medical model of gender dysphoria to morphological self-determination. *Lahey Clinic Medical Ethics Journal*, Winter. Available from: https://ieet.org/index.php/IEET2/more/hughes20060401/

Hyde, J.S. (2005) The gender similarities hypothesis. *American Psychologist*, 60(6): 581.

Hyde, J.S., Bigler, R.S., Joel, D., Tate, C.C. and van Anders, S.M. (2019) The future of sex and gender in psychology: Five challenges to the gender binary. *American Psychologist*, 74(2): 171–193.

Illich, I. (1977) *The limits to medicine*. Harmondsworth: Penguin.

Irving, D. (2008) Normalized transgressions: Legitimizing the transsexual body as productive. *Radical History Review*, 2008(100): 38–59.

Ivanović, S., Stanojević, Č, Jajić, S., Vila, A. and Nikolić, S. (2013) Medical law and ethics. *Etika I Medicinsko Pravo*, 52(3): 67–74.

Ivers, N., Jamtvedt, G., Flottorp, S., Young, J.M., Odgaard-Jensen, J., French, S.D. et al (2012) Audit and feedback: Effects on professional practice and healthcare outcomes. *Cochrane Database of Systematic Reviews*, 6. Available from: www.cochranelibrary.com/cdsr/doi/10.1002/14651858.CD000259.pub3/full

Jackson, S. and Rees, A. (2007) The appalling appeal of nature: The popular influence of evolutionary psychology as a problem for sociology. *Sociology*, 41(5): 917–930.

Jackson, S. and Scott, S. (2001) Putting the body's feet on the ground: Towards a sociological reconceptualization of gendered and sexual embodiment. In K. Backett-Milburn and L. McKie (eds), *Constructing gendered bodies* (pp 9–24). Harlow: Palgrave.

Jacob, M. (2019) *'Cold, calculated, institutionalized child abuse': Experts comment on gender 'transitions' for kids*. Available from: www.lifesitenews.com/news/cold-calculated-institutionalized-child-abuse-experts-comment-on-child-gender-transitions

Jacobson, D. (1997) *Rights across boarders: Immigration and the decline of citizenship*. Baltimore, MD: Johns Hopkins University Press.

James, S.E., Herman, J.L., Rankin, S., Keisling, M., Mottet, L. and Anafi, M. (2016) *The report of the 2015 U.S. transgender survey*. Washington, DC: National Center for Transgender Equality.

Jameson, F. (1991) *Postmodernism, or, the cultural logic of late capitalism*. Durham, NC: Duke University Press.

Janicka, A. and Forcier, M. (2016) Transgender and gender nonconforming youth: Psychosocial and medical considerations. *Rhode Island Medical Journal*, 99(9): 31–34.

Jeffreys, S. (1997) Transgender activism. *Journal of Lesbian Studies*, 1(3–4): 55–74.

Jeffreys, S. (2005) *Beauty and misogyny: Harmful cultural practices in the west*. London: Routledge.

Jeffreys, S. (2006) Judicial child abuse: The family court of Australia, gender identity disorder, and the 'Alex' case. *Women's Studies International Forum*, 29(1): 1–12.

Jeffreys, S. (2012) The transgendering of children: Gender eugenics. *Women's Studies International Forum*, 35(5): 384–393.

Jeffreys, S. (2014) *Gender hurts: A feminist analysis of the politics of transgenderism*. London: Routledge.

Jeffreys, S. and Davy, Z. (2014) *Women's hour*, 7th August. London: Radio 4.

Jennings, I. (1956) *The approach to self-government*. Cambridge: Cambridge University Press.

Jewson, N.D. (1974) Medical knowledge and the patronage system in 18th-century England. *Sociology*, 8(3): 369–385.

Johnson, S.L. and Benson, K.E. (2014) 'It's always the mother's fault': Secondary stigma of mothering a transgender child. *Journal of GLBT Family Studies*, 10(1–2): 124–144.

Jordan, E. (1991) 'Making good wives and mothers'? The transformation of middle-class girls' education in nineteenth-century Britain. *History of Education Quarterly*, 31(4): 439–462.

Joseph, J.A., Pitagora, D., Tworecke, A. and Roberts, K.E. (2013) Peering into gaps in the diagnostic and statistical manual of mental disorders: Student perspectives on gender and informing education. *Society for International Education Journal: Engaging with Difference, Gender and Sexuality in Education*, 7(1): 104–127.

Jutel, A. (2011) *Putting a name to it: Diagnosis in contemporary society.* Baltimore, MD: Johns Hopkins University Press.

Jutel, A. (2019) 'The expertness of his healer': Diagnosis, disclosure and the power of a profession. *Health (London)*, 23(3): 289–305.

Kamens, D.H., Meyer, J.W. and Benavot, A. (1996) Worldwide patterns in academic secondary education curricula. *Comparative Education Review*, 40(2): 116–138.

Kapp, M.B. (2007) Patient autonomy in the age of consumer-driven health care: Informed consent and informed choice. *Journal of Legal Medicine*, 28(1): 91–117.

Kara, S. and Cabral Grinspan, M. (2017) *Gender is not illness: How pathologizing trans people violates international human rights law.* Berlin: GATE.

Karkazis, K. (2019) The misuses of 'biological sex'. *The Lancet*, 394(10212): 1898–1899.

Kennedy, N. and Hellen, M. (2010) Transgender children: More than a theoretical challenge. *Graduate Journal of Social Science*, 7(2): 25–43.

Kessler, S.J. (1998) *Lessons from the intersexed.* New Brunswick, NJ: Rutgers University Press.

Kim, N.S. and Ahn, W. (2002) Clinical psychologists' theory-based representations of mental disorders predict their diagnostic reasoning and memory. *Journal of Experimental Psychology: General*, 131(4): 451–476.

King, H. (2001) *Greek and Roman medicine.* London: Bristol Classical Press.

Knutson, D. and Goldbach, C. (2019) Transgender and non-binary affirmative approaches applied to psychological practice with boys and men. *Men and Masculinities*, 22(5): 921–925.

Kondakov, A. (2020) The queer epistemologies: Challenges to the modes about knowing sexuality in Russia. In Z. Davy, A.C. Santos, C. Bertone, R. Thoresen and S.E. Wieringa (eds), *Sage handbook of global sexualities* (pp 82–98). London: Sage Publications.

Kreukels, B.P.C. and Cohen-Kettenis, P.T. (2011) Puberty suppression in gender identity disorder: The Amsterdam experience. *Nature Reviews Endocrinology*, 7: 466–472.

Kreukels, B.P.C., Haraldsen, I.R., De Cuypere, G., Richter-Appelt, H., Gijs, L. and Cohen-Kettenis, P.T. (2012) A European network for the investigation of gender incongruence: The ENIGI initiative. *European Psychiatry*, 27(6): 445–450.

Kruijver, F.P.M., Zhou, J., Pool, C.W., Hofman, M.A., Gooren, L.J.G. and Swaab, D.F. (2000) Male to female transsexuals have female neuron numbers in a limbic nucleus. *Journal of Clinical Endocrinology and Metabolism*, 85(5): 2034–2041.

Kuhar, R. and Paternotte, D. (eds) (2017) *Anti-gender campaigns in Europe: Mobilizing against equality*. Lanham, MD: Rowman & Littlefield.

Kuvalanka, K.A., Allen, S.H., Munroe, C., Goldberg, A.E. and Weiner, J. L. (2018) The experiences of sexual minority mothers with trans★ children. *Family Relations*, 67(1): 70–87.

Kymlicka, W. (1990) *Contemporary political philosophy: An introduction*. Oxford: Clarendon Press.

Laclau, E. (2005) *On populist reason*. New York: Verso.

Laclau, E. and Mouffe, C. (1985) *Hegemony and socialist strategy: Towards a radical democratic politics*. London: Verso.

Lahti, A. (2020) Research perspectives on bisexuality. In Z. Davy, A.C. Santos, C. Bertone, R. Thoresen and S.E. Wieringa (eds), *Sage handbook of global sexualities* (pp 119–140). London: Sage Publications.

Lang, S. (1998) *Men as women and women as men: Changing gender in Native American cultures* (J.L. Vantine trans.). Austin, TX: University of Texas Press.

Laqueur, T.W. (1990) *Making sex: Body and gender from the Greeks to Freud*. Cambridge, MA: Harvard University Press.

Lash, S. (1984) Genealogy and the body: Foucault/Deleuze/Nietzsche. *Theory, Culture & Society*, 2(2): 1–17.

Latham, J.R. (2019) Axiomatic: Constituting 'transexuality' and trans sexualities in medicine. *Sexualities*, 22(1–2): 13–30.

Latour, B. (1988) *The pasteurization of France* (A. Sheridan, J. Law trans.). Cambridge, MA: Harvard University Press.

Lawrence, A.A. (2006) Clinical and theoretical parallels between desire for limb amputation and gender identity disorder. *Journal of Sexual Medicine*, 35(3): 263–278.

Le Fanu, J. (2011) *The rise and fall of modern medicine*. London: Abacus.

Lev, A.I. (2004) *Transgender emergence: Therapeutic guidelines for working with gender-variant people and their families*. Binghamton, NY: Haworth Clinical Practice Press.

Lindemann, M. (2010) *Medicine and society in early modern Europe* (2nd edn). Cambridge: Cambridge University Press.

Linstead, S. and Pullen, A. (2006) Gender as multiplicity: Desire, displacement, difference and dispersion. *Human Relations*, 59(9): 1287–1310.

Longino, H. and Doell, R. (1983) Body, bias, and behaviour: A comparative analysis of reasoning in two areas of biological science. In E. Fox Keller and H. Longino (eds), *Feminism and science* (pp 73–90). Oxford: Oxford University Press.

Lorber, J. (1994) *Paradoxes of gender*. New Haven, CT: Yale University Press.

Lorber, J. (2000) Using gender to undo gender: A feminist degendering movement. *Feminist Theory*, 1(1): 79–95.

Lord, J. and Littlejohns, P. (1997) Evaluating healthcare policies: The case of clinical audit. *British Medical Journal*, 315, 668–671.

Lourde, A. (2018) *The master's tools will never dismantle the master's house*. London: Penguin.

MacKinnon, C.A. (1987) *Feminism unmodified*. Cambridge, MA: Harvard University Press.

MacKinnon, K.R., Grace, D., Ng, S.L., Sicchia, S.R. and Ross, L.E. (2020) 'I don't think they thought I was ready': How pre-transition assessments create care inequities for trans people with complex mental health in Canada. *International Journal of Mental Health*, 49(1): 56–80.

Maguire, E.A., Woollett, K. and Spiers, H. J. (2006) London taxi drivers and bus drivers: A structural MRI and neuropsychological analysis. *Hippocampus*, 16(12): 1091–1101.

Mahalingam, R. (2003) Essentialism, culture, and beliefs about gender among the Aravanis of Tamil Nadu, India. *Sex Roles*, 49(9–10): 489–496.

Maharaj, N.R., Dhai, A., Wiersma, R. and Moodley, J. (2005) Intersex conditions in children and adolescents: Surgical, ethical, and legal considerations. *Journal of Pediatric and Adolescent Gynecology*, 18(6): 399–402.

Marecek, J. (1993) Disappearances, silences, and anxious rhetoric: Gender in abnormal psychology textbooks. *Journal of Theoretical and Philosophical Psychology*, 13(2): 114–123.

Marecek, J., Crawford, M. and Popp, D. (2004) On the construction of gender, sex, and sexualities. In A.H. Eagly, A.E. Beall, R.J. Sternberg and R. Robert (eds), *The psychology of gender* (2nd edn, pp 192–216). New York: Guilford Press.

Martin, E. (2002) The egg and the sperm. In S. Jackson and S. Scott (eds), *Gender: A sociological reader* (pp 385–391). London: Routledge.

Massumi, B. (2002) *Parables for the virtual: Movement, affect, sensation.* Durham, NC: Duke University Press.

May, K. (2002) Becoming women: Transgendered identities, psychosexual therapy and the challenge of metamorphosis. *Sexualities*, 5(4): 449–464.

McDonald, D.D. and Gary Bridge, R. (1991) Gender stereotyping and nursing care. *Research in Nursing & Health*, 14(5): 373–378.

McGlynn, E. A. (1997) Six challenges in measuring the quality of health care. *Health Affairs*, 16(3): 7–21.

McHugh, R.K. and Barlow, D.H. (2010) The dissemination and implementation of evidence-based psychological treatments. A review of current efforts. *American Psychologist*, 65(2): 73–84.

McNay, L. (2000) *Gender and agency: Reconfiguring the subject in feminist and social theory.* Cambridge: Polity Press.

McQueen, P. (2016) Authenticity, intersubjectivity and the ethics of changing sex. *Journal of Gender Studies*, 25(5): 557–570.

Merleau-Ponty, M. (2002) *Phenomenology of perception* (C. Smith trans.). London: Routledge.

Meyer, D. (2012) An intersectional analysis of lesbian, gay, bisexual, and transgender (LGBT) people's evaluations of anti-queer violence. *Gender & Society*, 26(6): 849–873.

Meyer-Bahlburg, H.F.L. (1999) Gender assignment and reassignment in 46XY pseudohermaphroditism and related conditions. *Journal of Clinical Endocrinology & Metabolism*, 84(10): 3455–3458.

Meyerowitz, J. (2002) *How sex changed: A history of transsexuality in the United States.* Cambridge, MA: Harvard University Press.

Miller, R.A. (2016) *The limits of bodily integrity: Abortion, adultery, and rape legislation in comparative perspective.* London: Routledge.

Miller, S.J. (2018) Reframing schooling to liberate gender identity. *Multicultural Perspectives*, 20(2): 70–80.

Millot, C. (1990) *Horsexe: Essay on transsexuality* (K. Hylton trans.). New York: Autonomedia.

Ministry of Health and Department of Health for Scotland (1944) *A national health service* (CMND 6502). London: HMSO.

Missé, M. and Coll-Planas, G. (eds) (2010) *El género desordenado. críticas en torno a la patologización de la transexualidad.* Barcelona: Egales.

Money, J. (2016) *Gendermaps: Social constructionism, feminism and sexosophical history.* London: Bloomsbury.

Money, J., Hampson, J.G. and Hampson, J.L. (1955) Hermaphroditism: Recommendations concerning assignment of sex, change of sex, and psychological management. *Bulletin of Johns Hopkins Hospital*, 97: 284–300.

Monro, S. and Richardson, D. (2010) Intersectionality and sexuality: The case of sexuality and transgender equalities work in UK local government. In Y. Taylor, S. Hines and M. Casey (eds), *Theorizing intersectionality and sexuality* (pp 99–118). London: Palgrave Macmillan.

Monro, S., Crocetti, D. and Yeadon-Lee, T. (2019) Intersex/variations of sex characteristics and DSD citizenship in the UK, Italy and Switzerland. *Citizenship Studies*, 23(8): 780–797.

Moore, M. (1997) On national self-determination. *Political Studies*, 45(5): 900–913.

Moore, M. and Brunskell-Evans, H. (eds) (2019) *Inventing transgender children and young people.* Newcastle: Cambridge Scholars Publishing.

Mouffe, C. (1992) Feminism, citizenship, and radical democratic politics. In J. Butler and J.W. Scott (eds), *Feminist theorize the political* (pp 369–384). New York: Routledge.

Mouffe, C. (1994) For a politics of nomadic identity. In G. Robertson, M. Mash, L. Tickner, J. Bird, B. Curtis and T. Putnam (eds), *Traveller's tales: Narratives of home and displacement* (pp 102–110). London: Routledge.

Mouffe, C. (1996) Deconstruction, pragmatism and the politics of democracy. In C. Mouffe (ed.), *Deconstructionism and pragmatism* (pp 1–12). New York: Routledge.

Muir Gray, J.A. (1999) Postmodern medicine. *The Lancet*, 354(9189): 1550–1553.

Muller, J.H. (1994) Anthropology, bioethics, and medicine: A provocative trilogy. *Medical Anthropology Quarterly*, 8(4): 448–467.

Murray, S.O. and Roscoe, W. (1998) *Boy-wives and female-husbands: Studies of African homosexualities.* New York: St Martin's Press.

Murray, S. (2009) Within or beyond the binary/boundary? *Australian Feminist Studies*, 24(60): 265–274.

Nagesh, A. (2017) Christian parents plan to sue school over son's transgender classmate. *The Metro*, 11 Sept. Available from: http://metro.co.uk/2017/09/11/christian-parents-plan-to-sue-school-over-sons-transgender-classmate-6918942/

Navarro, V. (1980) Work, ideology, and science: The case of medicine. *International Journal of Health Services*, 10(4): 523–550.

Neal, M. and Fovargue, S. (2016) Conscience and agent-integrity: A defence of conscience-based exemptions in the health care context. *Medical Law Review*, 24(4): 544–570.

Neal, M. and Fovargue, S. (2019) Is conscientious objection incompatible with healthcare professionalism? *The New Bioethics*, 25(3): 221–235.

Nealy, E.C. (2017) *Transgender children and youth*. New York: W.W. Norton and Co.

Nettleton, S. (2004) The emergence of E-scaped medicine? *Sociology*, 38(4): 661–679.

Newby, D. (2003) Personal development plans: Making them work, making them count. *Advances in Psychiatric Treatment*, 9(1): 5–10.

Newdick, C. and Derrett, S. (2006) Access, equity and the role of rights in health care. *Health Care Analysis*, 14(3): 157–168.

Ng, H., Lunn, M.R. and Obedin-Maliver, J. (2011) Lesbian, gay, bisexual, and transgender health and medical education. *Journal of the American Medical Association*, 306(21): 2326–2327.

NHS (National Health Service) (2016) *Guidelines – gender dysphoria*. Available from: www.nhs.uk/conditions/gender-dysphoria/guidelines/#

Nicholson, L. (1994) Interpreting gender. *Signs: Journal of Women in Culture and Society*, 20(1): 79–105.

Nicolson, P. (2014) *A critical approach to human growth and development*. Basingstoke: Palgrave Macmillan.

Nietzsche, F. (1997) *Twilight of the idols. or, how to philosophize with the hammer* (R. Polt, T. Strong trans.). Indianapolis, IN: Hackett Publishing Co. Inc.

Nowak, A., Vallacher, R.R., Tesser, A. and Borkowski, W. (2000) Society of self: The emergence of collective properties in self-structure. *Psychological Review*, 107(1): 39–61.

Norfolk and Norwich University Hospitals NHS Foundation Trust (2019) *Hypospadias*. Patient information leaflet. Available from: www.nnuh.nhs.uk/publication/hypospadias-v4/

Nwoko, K.C. (2012) Female husbands in Igbo land: Southeast Nigeria. *Journal of Pan African Studies*, 5(1): 69–82.

Oakley, A. (1993) *Essay on women, medicine and health.* Edinburgh: Edinburgh University Press.

Obedin-Maliver, J., Goldsmith, E.S., Stewart, L., White, W., Tran, E., Brenman, S. et al (2011) Lesbian, gay, bisexual, and transgender-related content in undergraduate medical education. *JAMA Journal of the American Medical Association,* 306(9): 971–977.

Office of the High Commissioner on Human Rights (1989) Convention on the rights of the child. Available from: www.ohchr.org/en/professionalinterest/pages/crc.aspx

Ogbu, J.U. (1992) Understanding cultural diversity and learning. *Educational Researcher,* 21(8): 5–14.

Olson, J. and Garofalo, R. (2014) The peripubertal gender-dysphoric child: Puberty suppression and treatment paradigms. *Pediatric Annals,* 43(6): e132–e137.

Olson-Kennedy, J., Cohen-Kettenis, P.T., Kreukels, B.P.C., Meyer-Bahlburg, H.F.L., Garofalo, R., Meyer, W.J. et al (2016) Research priorities for gender nonconforming/transgender youth: Gender identity development and biopsychosocial outcomes. *Current Opinion in Endocrinology, Diabetes and Obesity,* 23(2): 172–179.

O'Malley, C.D. (1970) *The history of medical education: An international symposium held February 5–9, 1968.* Berkeley, CA: University of California Press.

Oudshoorn, N. (2003) *Beyond the natural body: An archaeology of sex hormones.* London: Routledge.

Parry, N. and Parry, J. (2018) *The rise of the medical profession: A study of collective social mobility.* Abingdon: Routledge.

Pateman, C. (1970) *Participation and democratic theory.* Cambridge: Cambridge University Press.

Pearce, R. (2018) *Understanding trans health: Discourse, power and possibility.* Bristol: Policy Press.

Pearce, R., Erikainen, S. and Vincent, B. (2020) TERF wars: An introduction. *Sociological Review,* 68(4): 677–698.

Pepper, R. (2012) *Transitions of the heart: Stories of love, struggle and acceptance by mothers of transgender and gender variant children.* Berkeley, CA: Cleis Press.

Pescosolido, B.A. and Georgianna, S. (1989) Durkheim, suicide, and religion: Toward a network theory of suicide. *American Sociological Review,* 54(1): 33–48.

Pettan, S. (2003) Male, female, and beyond in the culture of music of Roma in Kosovo. In T. Magrini (ed.), *Music and gender: Perspectives from the Mediterranean* (pp 287–306). Chicago, IL: University of Chicago Press.

Pitts-Taylor, V. (2016) Medicine, governmentality and biopower in cosmetic surgery. In S.W. Smith and R. Deazley (eds), *The legal, medical and cultural regulation of the body* (pp 159–170). London: Routledge.

Platero, R.L. (2014) The influence of psychiatric and legal discourses on parents of gender-nonconforming children and trans youths in Spain. *Journal of GLBT Family Studies*, 10(1–2): 145–167.

Polanyi, M. (2009) *The tacit dimension* (revised edn). Chicago, IL: Chicago University Press.

Pouchelle, M. (1990) *The body and surgery in the middle ages*. New Brunswick, NJ: Rutgers University Press.

Prété, G., Couto-Silva, A.C., Trivin, C. and Brauner, R. (2008) Idiopathic central precocious puberty in girls: Presentation factors. *BMC Pediatrics*, 8(1). Available from: https://link.springer.com/article/10.1186/1471-2431-8-27

Preves, S.E. (2005) *Intersex and identity: The contested self*. New Brunswick, NJ: Rutgers University Press.

Probyn, E. (2004) Teaching bodies: Affects in the classroom. *Body & Society*, 10(4): 21–43.

Prosser, J. (1998) *Second skins: The body narratives of transsexuality*. New York: Columbia University Press.

Pryor, R.E. and Vickroy, W. (2019) 'In a perfect world, you wouldn't have to work the system to get the things you need to survive': A pilot study about trans health care possibilities. *Transgender Health*, 4(1): 18–23.

Pyne, J. (2014a) Gender independent kids: A paradigm shift in approaches to gender non-conforming children. *Canadian Journal of Human Sexuality*, 23(1): 1–8.

Pyne, J. (2014b) The governance of gender non-conforming children: A dangerous enclosure. *Annual Review of Critical Psychology*, 11: 79–96.

Pyne, J. (2016) 'Parenting is not a job ... it's a relationship': Recognition and relational knowledge among parents of gender non-conforming children. *Journal of Progressive Human Services*, 27(1): 21–48.

Quick, O. (2018) *Regulating patient safety: The end of professional dominance?* Cambridge: Cambridge University Press.

Qvortrup, M. (2014) *Referendums and ethnic conflict*. Philadelphia, PA: University of Pennsylvania Press.

Rabinow, P. and Rose, N. (2006) Biopower today. *BioSocieties*, 1(2): 195–217.

Rawls, J. (1971) *The theory of justice*. Cambridge, MA: Harvard University Press.

Raymond, J. (1980) *The transsexual empire: The making of the she male*. London: Women's Press.

Raymond, J. (1994) The politics of transgender. *Feminism & Psychology*, 4(4): 628–633.

Redfern, J.S. and Sinclair, B. (2014) Improving health care encounters and communication with transgender patients. *Journal of Communication in Healthcare*, 7(1): 25–40.

Reed, T. (2017) It's still not easy being a trans child. This is what schools can do to help. *The Guardian Online*, 5 June. Available from: www.theguardian.com/commentisfree/2017/jun/05/trans-child-schools-help-transition-prejudice

Reid-Smith, T. (2015) Is General Medical Council failing trans people as they clear top doctor after four year probe? General Medical Council accused of ignoring real trans concerns while wasting time on investigation they have now dropped. *Gay Star News*, 26 Feb. Available from: www.gaystarnews.com/article/general-medical-council-failing-trans-people-they-clear-top-doctor-after-four-year-probe2602/

Reis, E. (2007) Divergence or disorder? The politics of naming intersex. *Perspectives in Biology and Medicine*, 50(4): 535–543. Available from: https://muse.jhu.edu/article/222245

Reis, H.T. and Judd, C.M. (2014) *Handbook of research methods in social and personality psychology* (2nd edn). New York: Cambridge University Press.

Reisner, S.L., Bradford, J., Hopwood, R., Gonzalez, A., Makadon, H., Todisco, D. et al (2015) Comprehensive transgender healthcare: The gender affirming clinical and public health model of Fenway health. *Journal of Urban Health*, 92(3): 584–592.

Reisner, S.L., Poteat, T., Keatley, J., Cabral, M., Mothopeng, T., Dunham, E. et al (2016) Global health burden and needs of transgender populations: A review. *The Lancet*, 388(10042): 412–436.

Rekers, G.A., Bentler, P.M., Rosen, A.C. and Lovaas, O.I. (1977) Child gender disturbances: A clinical rationale for intervention. *Psychotherapy: Theory, Research & Practice*, 14(1): 2–11.

Rekers, G.A., Yates, C.E., Willis, T.J., Rosen, A.C. and Taubman, M. (1976) Childhood gender identity change: Operant control over sex-typed play and mannerisms. *Journal of Behavior Therapy and Experimental Psychiatry*, 7(1): 51–57.

Rendtorff, J. D. (2002) Basic ethical principles in European bioethics and biolaw: Autonomy, dignity, integrity and vulnerability – towards a foundation of bioethics and biolaw. *Medicine, Health Care and Philosophy*, 5(3): 235–244.

Rendtorff, J. D. and Kemp, P. (2000) *Basic ethical principles in European bioethics and biolaw*. Copenhagen: Centre for Ethics and Law.

Richards, C., Arcelus, J., Barrett, J., Bouman, W.P., Lenihan, P., Lorimer, S. et al (2015) Trans is not a disorder – but should still receive funding. *Sexual and Relationship Therapy*, 30(3): 309–313.

Richards, C., Bouman, W.P., Seal, L., Barker, M.J., Nieder, T.O. and T'Sjoen, G. (2016) Non-binary or genderqueer genders. *International Review of Psychiatry*, 28(1): 95–102.

Richardson, S.S. (2013) *Sex itself: The search for male and female in the human genome*. Chicago, IL: Chicago University Press.

Riley, E.A., Sitharthan, G., Clemson, L. and Diamond, M. (2011) The needs of gender-variant children and their parents according to health professionals. *International Journal of Transgenderism*, 13(2): 54–63.

Roberts, C. (2002) 'A matter of embodied fact': Sex hormones and the history of bodies. *Feminist Theory*, 3(1): 7–26.

Roberts, C. (2015) *Puberty in crisis: The sociology of early sexual development*. Cambridge: Cambridge University Press.

Roberts, R. (2017) Church of England tells schools to let children 'explore gender identity'. *Independent*, 13 Nov. Available from: www.independent.co.uk/news/uk/home-news/church-of-england-schools-let-children-explore-gender-identity-transgender-gender-fluid-a8051406.html

Roen, K. (2008) 'But we have to do something': Surgical 'correction' of atypical genitalia. *Body & Society*, 14(1): 47–66.

Rogol, A.D. (2005) New facets of androgen replacement therapy during childhood and adolescence. *Expert Opinion on Pharmacotherapy*, 6(8): 1319–1336.

Ronen, D. (1979) *The quest for self-determination*. New Haven, CT: Yale University Press.

Rose, N. (1988) Calculable minds and manageable individuals. *History of the Human Sciences*, 1(2): 179–200.

Rose, N. (1990a) *Governing the soul: The shaping of the private self*. Florence: Taylor & Francis.

Rose, N. (1990b) Of madness itself: Histoire de la folie and the object of psychiatric history. *History of the Human Sciences*, 3(3): 373–380.

Rose, N. (1996) Psychiatry as a political science: Advanced liberalism and the administration of risk. *History of the Human Sciences*, 9(2): 1–23.

Rose, N. (1998) Governing risky individuals: The role of psychiatry in new regimes of control. *Psychiatry, Psychology and Law*, 5(2): 177–195.

Rose, N. (1999) *Powers of freedom: Reframing political thought*. Cambridge: Cambridge University Press.

Rose, N. (2001) The politics of life itself. *Theory, Culture & Society*, 18(6): 1–30.

Rose, N. (2005) In search of certainty: Risk management in a biological age. *Journal of Public Mental Health*, 4(3): 14–21.

Roy, J.R., Chakraborty, S. and Chakraborty, T.R. (2009) Estrogen-like endocrine disrupting chemicals affecting puberty in humans – a review. *Medical Science Monitor*, 15(6): 137–145.

Royal College of Psychiatrists (2018) Your faculties. Website page. Available from: www.rcpsych.ac.uk/members/your-faculties

Rycroft-Malone, J., Seers, K., Titchen, A., Harvey, G., Kitson, A. and McCormack, B. (2004) What counts as evidence in evidence-based practice? *Journal of Advanced Nursing*, 47(1): 81–90.

Saeger, K. (2006) Finding our way. *Journal of GLBT Family Studies*, 2(3–4): 207–245.

Saini, A. (2018) *Inferior: The true power of women and the science that shows it*. London: HarperCollins.

Saks, M. (1983) Removing the blinkers? A critique of recent contributions to the sociology of professions. *Sociological Review*, 31(1): 3–21.

Salter, B. (2000) Change in the governance of medicine: The politics of self-regulation. In D. Gladstone (ed.), *Regulating Doctors* (pp 8–27). Bury St Edmunds: St Edmundsbury Press.

Santos, A.L. (2020) Trans athletes and the posthuman: A critical analysis of trans policies in sport. In Z. Davy, A.C. Santos, C. Bertone, R. Thoresen and S.E. Wieringa (eds), *Sage handbook of global sexualities* (pp 267–290). London: Sage Publications.

Savulescu, J. (2006) Conscientious objection in medicine. *British Medical Journal*, 332: 294–297.

Schlich, T. (ed.) (2018) *The Palgrave handbook of the history of surgery*. London: Palgrave Macmillan.

Schneider, C., Cerwenka, S., Nieder, T.O., Briken, P., Cohen-Kettenis, P.T., De Cuypere, G. et al (2016) Measuring gender dysphoria: A multicenter examination and comparison of the Utrecht gender dysphoria scale and the gender identity/gender dysphoria questionnaire for adolescents and adults. *Archives of Sexual Behavior*, 45(3): 551–558.

Schramme, T. (2008) Should we prevent non-therapeutic mutilation and extreme body modification? *Bioethics*, 22(1): 8–15.

Schulz, S.L. (2018) The informed consent model of transgender care: An alternative to the diagnosis of gender dysphoria. *Journal of Humanistic Psychology*, 58(1): 72–92.

Sellar, S. (2012) 'It's all about relationships': Hesitation, friendship and pedagogical assemblage. *Discourse: Studies in the Cultural Politics of Education*, 33(1): 61–74.

Sellu, D. (1996) Time to audit audit. *British Medical Journal*, 312: 128–129.

Serano, J. (2007) *Whipping girl: A transsexual woman on sexism and scapegoating.* Emeryville, CA: Seal Press.

Serano, J. (2010) The case against autogynephilia. *International Journal of Transgenderism*, 12(3): 176–187.

Serano, J. (2016) *Outspoken: A decade of transgender activism and trans feminism.* Oakland, CA: Switch Hitter Press.

Sharpe, A. (2015) Sexual intimacy, gender variance, and criminal law. *Nordic Journal of Human Rights*, 33(4): 380–391.

Sharpe, A. (2020) Will gender self-declaration undermine women's rights and lead to an increase in harms? *Modern Law Review*, 83(3): 539–557.

Sheldon, K.M., Williams, G. and Joiner, T. (2003) *Self-determination theory in the clinic: Motivating physical and mental health.* New Haven, CT: Yale University Press.

Shildrick, M. (2004) Genetics, normativity, and ethics: Some bioethical concerns. *Feminist Theory*, 5(2): 149–165.

Shildrick, M. (2005) Beyond the body of bioethics: Challenging the conventions. In M. Shildrick and R. Mykitiuk (eds), *Ethics of the body: Postconventional challenges* (pp 1–26). Cambridge, MA: MIT Press.

Shildrick, M. (2015) 'Why should our bodies end at the skin?' Embodiment, boundaries, and somatechnics. *Hypatia*, 30(1): 13–29.

Shildrick, M. and Mykitiuk, R. (eds) (2005) *Ethics of the body: Postconventional challenges.* Cambridge, MA: MIT Press.

Shonkoff, J.P. and Phillips, D.A. (eds) (2000) *From neurons to neighborhoods: The science of early childhood development.* Washington, DC: National Academy Press.

Siedlberg, S. (2006) 'Games people play', 17 May. Available from: http://oii-uk.blogspot.com/2006/09/games-people-play.html

Siegworth, G. J. and Gregg, M. (2010) An inventory of shimmers. In M. Gregg and G. J. Siegworth (eds), *The affect theory reader* (pp 1–27). Durham, NC: Duke University Press.

Simmel, G. (1955) *Conflict and the web of group affiliation.* New York: Free Press.

Singh, A. A. (2016) Moving from affirmation to liberation in psychological practice with transgender and gender nonconforming clients. *American Psychologist*, 71(8): 755–762.

Smith, A.M. (1998) *Laclau and Mouffe: The radical democratic imaginary.* London: Routledge.

Smith, D.W. (2007) Deleuze and the question of desire: Toward an immanent theory of ethics. *Parrhesia*, 2: 66–78.

Smith Cross, J. (2015) Outcry prompts CAMH to review its controversial treatment of trans youth. Metro, 18 March. Available from: https://web.archive.org/web/20150320203815/http://metronews.ca/news/toronto/1315743/outcry-prompts-camh-to-review-its-controversial-treatment-of-trans-youth/

Sontag, S. (1979) *Illness as metaphor* and *AIDS and its metaphors.* London: Allen Lane.

Spade, D. (2006) Mutilating gender. In S. Stryker and S. Whittle (eds), *Transgender studies reader* (pp 315–332). New York: Routledge.

Speer, S.A. (2013) Talking about sex in the gender identity clinic: Implications for training and practice. *Health*, 17(6): 622–639.

Spielhofer, T., Benton, T. and Schagen, S. (2004) A study of the effects of school size and single-sex education in English schools. *Research Papers in Education*, 19(2): 133–159.

Squier, S. (1996) Fetal subjects and maternal objects: Reproductive technology and the new fetal/maternal relation. *Journal of Medicine and Philosophy: A Forum for Bioethics and Philosophy of Medicine*, 21(5): 515–535.

Stacey, M. (1992) *Regulating British medicine: The general medical council.* London: Wiley-Blackwell.

Stafford, A. (2012) Departing shame: Feinberg and queer/transgender counter-cultural remembering. *Journal of Gender Studies*, 21(3): 301–312.

Steensma, T.D., Kreukels, B.P.C., de Vries, A.L.C. and Cohen-Kettenis, P.T. (2013) Gender identity development in adolescence. *Hormones and Behavior*, 64(2): 288–297.

Steinmetz, K. (2014) The transgender tipping point: America's next civil rights frontier. *Time Magazine*, 29 May. Available from: http://time.com/magazine/us/135460/june-9th-2014-vol-183-no-22-u-s/

Stern, D.T. (2006) *Measuring medical professionalism.* New York: Oxford University Press.

Stewart, K. (2007) *Ordinary affects.* Durham, NC: Duke University Press.

Stryker, S. and Whittle, S. (eds) (2006) *Transgender studies reader.* New York: Routledge.

Suess Schwend, A. (2020) Questioning pathologization in clinical practice and research from trans and intersex perspectives. In Z. Davy, A.C. Santos, C. Bertone, R. Thoresen and S.E. Wieringa (eds), *Sage handbook of global sexualities* (pp 798–821). London: Sage Publications.

Suess Schwend, A., Winter, S., Chiam, Z., Smiley, A. and Cabral Grinspan, M. (2018) Depathologising gender diversity in childhood in the process of *ICD* revision and reform. *Global Public Health*, 13(11): 1585–1598.

Sureda, A.R. (1973) *The evolution of the right of self-determination: A study of United Nations practice*. Leiden: Sijthoff & Noordhoff International Publishers.

Suzuki, B.H. (1984) Curriculum transformation for multicultural education. *Education and Urban Society*, 16(3): 294–322.

Szasz, T.S. (2009) *Antipsychiatry: Quakery squared*. Syracuse, NY: Syracuse University Press.

Taylor, C.A. (2016) Edu-crafting a cacophonous ecology: Posthumanist research practices for education. In C.A. Taylor and C. Hughes (eds), *Posthumanist research practices for education* (pp 5–24). London: Palgrave.

Temple Newhook, J., Winters, K., Pyne, J., Jamieson, A., Holmes, C., Feder, S. et al (2018) Teach your parents and providers well: Call for refocus on the health of trans and gender-diverse children. *Canadian Family Physician*, 64(5): 332–325. Available from: www.cfp.ca/content/64/5/332.short

Tilly, C. (1984) *Big structures, large processes, huge comparisons*. New York: Russell Sage Foundation.

Transgender London (2011) *Not a choice? what causes it?* Available from: www.transgenderlondon.com/What%20Causes%20It.htm

Tronto, J.C. (2013) *Caring democracy: Markets, equality, and justice*. New York: New York University Press.

Turner, B.S. (1995) *Medical power and social knowledge* (2nd edn). London: Sage Publications.

United Nations (1966) International Covenant on Civil and Political Rights. Available from: www.ohchr.org/en/professionalinterest/pages/ccpr.aspx

United Nations General Assembly (1960) Resolution 1514: Declaration on the granting of independence to colonial countries and peoples. Available from: www.un.org/ga/search/view_doc.asp?symbol=A/RES/1514(XV)

United Nations Office of the High Commissioner for Human Rights (2019) Victor Madrigal-Borloz. Available from: www.ohchr.org/EN/Issues/SexualOrientationGender/Pages/VictorMadrigalBorloz.aspx

Vaccaro, J. (2013) Felt matters. In S. Stryker and A.Z. Aizura (eds), *The transgender studies reader 2* (pp 91–100). New York: Routledge.

Veatch, R.M. (1987) *Patient as partner: Theory of human experimentation ethics*. Bloomington, IN: Indiana University Press.

Veatch, R.M. (1991) *The patient–physician relation: The patient as partner, part 2*. Bloomington, IN: Indiana University Press.

Venkatesan, P. and Peters, M.A. (2010) Biocapitalism and the politics of life. *Geopolitics, History and International Relations*, 2(2): 100–122.

Waites, M. (2009) Critique of 'sexual orientation' and 'gender identity' in human rights discourse: Global queer politics beyond the Yogyakarta Principles. *Contemporary Politics*, 15(1): 137–156.

Waldby, C. (2002) Stem cells, tissue cultures and the production of biovalue. *Health*, 6(3): 305–323.

Walker, M. and Unterhalter, E. (eds) (2007) *Amartya Sen's capability approach and social justice in education.* New York: Palgrave Macmillan.

Wallis, F. (2010) *Medieval medicine: A reader.* Toronto: University of Toronto.

Walsh, J. and Griffiths, S. (2019) Parents battle 'state-sponsored sterilisation' of trans children: A new group says the NHS is steering confused youngsters towards treatments that can leave them infertile. *The Sunday Times*, 26 Oct. Available from: www.thetimes.co.uk/article/parents-battle-state-sponsored-sterilisation-of-trans-children-mb55fxt60

Waskul, D.D. and van der Riet, P. (2002) The abject embodiment of cancer patients: Dignity, selfhood, and the grotesque body. *Symbolic Interaction*, 25(4): 487–513.

Watson, S.E., Greene, A., Lewis, K. and Eugster, E.A. (2015) Bird's-eye view of GnRH analog use in a pediatric endocrinology referral center. *Endocrine Practice*, 21(6): 586–589.

Weatherall, D. (1996) *Science and the quiet art: The role of medical research in health care.* New York: W.W. Norton and Co.

Webster, A. (2007) *Health, technology and society: A sociological critique.* Basingstoke: Palgrave Macmillan.

Wehmeyer, M.L. (2014) Framing the future: Self-determination. *Remedial and Special Education*, 36(1): 20–23.

Wehmeyer, M.L., Abery, B.H., Mithaug, D.E. and Stancliffe, R.J. (2003) *Theory in self-determination: Foundations for educational practice.* Springfield, IL: Charles C. Thomas Publisher.

Weinhardt, L.S., Xie, H., Wesp, L.M., Murray, J.R., Apchemengich, I., Kioko, D. et al (2019) The role of family, friend, and significant other support in well-being among transgender and non-binary youth. *Journal of GLBT Family Studies*, 15(4): 311–325.

Weinstock, D. (2014) Conscientious refusal and health professionals: Does religion make a difference? *Bioethics*, 28(1): 8–15.

Weitz, E.D. (2015) Self-determination: How a German enlightenment idea became the slogan of national liberation and a human right. *American Historical Review*, 120(2): 462–496.

West, P. (2004) *Report into the medical and related needs of transgender people in Brighton and hove: The case for a local integrated service.* Available from: www.pfc.org.uk/files/medical/spectrum.pdf

Westbrook, L. and Schilt, K. (2014) Doing gender, determining gender: Transgender people, gender panics, and the maintenance of the sex/gender/sexuality system. *Gender & Society*, 28(1): 32–57.

Whittle, S. (1999) Transgender rights: The European Court of Human Rights and new identity politics for the new age. In A. Hegarty and S. Leonard (eds), *Human rights: An agenda for the 21st century* (pp 201–216). London: Cavendish.

Whittle, S. (2002) *Respect and equality: Transsexual and transgender rights*. London: Cavendish.

Whittle, S., Turner, L., Combs, R. and Rhodes, S. (2008) *Transgender EuroStudy: Legal survey and focus on the transgender experience of health care*. Available from: www.pfc.org.uk/pdf/eurostudy.pdf

WHO (1975) *The ICD-9 Classification of Mental and Behavioural Disorders: Clinical Descriptions and Diagnostic Guidelines*. Geneva: WHO Publications.

WHO (1993) *The ICD-10 Classification of Mental and Behavioural Disorders: Clinical Descriptions and Diagnostic Guidelines*. Geneva: WHO Publications.

WHO (2015) *ICD-11 beta draft*. World Health Organization. Available from: http://apps.who.int/classifications/icd11/browse/l-m/en

WHO (2018) *ICD-11*. Available from: www.who.int/classifications/icd/en/

Wicclair, M.R. (2000) Conscientious objection in medicine. *Bioethics*, 14(3): 205–227.

Wilkerson, A.L. (1998) *Diagnosis. Difference: The moral authority of medicine*. Ithaca, NY: Cornell University Press.

Wilkerson, J.M., Rybicki, S., Barber, C.A. and Smolenski, D.J. (2011) Creating a culturally competent clinical environment for LGBT patients. *Journal of Gay and Lesbian Social Services*, 23(3): 376–394.

Winter, S. (2017) Gender trouble: The World Health Organization, the International Statistical Classification of Diseases and Related Health Problems (ICD)-11 and the trans kids. *Sexual Health*, 14(5): 423–430.

Winter, S., Chalungsooth, P., Teh, Y.K., Rojanalert, N., Maneerat, K., Wong, Y.W. et al (2009) Transpeople, transprejudice and pathologization: A seven-country factor analytic study. *International Journal of Sexual Health*, 21(2): 96–118.

Winter, S., Settle, E., Wylie, K., Reisner, S. L., Cabral, M., Knudson, G. et al (2016) Synergies in health and human rights: A call to action to improve transgender health. *The Lancet*, 388(10042): 318–321. Available from: www.thelancet.com/journals/lancet/article/PIIS0140-6736(16)30653-5/fulltext?rss=yes

Winters, K. (2008) *Gender madness in American psychiatry: Essays from the struggle for dignity.* Dillon, CO: GID Reform Advocates.

Winters, K. (2013) *GID reform in the DSM-5 and ICD-11: A status update.* Available from: https://gidreform.wordpress.com/category/dsm-5-2/

Winters, K., Temple Newhook, J., Pyne, J., Feder, S., Jamieson, A., Holmes, C. et al (2018) Learning to listen to trans and gender diverse children: A response to Zucker (2018) and Steensma and Cohen-Kettenis (2018). *International Journal of Transgenderism*, 19(2): 246–250.

WMA (2015) WMA statement on transgender people: Adopted by the 66th WMA general assembly, Moscow, Russia, October 2015. Available from: www.wma.net/policies-post/wma-statement-on-transgender-people/

Women's Hour (2014) *Transgender children.* London: BBC Radio 4. Available from: www.bbc.co.uk/programmes/b04v2ynv

Woollett, K. and Maguire, E. (2011) Acquiring 'the knowledge' of London's layout drives structural brain changes. *Current Biology*, 21(24): 2109–2114.

WPATH (World Professional Association for Transgender Health) (2012) *Standards of care for the health of transsexual, transgender, and gender nonconforming people (SOC 7)*, Version 7. Available from: www.wpath.org/documents/SOC%20V7%2003-17-12.pdf

Wylie, K., Barrett, J., Besser, M., Bouman, W.P., Bridgman, M., Clayton, A. et al (2014) Good practice guidelines for the assessment and treatment of adults with gender dysphoria. *Sexual and Relationship Therapy*, 29(2): 154–214.

Yack, B. (2012) *Nationalism and the moral psychology of community.* Chicago, IL: University of Chicago Press.

Young, I.M. (1990) *Throwing like a girl and other essays in feminist philosophy and social theory.* Bloomington, IN: Indiana University Press.

Zhou, J.-N., Hofman, M.A., Gooren, L.J.G. and Swaab, D.F. (1995) A sex difference in the human brain and its relation to transsexuality. *Nature*, 378(6552): 68–70.

Zucker, K.J. (2008) Children with gender identity disorder: Is there a best practice? *Neuropsychiatrie de l'enfance et de l'adolescence*, 56(6): 358–364.

Zucker, K.J. (2013) The science and politics of DSM-5. Paper presented at the Classifying Sex: Debating DSM-5 conference, University of Cambridge, UK, 4 July.

Zucker, K.J. and Bradley, S.J. (1995) *Gender identity disorder and psychosexual problems in children and adolescents.* New York: Guilford Press.

Zucker, K. J. and Seto, M.C. (2015) Gender dysphoria and paraphilic sexual disorders. In D.S. Pine, J.F. Leckman, S. Scott, M.J. Snowling and E. Taylor (eds), *Rutter's child and adolescent psychiatry* (pp 983–998). Chichester: John Wiley & Sons.

Zucker, K.J., Bradley, S.J. and Ipp, M. (1994) Delayed naming of a newborn boy. *Journal of Psychology & Human Sexuality*, 6(1): 57–68.

Index

References to endnotes show both the page number and the note number (e.g. 231n3).